USING AI TO POWER PRIMARY LITERACY

Artificial intelligence (AI) is transforming the world around us and education is no exception. But how can AI help in the primary classroom, particularly with teaching reading, writing and comprehension? This practical guide demystifies AI for teachers, offering clear, accessible and practical strategies to enhance literacy teaching in a way that is both effective and engaging.

Written specifically for primary school teachers, this book explores how AI-powered tools can support children's literacy development. It provides step-by-step guidance on using AI to enrich reading activities, improve comprehension skills, inspire creative writing, make poetry analysis and writing easier, and make non-fiction research more engaging. The book is packed with real-world, tried and tested examples with easy-to-follow lesson ideas, and thoughtful discussion points to help teachers integrate AI into their teaching while maintaining the human connection that is central to learning.

This practical resource is for anyone looking for innovative ways to engage young learners with their reading and writing. It is particularly relevant for teachers and school leaders and offers hands-on support on how to use AI ethically and effectively in the classroom, whilst also suggesting ways to enhance learning and pupil engagement within an ever-evolving educational landscape.

Adam Bushnell is an award-winning author of fictional and academic books. He has had over fifty books published including *Descriptosaurus: Story Writing* and *Modelling Exciting Writing*. He works in the UK and internationally in both state and private education delivering creative writing workshops to all ages. Previously a teacher, Adam also delivers Continuous Professional Development to teachers on how to inspire reading and writing in the classroom.

"As with any new innovation or teaching and learning tool, it is the fear of the unknown or the lack of an infrastructure to navigate the resource that inhibits its effective adoption. This new and groundbreaking publication is a timely and comprehensive guide on how to harness the power of AI to enhance the teaching and learning of literacy in primary classrooms."

Alison Wilcox, *creator of* Descriptosaurus

"Wow… I never realised how much I could do with AI to enhance my teaching and save huge amounts of time. Reading and writing is about to be supercharged! Adam has carefully crafted a book of AI gold-dust to help enhance your teaching and revolutionise the way you plan, resource and deliver your lessons. This book is filled with a variety of simple, yet mind blowing ideas that AI can do that will save endless hours, while enhancing every lesson!"

Andrew Jennings, *Vocabulary Ninja*

USING AI TO POWER PRIMARY LITERACY

A Classroom Guide for Teachers

Adam Bushnell

LONDON AND NEW YORK

Designed cover image: © Getty Images

First published 2026
by Routledge
4 Park Square, Milton Park, Abingdon, Oxon OX14 4RN

and by Routledge
605 Third Avenue, New York, NY 10158

Routledge is an imprint of the Taylor & Francis Group, an informa business

© 2026 Adam Bushnell

The right of Adam Bushnell to be identified as author of this work has been asserted in accordance with sections 77 and 78 of the Copyright, Designs and Patents Act 1988.

All rights reserved. No part of this book may be reprinted or reproduced or utilised in any form or by any electronic, mechanical, or other means, now known or hereafter invented, including photocopying and recording, or in any information storage or retrieval system, without permission in writing from the publishers.

Trademark notice: Product or corporate names may be trademarks or registered trademarks, and are used only for identification and explanation without intent to infringe.

British Library Cataloguing-in-Publication Data
A catalogue record for this book is available from the British Library

ISBN: 978-1-041-02906-9 (hbk)
ISBN: 978-1-041-02905-2 (pbk)
ISBN: 978-1-003-62137-9 (ebk)

DOI: 10.4324/9781003621379

Typeset in Interstate
by KnowledgeWorks Global Ltd.

CONTENTS

Introduction ix

Part 1 Reading 1

 1 **Personalised Texts and Reading Lists** 3

 2 **Speech-to-Text** 8

 3 **Phonics** 11

 4 **Interactive Storytelling** 16

 5 **Reading Fluency** 19

 6 **Virtual Reading Buddies** 23

 7 **Reading Games** 27

 8 **Audiobooks** 31

 9 **Simplifying and Extending Texts** 34

10 **Summarising Texts** 38

Part 2 Comprehension Skills 43

11 **Quizzes** 45

12 **Key Moments** 50

13 **Vocabulary Expansion and Building** 54

14	Emotion Analysis	59
15	Book Discussions	64
16	Reading Aloud to Avatars	68
17	Reading Challenges	73
18	Flashcards	79
19	Guess the Ending	83
20	Clarify the Confusion	87

Part 3 Character Descriptions 91

21	Checking Book Character Descriptions	93
22	Character Analysis	96
23	Context of Characters	100
24	Appearance and Personality	104
25	Revealing Character through Actions	109
26	Character Development	114
27	Sentence Starters	119
28	Opposites and Comparisons	123
29	Emotive Language	127
30	Dialogue	131

Part 4 Setting Descriptions 135

31	Example Texts	137
32	Change the Timeline	141
33	Adding Sensory Detail	145

34 Developmental Prompts	149
35 Weather and Other Influences	152
36 Colour and Tone	156
37 Feedback on Descriptions	160
38 Movement	163
39 Other Worlds	167
40 Contrasting Places	171

Part 5 Poetry — 177

41 Explaining Literary Devices	179
42 More Figurative Language	184
43 Writing Ballads	188
44 Structured Poetry	192
45 Free Verse	197
46 Poetry Prompts	202
47 Rhyme	206
48 Thematic Ideas	210
49 Collaborative Ideas	214
50 Poetry Analysis	218

Part 6 Non-Fiction — 223

51 Structure	225
52 Research	229
53 Captions and Headings	234

54	Lesson Planning	238
55	Topic-Related Vocabulary	242
56	Fact vs. Opinion	246
57	Summarising	250
58	Explaining Features	254
59	Creating Narrative Non-Fiction	258
60	Writing Conclusions	262

References   265

INTRODUCTION

> Artificial Intelligence (AI) is transforming education, offering us time-saving tools, personalised learning opportunities and innovative ways to support literacy development. This guide, Using AI to Power Primary Literacy: A Classroom Guide for Teachers, is designed to help primary educators harness the power of AI to enhance reading, writing, comprehension and research skills in the classroom.

Change is the law of life. As educators, we need to embrace the future but not forget the past. This is especially true with technology. A lot of us might be wary of AI but let us remember that it is simply a tool. A resource for the classroom. The use of interactive boards has not completely replaced flipcharts and whiteboards in classrooms. Tablets have not replaced workbooks for children. Rather new technology is used in conjunction with what we already have. AI is no exception.

In my role, I work as a visiting author in schools, running creative writing workshops. The first time I experimented with AI in the classroom, I wasn't sure what to expect. I'd heard of ChatGPT but didn't really know where to start with using it in my sessions. Then, out of curiosity, I started playing around with image generation platforms to see what the characters from my own books might look like. Seeing a visual version of a character I'd only pictured in my head sparked new ideas and made me rethink how I described them in my writing. That got me thinking; if AI could help me see my own stories in a new way, how could it be used to inspire writing in the classroom? Could it spark children's creativity, boost their confidence or help them develop new ideas for their own stories? I firmly believe that it can and does. I use a variety of AI platforms every day in primary schools and have seen how it inspires, educates and engages children in ways I hadn't expected. AI can help reluctant writers find their voice, give confident writers new challenges and provide all children with fresh perspectives on storytelling. Whether it's generating unique story prompts, creating vivid character descriptions or helping young writers refine their ideas, AI offers an exciting new tool to support creativity in the classroom. Most importantly, it encourages children to experiment, take risks and see writing as an enjoyable, dynamic process rather than a fixed task with only one right answer.

In this book, the ideas and suggestions are all tried and tested in real classrooms with primary-aged children. They are designed to be practical, engaging and adaptable to different teaching styles and needs. Whether you're looking to introduce AI into your literacy lessons for the first time or expand on what you're already doing, you'll find a range of activities, tips and insights to help you make the most of these tools. The aim is to show how AI can enhance, rather than replace, traditional teaching methods, supporting creativity, building confidence and making writing an exciting, accessible experience for all children.

This book is organised into clear, practical chapters covering the key aspects of primary literacy development. Each chapter focuses on a specific skill, such as summarising, researching, writing conclusions and developing vocabulary, and demonstrates how AI can support both teachers and pupils.

Throughout the guide, you'll find:

- ☑ Practical examples from real primary school texts to show how AI can enhance traditional teaching methods.
- ☑ AI-generated prompts and responses, allowing teachers to see how AI can be used in real classroom scenarios.
- ☑ Engaging classroom activities that blend AI with hands-on learning to keep pupils actively involved.
- ☑ Caution and consideration sections to help teachers critically assess AI-generated content and encourage pupils to think independently.

This guide is not a rigid curriculum but rather a toolkit of ideas that teachers can adapt based on their pupils' needs, school policies, and personal teaching style.

Not all schools have access to premium AI software, so this guide includes a mix of free and freemium tools that teachers can explore at no cost or with minimal investment. Some of the recommended AI tools include:

- ChatGPT (free/paid) – Generates lesson ideas, summarises text, and provides writing support.
- DeepL Write (free) – Helps improve sentence clarity and refine pupils' writing.
- CommonLit (free) – Offers structured non-fiction texts for reading and analysis.
- Book Creator (freemium) – Enables pupils to structure and publish their own books.

These tools provide instant access to resources, lesson planning support and personalised feedback, allowing teachers to spend more time on teaching and pupil interaction rather than administrative tasks.

It is worth noting that a lot of these platforms are for teachers only, as Chat GPT, Deep Seek and Gemini, etc. are 13+. Under 13's are not allowed to use them; 13 to 17 year olds are allowed to use them with parental or guardian permission; those 18 years and over can use them freely without restrictions. Microsoft Copilot is also for users aged 13 and older; however, in an educational setting, parental or school consent may be given.

Here are some recommended AI platforms for children under 13:

- Google's Read Along – AI-powered reading app with real-time feedback (ages 5-12)
- Khanmigo (by Khan Academy) – AI tutor for maths, reading, and other subjects (ages 7+)
- Duolingo – Language learning with AI-driven lessons and feedback (ages 4+)
- Replika for Kids – AI chatbot for emotional support and communication (ages 7+)

- Woebot – AI mental health support and emotional regulation (ages 10+)
- Scratch (by MIT) – Teaches coding through drag-and-drop blocks (ages 8+)
- Tynker – Coding platform with AI support (ages 5+)
- Osmo – AI-enhanced educational games with physical interaction (ages 4+)

Every classroom is unique and every teacher has their own approach to literacy instruction. This guide is not a one-size-fits-all model, it's a flexible framework that you can modify, expand upon and integrate into your existing teaching practices.

I would encourage you to:

✓ Experiment with AI tools to see how they fit into your lessons.
✓ Encourage pupils to think critically about AI-generated content rather than passively accepting responses.
✓ Use AI as a time-saving assistant, not as a replacement for professional judgement and creativity.

As AI continues to evolve, its role in education will grow, offering new opportunities for literacy development. This guide provides a foundation for using AI purposefully and effectively in primary classrooms, helping pupils develop strong literacy skills while maintaining creativity, independence and critical thinking.

Let's together explore how AI can empower our teaching, engage pupils and enhance literacy education for the next generation.

PART 1
Reading

This section explores how AI can revolutionise reading experiences in primary classrooms, offering tools and strategies to personalise, engage and support all learners. From generating customised reading lists based on children's interests to creating simplified or extended texts, AI enables inclusive, differentiated instruction. Chapters cover practical uses of tools such as speech-to-text for reluctant writers, interactive storytelling platforms to boost creativity and virtual reading buddies that provide real-time feedback on fluency and expression. The section also highlights how AI can support phonics through personalised sound recognition activities, and how audiobooks can develop listening skills and enjoyment of literature. Whether you're helping early readers decode words or providing enrichment for fluent pupils, these chapters present adaptable approaches that save teacher time while deepening children's reading confidence and comprehension. It's ideal for teachers wanting to make reading more interactive, accessible and enjoyable through technology.

1 Personalised Texts and Reading Lists

> AI tools can generate personalised reading lists and even create customised texts to engage and inspire children. This approach ensures every pupil is met where they currently are in their reading journey, helping to build confidence, comprehension and a love of books.
>
> Many platforms and resources are available to help teachers create customised reading experiences. Some tools are free, offering limited features, while others may require a subscription for full access. A list of recommended options will be included at the end of this chapter.

Every child is unique. While some pupils devour every book they can get their hands on, others may struggle to connect with traditional texts. Personalising reading lists acknowledges the diversity in a classroom and aims to meet pupils where they are in their literacy journey, and one of the most exciting ways artificial intelligence (AI) can revolutionise literacy in the classroom is by tailoring reading experiences to suit individual pupils' needs, interests and abilities.

Creating Reading Lists – AI-Powered Book Recommendations

AI platforms designed for literacy can make personalised reading lists easy to create. For instance, if a pupil mentions liking animals, you could generate a list that includes books such as *Charlotte's Web* by E.B. White or *The Butterfly Lion* by Michael Morpurgo.

For example, I asked AI to "generate a list of 10 recommended books for a Year 3 child who enjoys reading animal books such as Charlotte's Web by E.B. White and The Butterfly Lion by Michael Morpurgo." The response I got was:

> Here's a list of 10 recommended books for a Year 3 child who enjoys animal-themed stories like *Charlotte's Web* by E.B. White and *The Butterfly Lion* by Michael Morpurgo:
>
> 1. The Tale of Despereaux by Kate DiCamillo
>   - The adventurous story of a brave mouse, a princess, and a mission to rescue a kingdom.

DOI: 10.4324/9781003621379-2

2. The Wind in the Willows by Kenneth Grahame
   - A classic tale of friendship and adventure featuring Mole, Rat, Toad, and Badger.
3. Fantastic Mr Fox by Roald Dahl
   - A clever fox outsmarts farmers to provide for his family in this witty and exciting tale.
4. Mrs. Frisby and the Rats of NIMH by Robert C. O'Brien
   - A courageous field mouse seeks the help of intelligent rats to save her home and family.
5. The Sheep-Pig (or *Babe: The Gallant Pig*) by Dick King-Smith
   - The charming story of a pig who learns to herd sheep and wins the hearts of all.
6. The Jungle Book by Rudyard Kipling
   - A collection of stories about Mowgli, a boy raised by wolves, and his adventures in the jungle.
7. Varjak Paw by S.F. Said
   - A mesmerising tale of a cat who must leave home to learn the ways of his ancestors and save his family.
8. The One and Only Ivan by Katherine Applegate
   - A moving story told from the perspective of a gorilla living in captivity who dreams of freedom.
9. Stuart Little by E.B. White
   - Another delightful story by the author of Charlotte's Web, following a small mouse with big adventures.
10. Pax by Sara Pennypacker
    - A touching story about a boy and his fox, separated during wartime but connected by their enduring bond.

Would you like to include these titles in a reading list template or add any additional notes for the Year 3 classroom?

So not only does AI generate the list but it also asks if you would like any additional support on these texts, which is both time-saving for you and fantastic for enhancing the reading experience for a child.

Similarly, for a pupil interested in space, you might ask an AI platform to recommend texts for a child who has read *Look Up!* by Nathan Bryon or *George's Secret Key to the Universe* by Stephen and Lucy Hawking to see what other recommended texts are suggested for this theme, and countless other themes too.

You could start this personalised list by collecting some basic information from your class:

- What are their favourite hobbies or topics?
- Do they prefer adventure stories, mysteries, or funny books?
- Who are their favourite authors or characters?

Input this information into an AI-powered reading platform that generates recommendations. Show pupils how the tool works by creating an example list for a fictional character, such as "A nine-year-old who loves animals and magic." Compare the suggested books with the class's ideas to spark discussion about how AI can match texts to readers.

Once pupils understand how personalised reading works, link it to your current classroom texts. For example, if you're studying *The Lion, the Witch and the Wardrobe* by C.S. Lewis, you can use AI tools to recommend similar fantasy books, such as *The Wizards of Once* by Cressida Cowell or *The Chronicles of Prydain* by Lloyd Alexander. This reinforces thematic connections while broadening pupils' literary horizons.

Customised Texts for Every Reader

Beyond recommending existing books, some AI tools can create personalised texts tailored to individual pupils. Imagine a child who loves dinosaurs but struggles with long paragraphs. With the right AI platform, you could generate a short story about a dinosaur adventure, written in simple sentences with appropriate vocabulary for their level. These customised texts can also include elements that make the child feel directly connected to the story, such as using their name as a character or referencing their favourite activities.

You do need to be specific though. I'd recommend not only inputting the age of the child but also the word length of the story you would like and any specific vocabulary you would like them to use. I asked an AI platform to "write a 200 word story for a 6 year old child about dinosaurs with UK spelling including the nouns 'volcano', 'Spinosaurus' and 'Velociraptor' and also include the adjectives 'massive', 'scary' and 'crimson'."

It made this story:

Dino Trouble

In a land of roaring dinosaurs, a **massive** volcano stood tall, its top glowing with **crimson** lava. Nearby, a **Spinosaurus** waded through a river, its sail-like back glinting in the sunlight. It was the biggest dinosaur in the valley, and most creatures stayed out of its way.

One day, a clever **Velociraptor** spotted the Spinosaurus. The raptor was smaller but very quick, with sharp claws and a curious mind. The **Velociraptor** wanted to find out what made the Spinosaurus so special.

"Why do you always stay near the river?" the raptor asked.

The Spinosaurus smiled. "The river cools me down, and it's full of fish! But beware, the volcano is **scary** today."

Just as the Spinosaurus warned, the ground began to rumble. The **massive** volcano shook, and hot ash puffed into the sky. The raptor froze, staring at the glowing lava spilling down the mountain.

"Quick!" shouted the Spinosaurus. "Follow me!"

The Spinosaurus led the raptor to safety by splashing through the river, the water cooling the fiery danger behind them.

From that day on, the Velociraptor respected the **massive** Spinosaurus and its wise advice. They became the best of friends, exploring their wild, prehistoric world together.

You might also input more specific and wide-ranging topics such as: "Write a story for an 8-year-old about a brave astronaut who loves football and discovers a secret alien match on Mars." The AI can then create a text specifically designed to capture the imagination of that child while ensuring the language and content are suitable.

Once generated, read the AI-generated story aloud and discuss:

- Does the story match the input details?
- What elements make it engaging or fun?
- How could pupils add their own ideas to improve it?

One of the key benefits of personalised texts is how they empower pupils to take ownership of their learning. They can generate their own texts based upon an interest in gymnastics, Minecraft or fairies. When children see their interests and ideas reflected in a story, they become more invested in reading and writing. Encourage pupils to personalise further by:

- Illustrating scenes from the story.
- Adding their own twists or alternative endings.
- Writing a sequel or prequel to the AI-generated story.

In small groups, pupils can work together to create a personalised story. Provide a framework for the story (e.g. "A group of friends discover a secret portal in their school library") and let each pupil contribute a character or plot point. Use an AI tool to combine their ideas into a cohesive text, then refine it as a class. This activity not only fosters creativity but also teaches pupils how to collaborate and edit.

Benefits for Differentiation

Personalised texts and reading lists are particularly valuable in differentiated instruction. AI tools can help you provide:

- Simplified texts for struggling readers, ensuring they can engage with the same themes as their peers.
- Advanced texts or challenges for gifted readers to deepen their learning.
- Culturally relevant texts that reflect diverse backgrounds and experiences.

For instance, if a pupil is learning English as an additional language, AI can simplify a story's vocabulary or structure while retaining its essence. Similarly, if a pupil has a keen interest in science, the tool can generate texts that integrate their interests into literacy activities.

Caution and Consideration

- While AI offers incredible opportunities, it's important to use these tools thoughtfully. Ensure that the content generated is age-appropriate and accurate.
- Always review AI-generated texts before sharing them with pupils, as the output might occasionally include errors or unsuitable language.
- Additionally, remind pupils that AI is a tool to support their learning, not a replacement for their own creativity and effort. Balance activities involving AI with traditional reading and writing tasks to ensure a well-rounded literacy experience.

Recommended Tools

1. ChatGPT (free/paid) – Generates personalised texts and reading lists tailored to pupils' needs.
2. Monsha (free/paid) – AI-powered recommendations and customised reading materials.
3. Perplexity (free/paid) – Provides AI-driven reading suggestions and research support.
4. Appaca (free/paid) – Curates personalised reading lists and educational content.

2 Speech-to-Text

Speech-to-text technology is transforming how children approach literacy. By allowing pupils to dictate their thoughts and have them converted into written text, this tool opens up new ways to engage with language, develop storytelling skills and overcome barriers to traditional writing. Whether it's helping a reluctant writer find their voice or assisting pupils with additional needs, speech-to-text tools can make literacy more inclusive and exciting for everyone.

How Does Speech-to-Text Work?

Speech-to-text tools use voice recognition technology to transcribe spoken words into written text. Many platforms, including those built into devices like tablets and laptops, offer this feature. Tools such as Google Docs' Voice Typing or Microsoft Word's Dictate function are readily available, making it easy for classrooms to integrate this technology into daily activities. Pupils simply speak into a microphone and the software converts their words into text on the screen.

For example, a pupil might say, "Once upon a time, a brave knight found a hidden treasure," and watch as these words appear instantly. The ability to see their spoken ideas transformed into text is both empowering and motivating, especially for those who struggle with handwriting or spelling.

Benefits of Speech-to-Text in the Classroom

1. **Inclusivity:**
   - Speech-to-text provides a way for pupils with physical disabilities, dyslexia or motor challenges to express themselves without the frustration of traditional writing.
   - For pupils learning English as an additional language (EAL), it's a helpful tool to practise pronunciation and build confidence.
2. **Encouraging Reluctant Writers:**
   - Some children may have great ideas but struggle to get them onto paper. Speech-to-text allows them to focus on expressing their thoughts without worrying about spelling or handwriting.

3. **Boosting Creativity:**
   - By removing the mechanics of writing, pupils can let their ideas flow more freely, leading to richer and more imaginative storytelling.
4. **Immediate Feedback:**
   - Many tools offer real-time transcription, allowing pupils to see how their words translate into text. This helps them identify errors in grammar, punctuation, or word choice as they go.

Exploring Speech-to-Text

Introduce pupils to speech-to-text by demonstrating how it works. Choose a simple story prompt such as, "Describe your favourite animal." Speak into the tool and show how it instantly transcribes your words.

Ask pupils to pair up and practise dictating short sentences. Provide prompts like:

- "Tell me about your dream holiday."
- "Describe what you see outside the classroom window."
- "What would be your perfect pet?"

Encourage them to explore different types of sentences, from descriptive to action-packed, and watch their words come to life on the screen.

Using Speech-to-Text for Storytelling

Once pupils are comfortable with the technology, guide them to use speech-to-text for storytelling. Provide a loose framework to help them structure their ideas. For example:

- **Beginning:** Who is your main character? Where are they?
- **Middle:** What problem do they face?
- **End:** How is the problem solved?

Encourage pupils to speak freely, reminding them that they can always edit their story once it's on the screen. Seeing their spoken ideas written down can boost confidence and inspire further creativity.

Ask pupils to create a story using a speech-to-text tool. Provide a prompt such as, "Imagine you find a mysterious key. What does it unlock?" Once they've dictated their story, ask the children to read through the text and identify areas to improve. They can then add punctuation or adjust phrasing where needed. You could also ask them to share their final story with the rest of the class.

Helping with Editing and Revision

Speech-to-text doesn't just assist with the initial writing process; it's also a valuable tool for editing. Pupils can use the tool to:

- Read their text aloud and listen for errors or areas that need improvement.
- Dictate additional details or refine existing sentences.
- Experiment with rephrasing ideas to make their writing stronger.

For instance, a pupil might dictate, "The dog ran fast across the field," but decide to revise it to, "The golden retriever sprinted joyfully through the sunlit meadow."

You could provide pupils with a basic paragraph, either one they've created or a prepared example, then ask them to use speech-to-text to expand the paragraph by adding descriptive details. They can also rearrange sentences to improve clarity or flow and also replace simple words with more vivid vocabulary.

At the end of any lesson using speech-to-text, ask your class what they enjoyed about using speech-to-text, and how did it help them express their ideas. Encourage them to think about when they might use speech-to-text in the future, whether for creative writing, school projects or even just getting down some ideas.

By incorporating speech-to-text technology into the classroom, you can unlock new ways for your pupils to connect with language and express themselves. This tool is particularly valuable for those who find traditional writing tasks daunting, offering a bridge between spoken ideas and the written word. When used thoughtfully, speech-to-text can inspire confidence, boost creativity and make literacy accessible to all.

Caution and Consideration

While speech-to-text is a powerful tool, it's not without its challenges. For example:

- Accuracy: The tool may struggle with strong accents or misinterpret words. Encourage pupils to speak clearly and at a steady pace.
- Over-reliance: Remind pupils that this is a support tool, not a replacement for traditional writing. Balance speech-to-text activities with handwriting and typing tasks.
- Technical Issues: Ensure devices are properly set up and tested before use. Having a backup plan for when technology fails is always wise.

Recommended Tools

1. Google Docs Voice Typing
   - Found under Tools > Voice Typing in Google Docs. It's free, easy to use and works in real time.
2. Microsoft Word Dictate
   - Available in Microsoft 365. You can find the Dictate button on the toolbar.
3. Built-in Device Features
   - iOS (Apple): The microphone icon on the keyboard activates dictation.
   - Android: The Google voice typing feature allows easy transcription.
4. Dedicated Apps
   - Otter.ai: Ideal for transcribing long conversations or lessons. (There's a free trial on this but then it is subscription based.)
   - Dragon NaturallySpeaking: A premium tool with advanced accuracy and features which is not free, but there is a free trial of the Dragon Anywhere dictation app for iOS and Android.

3 Phonics

> Phonics is a cornerstone of literacy instruction in primary schools. It equips children with the skills to decode words, recognise letter-sound relationships and develop confidence in reading and spelling. With artificial intelligence (AI), phonics teaching can be personalised, interactive and engaging, helping every child work towards success on their literacy journey. In this chapter we'll explore some practical, workable ideas in using AI to help with the teaching and learning of phonics.

The Importance of Phonics

Phonics has its roots in the ancient Phoenician alphabet, one of the earliest systems to link symbols with sounds. The Phoenicians had created something revolutionary because for the first time in human history any language could be written down according to sound. This phonetic approach laid the foundation for modern alphabets and the teaching of letter-sound relationships.

Phonics in primary schools focuses on teaching children how to connect sounds (phonemes) with letters or groups of letters (graphemes) and blend them to read and write words. For example, understanding that the letters "ch" produce the sound in "chat" or that "e" at the end of "hop" changes the vowel sound to make "hope."

Phonics instruction helps children to develop decoding skills to read unfamiliar words, builds a foundation for spelling and also improves fluency and comprehension.

AI can enhance phonics teaching by providing personalised activities, instant feedback and engaging ways to practise, which we will explore throughout this chapter. This technology ensures that pupils progress at their own pace, reinforcing their strengths and addressing gaps in understanding.

Exploring AI Phonics Tools

Introduce pupils to an AI phonics tool. Websites like ChatGPT can support your phonics teaching by generating resources, adapting materials and offering tailored advice, but do not have audio prompts. Read Naturally's Phonics Sounds, Kumon's Phonics Practice and Teach

Your Monster's digital flashcards all do offer audio prompts. Demonstrate these features to children by showing them how the tool provides these audio prompts for a sound, such as "sh," and asks pupils to identify or build words that include it. Let pupils take turns using the tool to practise specific sounds, blending skills or tricky words.

Using AI to Personalise Phonics Instruction

AI tools can analyse a pupil's performance and identify areas where they need more practice. For instance, if a child struggles with digraphs like "ch" or "sh," you can ask the tool to provide extra activities focused on those sounds. For example, I asked an AI website to "provide 5 extra activities for a five year old child who struggles with the digraphs 'ch' or 'sh'." It said:

> Here are 5 engaging activities designed to help a five-year-old child who struggles with the digraphs "ch" and "sh":
>
> ### 1. Digraph Detective
>
> **Materials:** Flashcards with pictures and words (e.g. chair, ship, cheese, shell).
> **Instructions:**
>
> - Spread out the cards on a table or floor.
> - Say a word containing "ch" or "sh" (e.g. "chair").
> - Ask the child to find the matching picture or word card.
> - Celebrate when they find the right card and emphasise the digraph sound: "Ch-air, chair!"
>
> **Variation:** Include non-digraph cards to increase the challenge.
>
> ### 2. Digraph Hopscotch
>
> **Materials:** Outdoor chalk or masking tape for indoors.
> **Instructions:**
>
> - Draw a hopscotch grid with "ch" and "sh" written in different squares alongside simple words (e.g. chip, shop, chat, ship).
> - Call out a word, and the child hops to the square with the corresponding digraph or word.
> - Once they land, have them say the word aloud, emphasising the digraph sound.
>
> ### 3. Digraph Sorting Game
>
> **Materials:** Two boxes or baskets labelled "ch" and "sh" and small objects or pictures (e.g. chalk, shoe, chair, shell).
> **Instructions:**
>
> - Mix the items in a pile.
> - Ask the child to sort them into the correct box based on whether they start with "ch" or "sh."
> - Reinforce by having the child say each word as they sort.

4. Silly Digraph Sentences

Materials: None.
Instructions:

- Create silly sentences using words with "ch" and "sh." For example, "The chicken ate chocolate on a chair" or "The shark wore shiny shoes."
- Say the sentences aloud together, exaggerating the digraph sounds.
- Encourage the child to come up with their own silly sentences.

5. Digraph Fishing

Materials: Paper fish with "ch" and "sh" words written on them, a fishing net (or DIY using string and a paperclip).
Instructions:

- Scatter the paper fish on the floor or in a container.
- Have the child fish for words with the rod.
- When they catch a fish, they read the word aloud, emphasising the digraph sound.
- Bonus: Let them "release" the fish into a "ch pond" or "sh pond" based on the digraph.

These activities combine movement, hands-on learning, and auditory reinforcement to make practising digraphs fun and engaging! Let me know if you'd like further ideas.

Similarly, if a pupil is excelling, the tool can introduce more advanced phonics patterns to keep them challenged.

Integrating AI into Phonics Lessons

AI can also be seamlessly integrated into daily phonics instruction. Here are some examples:

- **Blending Practice:** Use AI to provide blending exercises, such as combining "str" and "eet" to form "street."
- **Sound Recognition:** Pupils listen to a sound and select the correct grapheme from multiple choices.
- **Tricky Words:** Practise recognising and spelling tricky words like "one," "would," or "said."
- **Assessments:** AI tools can administer quick phonics quizzes, providing immediate feedback and tracking pupil progress.

Creating Words

Provide pupils with a list of phonemes, such as "sh," "ch," "ai," and "igh." Use an AI tool to help them build words using these sounds. For instance:

- "sh" + "ark" = "shark"
- "ch" + "est" = "chest"

Ask pupils to create their own sentences using the words they've built, reinforcing their understanding of phonics and vocabulary.

One of the benefits of AI phonics tools is that they enable independent practice. Set up phonics stations where pupils can work on specific activities, such as listening to sounds and matching them to the correct letters using audio prompts. There are online interactive phonics games on AI websites that offer this (a list is provided at the end of the chapter).

Encourage pupils to set personal goals, such as mastering a certain number of sounds or words within a week. Celebrate their achievements to keep them motivated.

Creating Personalised Phonics Stories

Use an AI platform to generate short stories that incorporate specific phonics patterns. For example, if the class is learning about the "ai" sound, input a prompt like: "Write a 100 word story for a Year 1 pupil using the words 'rain,' 'train,' and 'pain'."

Read the story aloud and ask pupils to identify and highlight the target sounds. Then, encourage them to write their own short story or sentence using the same phonics pattern.

I tried this with ChatGPT and it created the following:

> **The Rainy Train Ride**
>
> Lily loved riding the train, even when it rained. One stormy afternoon, raindrops tapped on the windows as the train chugged through the countryside.
>
> "Look at the rainbow!" Lily shouted, pointing out of the window. It stretched across the sky like magic.
>
> But then, the train jolted. "Ouch!" Lily cried as she bumped her knee. "What a pain!"
>
> The kind conductor came by. "Don't worry, little one," he said, handing her a plaster and a smile.
>
> Soon, Lily was happy again, watching the rain and dreaming of riding the train all the way to the rainbow.

Caution and Consideration

- While AI tools are highly effective, they may occasionally misinterpret input or provide content that needs adjustment.
- Always review activities and outputs before presenting them to pupils.
- Additionally, balance AI-based activities with hands-on phonics instruction to ensure pupils are engaging with a variety of learning methods.

Recommended Tools

1. Teach Your Monster to Read - An interactive game where children create a monster and take it on adventures while practising phonics skills. (Free to play online)
2. Reading Eggs - A comprehensive platform that includes phonics lessons, games and assessments tailored to individual progress. (30-day free access)
3. Phonics Hero - A structured program with engaging activities focusing on blending, segmenting, and tricky words. (Six-month recurring subscription of £29.99)
4. Read Naturally's Phonics Sounds - This comprehensive collection provides audio examples of various phonics sounds, aiding in correct pronunciation and phonemic awareness. (While the full Read Naturally program is not free, they do offer a collection of free phonics sounds and audio examples on their website, which can be used to support phonics teaching without purchasing the full program; additionally, Read Naturally provides a free phonics assessment tool called "Signs for Sounds" to help identify students who might need phonics intervention.)
5. Kumon's Phonics Practice - Kumon offers printable phonics charts accompanied by MP3 audio files, covering alphabet sounds, consonant combinations, vowel combinations and more. (Free to download or print)

4 Interactive Storytelling

Interactive storytelling is a dynamic way to engage pupils in literacy, combining the imaginative world of narrative with technology's interactive possibilities. Through AI tools and digital platforms, we can inspire creativity, improve comprehension and foster a deeper connection to stories. In this chapter, we'll explore some practical ways to implement interactive storytelling in the classroom.

What Is Interactive Storytelling?

Interactive storytelling allows pupils to shape the narrative, make decisions for characters or even create their own stories with the help of digital tools. This approach gives children agency in the storytelling process, making it more immersive and personal. Instead of passively reading, pupils actively participate in crafting the story's direction.

For example, an AI-powered platform might ask a pupil to decide, "Does the hero enter the cave or climb the mountain?" The story unfolds based on their choice, providing a unique experience every time. This process encourages critical thinking, creativity, and engagement, as children feel a sense of ownership over the narrative.

The Benefits of Interactive Storytelling

1. **Fostering Creativity:** Pupils develop their imagination by creating characters, settings and plot twists.
2. **Improving Comprehension:** Actively engaging with the story helps pupils understand narrative structure and character development.
3. **Enhancing Decision-Making Skills:** Choosing paths or outcomes teaches pupils to evaluate options and consider consequences.
4. **Supporting Reluctant Writers:** Interactive formats lower the pressure of traditional writing tasks, making storytelling accessible and fun.
5. **Building Collaboration:** Group activities in interactive storytelling encourage teamwork and communication.

Create a Collaborative Adventure Story

Begin by introducing pupils to an interactive storytelling tool like Twine or ChatGPT. Explain that they will work together to create a story where the class decides what happens at key moments.

1. Start with a simple prompt: "You are exploring a mysterious forest and find a hidden door in a tree. Do you open it or keep walking?"
2. Divide pupils into small groups and assign each group a different branch of the story to develop.
3. Use the AI tool to weave the branches together, creating a cohesive adventure.
4. Read the final story aloud as a class, celebrating the collective creativity.

Here's an example I made using ChatGPT. I typed, "Let's make a story... 'You are exploring a mysterious forest and find a hidden door in a tree. Do you open it or keep walking?' I open the door. What happens next?"

Its response was:

> You push the hidden door gently, and it creaks open to reveal a swirling, golden mist. As you step through, the air feels warmer, like stepping into a dream. The mist clears, and you find yourself in a glowing glade, filled with enormous flowers as tall as trees. The petals shimmer with colours you've never seen before, and their sweet scent fills the air.
>
> In the centre of the glade stands a peculiar figure: a talking fox wearing a tiny satchel across its chest. The fox bows and says, "Welcome, brave traveller. Only those with curious hearts may enter this realm. You've unlocked the Door of Whimsy."
>
> Before you can reply, the fox opens its satchel and pulls out a map. "There is much to explore," it says. "This map shows treasures hidden deep within this forest, but beware – each treasure is guarded by a riddle or a challenge. Do you seek the treasure, or do you wish to return to your world?"
>
> What will you do next? Do you take the map and embark on the quest, or ask the fox for more details about this magical place?

I would then expand this story as far as I wanted to.

Writing with Prompts

AI tools like ChatGPT can generate prompts to spark ideas. For example, ask the AI to: "Write a story where a magical animal helps a child solve a big problem." Pupils can use the prompt to begin their stories, then return to the AI for guidance or inspiration if they get stuck. For example:

> Prompt: *Write a story about a time-travelling robot who visits ancient Egypt.*
> Generated Story Opening: *Zara the robot's gears whirred as she stepped out of her time machine into the sandy streets of ancient Egypt. The Great Pyramid loomed in the distance, and she couldn't wait to explore. But first, she needed to help a young scribe find his lost scroll.*

Encourage pupils to continue the story, adding their own twists and turns.

Digital Storybooks

Use a platform like Book Creator to help pupils design interactive storybooks. They can write the text for each page, add illustrations or photographs and record their voices narrating the story. This activity allows pupils to combine writing, art, and technology, resulting in a finished product they can share with classmates and family.

Interactive Group Storytelling

1. Start with a class-wide brainstorming session to create characters, setting and a central conflict.
2. Assign each group a specific part of the story: beginning, middle, or end.
3. Use an AI tool to help refine each section or suggest ideas for transitions.
4. Combine the parts into a single narrative and perform it as a class, with pupils acting out scenes or narrating the story.

Encouraging Personalisation

Interactive storytelling tools often allow for personalisation, which makes the experience more engaging. Encourage pupils to:

- Include their names or favourite hobbies in the story.
- Base characters on themselves or their friends.
- Create settings inspired by places they love or dream about visiting.

Caution and Consideration

While interactive storytelling tools are powerful, it's essential to use them thoughtfully:

- Age Appropriateness: Ensure the prompts and content are suitable for the pupils' age group.
- Privacy: Use platforms that comply with data protection regulations and avoid storing sensitive information.
- Balance: Combine digital storytelling with traditional methods to provide a well-rounded literacy experience.

Recommended Tools

1. Twine – A free tool for creating interactive, choose-your-own-adventure stories. (completely free)
2. ChatGPT – An AI tool that can act as a dynamic storyteller, allowing pupils to contribute ideas and guide the narrative. (free with basic features and you get more features with a paid subscription)
3. Storybird – A platform that combines storytelling with artwork to inspire creativity. (There are both free and paid options for storytelling.)
4. Book Creator – A digital book-making tool where pupils can write, illustrate, and narrate their stories. (Teachers can create one library for free with up to 40 books, accessible to an unlimited number of pupils.)
5. Night Zookeeper – An engaging platform where pupils create stories about fantastical creatures in a magical zoo. (A seven-day free trial is available for new users.)

5 Reading Fluency

Reading fluency is a vital skill that bridges the gap between decoding words and comprehending text. It enables pupils to read smoothly, accurately, and with expression, making the experience of reading more enjoyable and meaningful. By incorporating artificial intelligence (AI) into teaching strategies, educators can provide personalised support, track progress, and create engaging ways to practise fluency.

What Is Reading Fluency?

Reading fluency encompasses three main components:

1. **Accuracy**: Reading words correctly without mispronunciations or errors.
2. **Rate**: Reading at an appropriate speed for the level of the text.
3. **Expression**: Using intonation, pauses, and emphasis to convey meaning and engage listeners.

Fluency is essential for comprehension. When pupils read fluently, they can focus on understanding the text rather than decoding individual words. This chapter explores how free AI tools can support fluency development and practical activities for the classroom.

Why Focus on Reading Fluency?

Fluency is often a challenge for early readers and those who struggle with confidence or literacy skills. Pupils who read fluently are more likely to:

- Understand and enjoy what they read.
- Build vocabulary and general knowledge.
- Develop a positive attitude toward reading.

Free AI tools provide a unique opportunity to practise fluency in a supportive, non-judgemental environment, allowing pupils to progress at their own pace.

Recording and Reflecting

Introduce pupils to a tool like Google Docs Voice Typing or Microsoft Immersive Reader. Have them:

1. Choose a passage to read aloud.
2. Record themselves reading the passage using the tool.
3. Listen to the recording and reflect on their pace, accuracy, and expression.

Encourage pupils to consider:

- How well they matched the tone of the passage.
- Whether they read at a comfortable and appropriate speed.
- What they would like to improve for their next attempt.

Echo Reading

Echo reading involves the teacher or AI tool reading a sentence or short passage aloud, and the pupil repeating it back with the same expression and pace. This activity helps pupils internalise proper phrasing and intonation.

For example:

1. Read a sentence aloud with expression: "The little bird chirped happily in the bright morning sun."
2. Have the pupil repeat the sentence, mirroring your tone and emphasis.

Pair this with a resource like Storyline Online for professional examples of expressive reading.

Building Fluency through Repeated Reading

Repeated reading is a proven method for improving fluency. By reading the same passage multiple times, pupils become more familiar with the text, allowing them to focus on pace and expression.

You could try this:

1. Select a short, engaging passage.
2. Time the pupil as they read it aloud the first time.
3. Have them practise reading the passage two or three more times, aiming to improve their speed and accuracy with each attempt.
4. Record their final attempt and celebrate their progress.

It's important to distinguish between speed and fluency. Fluency isn't just reading fast, it is reading at a pace that feels comfortable. The passage that you read could include a mixture of familiar and unfamiliar words. You could try and use a child's area of interest for the familiar and relevant vocabulary related to a topic you are studying. I created a passage using ChatGPT. This was the prompt: "Write a short passage with a Minecraft theme. Include the vocabulary 'energy', 'wildly', 'friction' and 'source'."

This was the response:

> Steve sprinted through the dense jungle, his pickaxe swinging **wildly** as he cleared a path. He needed to reach the lava pool before nightfall – his only **source** of energy to smelt the iron ore he'd gathered earlier. As he descended into the cave, the air grew cooler, and he felt the **friction** of his boots against the rocky floor. Finally, the glowing pool came into view, bubbling and hissing like a living thing. He quickly built a furnace, feeding it coal and watching the flames dance with renewed **energy**. The hiss of the lava reminded him to hurry – creepers weren't far behind.

Using AI for Feedback and Support

Free AI tools can provide helpful feedback and guidance. For example:

- **Pronunciation Practice**: Microsoft Immersive Reader highlights words as it reads them aloud, allowing pupils to follow along and practise.
- **Expression Inspiration**: Storyline Online offers examples of expressive reading for pupils to emulate.
- **Text Adaptation**: ChatGPT can simplify or adjust the difficulty of a passage to match a pupil's level.

Fluency Games

Make fluency practice fun by incorporating games. For example:

- **Fluency Dice**: Roll a die to determine how to read a passage (e.g. in a whisper, with excitement, or like a robot).
- **Expression Cards**: Draw a card that describes a tone or mood (e.g. happy, sad, angry) and read the passage accordingly.
- **Fluency Relay**: In groups, pupils take turns reading one sentence at a time, aiming for smooth transitions and consistent expression.

You can ask your chosen AI platform to create more games similar to these examples. These can be made bespoke to your own particular class too.

Caution and Consideration

When using AI tools for fluency practice, keep the following in mind:

- Accessibility: Ensure tools are user-friendly and suitable for the pupils' age and ability levels.
- Privacy: Use platforms that comply with data protection regulations and avoid storing sensitive information about pupils.
- Balance: Combine AI-based activities with teacher-led and peer-to-peer practice to provide a well-rounded experience.

Recommended Tools

1. ChatGPT (free version) - While primarily a text-based tool, ChatGPT can engage pupils in interactive reading and comprehension activities by generating customised passages and questions.
2. Google Docs Voice Typing - A built-in, free tool that allows pupils to read aloud while transcribing their words, helping them practise fluency and self-monitor errors.
3. Microsoft Immersive Reader - A free tool integrated into many Microsoft apps, offering text-to-speech features and visual aids to improve reading fluency and comprehension.
4. Storyline Online - A platform where professional actors read children's books aloud. Pupils can listen and practise mimicking the expression and pacing.
5. ReadWorks - Offers free reading passages with accompanying questions to support fluency and comprehension practice.

6 Virtual Reading Buddies

Virtual reading buddies are a creative and interactive way to enhance pupils' literacy skills. By pairing children with AI-driven reading companions, we can provide a supportive, engaging environment for reading practice. These tools offer instant feedback, encouragement and opportunities for independent learning, making them a valuable resource in the classroom.

What Are Virtual Reading Buddies?

Virtual reading buddies are AI-based tools designed to simulate a reading partner. These companions read along with pupils, listen to them read aloud and offer guidance to improve accuracy, fluency and comprehension. Pupils can interact with these tools in a safe, pressure-free setting, which helps build confidence and motivation.

Examples include AI apps like ChatGPT, which can generate reading prompts and respond to questions, and specialised platforms like Microsoft Immersive Reader or Google Read Along, which provide audio feedback and personalised support.

Why Use Virtual Reading Buddies?

Reading buddies create a dynamic learning experience, offering benefits such as:

- **Individualised Attention:** Pupils receive personalised feedback tailored to their reading level.
- **Increased Engagement:** Interactive elements make reading fun and encourage active participation.
- **Confidence Building:** Pupils can practise without fear of judgement, fostering a positive attitude toward reading.
- **Flexible Learning:** Virtual buddies are available anytime, allowing pupils to practise at their own pace.

How Virtual Reading Buddies Work

Most virtual reading buddies function by:

1. Listening to the pupil read aloud.
2. Offering corrections for mispronunciations or missed words.
3. Providing encouragement and celebrating achievements.
4. Suggesting vocabulary or comprehension questions to deepen understanding.

These tools often include additional features like highlighting text as it's read, recording progress, and offering recommendations for future practice.

Meet Your Virtual Buddy

Introduce pupils to a virtual reading buddy platform such as Google Read Along. You can guide them through the following process:

1. Open the app and select a story or passage to read.
2. Begin reading aloud while the virtual buddy listens.
3. Respond to feedback, such as correcting a mispronounced word or answering a comprehension question.

Encourage pupils to explore the platform independently and share their thoughts about the experience.

Virtual reading buddies are especially effective for improving fluency. Pupils can practise reading aloud with immediate feedback on their pace, accuracy and expression.

Building Comprehension with Virtual Buddies

Many virtual buddies integrate comprehension questions into the reading experience, helping pupils engage more deeply with the text. For example:

- After reading a paragraph, the buddy might ask, "What do you think will happen next?" or "What did this character do?" or "Where did they go first?"
- Pupils can respond aloud or type their answers, encouraging critical thinking.

Virtual reading buddies often include gamified elements to keep pupils engaged. For example:

- Earning badges for completing stories.
- Unlocking new levels by achieving reading goals.
- Participating in mini-games that reinforce vocabulary and comprehension.

You could set up a classroom competition where the pupils complete reading challenges with their virtual buddies and earn points for achievements like fluency improvements or answering comprehension questions. You can celebrate their progress with certificates or small prizes.

Encouraging Independent Practice

Virtual buddies empower pupils to practise reading outside of structured lessons. Therefore, you could encourage pupils to choose stories they find interesting and read them with their buddy at home. In doing this the children can set personal goals, such as reading a certain number of pages or mastering tricky words. You could give the children opportunities to share their experiences with the class, fostering a sense of accomplishment.

Have your pupils record their daily reading sessions with their virtual buddy. Note what they enjoyed, what they found challenging and how they improved, in order to reflect on their progress at the end of the week.

Using AI for Personalised Feedback

Virtual reading buddies use AI to adapt to each pupil's needs, offering:

- **Pronunciation Support:** Correcting errors and modelling accurate sounds.
- **Pacing Guidance:** Highlighting whether the pupil is reading too quickly or slowly.
- **Expression Tips:** Encouraging pupils to add emotion and emphasis to their reading.

Personalised Story Adventures

Ask pupils to use a virtual buddy like ChatGPT to create a customised story. For example, the prompt I used was: "Write a story about a brave fox who saves a village, and include the words 'forest', 'courage', and 'celebration'."

This was the response I was given:

The Brave Fox

Deep in the heart of the **forest**, a small village of woodland creatures thrived. But one fateful day, dark smoke billowed through the trees, and the villagers discovered that a fire was spreading rapidly toward their homes.

The animals panicked, unsure of what to do. "We need help!" cried a squirrel. But no one dared to face the roaring flames – no one, except Felix, the fox.

With boundless **courage**, Felix leapt into action. He raced through the woods, his keen nose guiding him to the river. Grabbing a large hollow log, he pushed it into the water, creating a makeshift channel. He then dug trenches with his swift paws, diverting the river toward the fire.

The water gushed through the dry brush, dousing the flames just as they reached the village. Felix, though exhausted and singed, stood proudly as the villagers cheered.

"You've saved us, Felix!" the owl declared, spreading his wings in gratitude.

That evening, the animals gathered in a joyful **celebration**. Lanterns glowed, music filled the air, and Felix was crowned the hero of the forest. Though he felt shy from all the attention, Felix knew that his bravery had made a difference – and that courage could always conquer fear.

The children could read the story aloud with their buddy, practising fluency and expression. They could then discuss how the story's elements made reading enjoyable.

After a session with virtual reading buddies, encourage pupils to reflect on their experience:

- What did you enjoy most about reading with your buddy?
- How did the buddy's feedback help you improve?
- What would you like to read with your buddy next?

Caution and Consideration

While virtual reading buddies offer valuable support, it's important to:

- Monitor Usage: Ensure pupils are using the tools correctly and staying on task.
- Balance Activities: Combine virtual buddy sessions with teacher-led and peer-to-peer reading to provide a comprehensive learning experience.
- Protect Privacy: Choose platforms that comply with data protection regulations and safeguard pupil information.

Recommended Tools

1. Google Read Along (free) – A child-friendly app that listens to pupils read aloud and provides real-time feedback.
2. ChatGPT (free version) – Generates customised stories and reading prompts for pupils to practise with.
3. Microsoft Immersive Reader (free) – Offers text-to-speech and highlighting features to support fluency and comprehension.
4. Storyline Online (free) – Features videos of actors reading children's books aloud, providing excellent examples of expressive reading.
5. ReadWorks (free) – Provides a library of passages and comprehension questions to support reading practice.

7 Reading Games

> Reading games are a powerful way to make literacy lessons engaging, interactive, and effective. By incorporating play into learning, teachers can foster a love of reading while helping pupils develop essential skills such as fluency, comprehension, and vocabulary. This chapter explores how to use AI-driven and traditional reading games in the classroom, offering practical ideas and strategies to enhance primary literacy.

What Are Reading Games?

Reading games are activities designed to make reading practice fun and interactive. They can be digital or physical, competitive or collaborative, and tailored to suit different reading levels and interests. AI-powered reading games, in particular, offer personalised experiences that adapt to each pupil's abilities, providing instant feedback and challenges that keep the children motivated.

Examples of reading games include:

- **Digital Platforms:** Apps like Reading Eggs, Teach Your Monster to Read and Kahoot!
- **AI Tools:** ChatGPT for creating customised word puzzles or interactive story adventures.
- **Classroom Activities:** Traditional games like word bingo, scavenger hunts, or role-playing story characters.

Why Use Reading Games?

Reading games offer a range of benefits for primary pupils such as increased motivation, as games can make learning feel like play, encouraging reluctant readers to participate. The interactive elements can also keep pupils focused and involved in the learning process. To reinforce the learning, the games provide opportunities to practise decoding, fluency and comprehension in a low-pressure environment. Also, many games encourage collaboration and communication, helping pupils learn from one another.

How to Use Reading Games in the Classroom

You could set up a "Reading Game Day" where pupils rotate through different digital games. For example, one group could play Teach Your Monster to Read, while another completes a Kahoot! quiz. (A list of recommended platforms is at the end of the chapter.)

After the session, discuss with the children what they learned and which games they enjoyed most.

1. AI-Generated Word Games

AI tools like ChatGPT can create customised word games to reinforce vocabulary and spelling. For example:

- **Word Scrambles:** Ask ChatGPT to generate a list of scrambled words related to a recent topic. Pupils unscramble the words and use them in sentences.
- **Crossword Puzzles:** Request a crossword puzzle with clues based on a story or theme. This encourages critical thinking and vocabulary recall.
- **Rhyming Challenges:** Use AI to create a list of rhyming words and challenge pupils to write a short poem or song.

Example Prompt for ChatGPT: "Create a word scramble with 10 words related to space exploration, suitable for Year 3 pupils."

ChatGPT Response:

1. TRSAS (STARS)
2. NPLATE (PLANET)
3. COKERT (ROCKET)
4. NOOM (MOON)
5. LAGAXY (GALAXY)
6. TRAOSNUAT (ASTRONAUT)
7. CESPA (SPACE)
8. ENUSV (VENUS)
9. RSAM (MARS)
10. LEOTCESEP (TELESCOPE)

2. Story-Based Role-Playing Games

Role-playing games allow pupils to step into the shoes of characters from a story, deepening their understanding and engagement.

- **Character Interviews:** Pupils take turns playing a character from a book while their classmates ask questions. For example, "Why did you decide to help the villagers, Felix the Fox?"
- **Story Retelling:** Use props and costumes to act out key scenes from a story. This helps pupils practise sequencing and comprehension.
- **Choose-Your-Own-Adventure:** Use ChatGPT to create an interactive story where pupils make decisions that affect the outcome.

Example Prompt for ChatGPT: "Write a short choose your own adventure story about a pirate searching for treasure, with three possible endings."

ChatGPT Response:

The Pirate's Quest for Treasure

You are Captain Flynn, sailing to Skull Isle in search of **The Emerald Crown**. As you step onto the beach, you spot a dark **cave** and an old **map** buried nearby.

- **Enter the Cave** → [Go to Path A]
- **Follow the Map** → [Go to Path B]

Path A: The Cave of Whispers
Inside, glowing symbols light up. A **ghostly pirate** appears, warning you to turn back.

- **Challenge the Ghost** → [Go to Ending 1]
- **Offer to Share the Treasure** → [Go to Ending 2]

Path B: The Map's Secret
The map leads you to a **stone serpent** with a hidden chest. Just as you open it, **rival pirates** appear!

- **Fight Them** → [Go to Ending 1]
- **Share the Treasure** → [Go to Ending 2]
- **Run With the Treasure** → [Go to Ending 3]

Ending 1: The Curse of the Crown
You defeat your enemy, but as soon as you claim the **Emerald Crown**, a storm rises. The sea swallows your ship - you are now cursed to sail forever!

Ending 2: A Pirate's Pact
Instead of fighting, you **share the treasure**. The ghost vanishes, the pirates shake hands, and you all **leave richer than before**.

Ending 3: Escape to the Sea
You **grab the chest and run**, barely reaching your ship. You've won the treasure - but now, every pirate wants it too!

3. Classroom Reading Challenges

Turn reading into a game by setting up challenges with rewards and milestones.

- **Reading Bingo:** Create bingo cards with reading tasks like "Read a poem," "Find a word with three syllables," or "Read a story to a friend." The first pupil to complete a row wins a prize.
- **Book Quest:** Hide books around the classroom or school with clues leading to each one. Pupils solve the clues to find the books and read them aloud.
- **Reading Olympics:** Set up a series of reading-related challenges, such as speed reading, dramatic readings, or creating a book trailer. Award medals for participation and achievement.

4. Fluency Jenga

A fun way to practise reading aloud with expression. Write different reading challenges on Jenga blocks (e.g. "Read this sentence in a whisper," "Read like a robot," "Use your best witch voice," etc.). Pupils then take turns pulling out a block, reading a sentence using the challenge and placing it back on the tower. This game makes fluency practice exciting and encourages expressive reading.

5. Speedy Synonyms and Antonyms

Write words on index cards and place them in two piles. One pile contains words; the other contains either synonyms or antonyms. Pupils race against the clock to match words correctly. Then encourage pupils to use AI tools like ChatGPT or DeepSeek to find additional synonyms and antonyms.

Caution and Consideration

While reading games are a valuable tool, it's important to:

- Monitor Screen Time: Balance digital games with offline activities to ensure a well-rounded learning experience.
- Adapt to Abilities: Choose games that match each pupil's reading level to avoid frustration or boredom.
- Encourage Reflection: After playing a game, ask pupils to reflect on what they learned and how they can apply it to their reading.

Recommended Tools

1. Teach Your Monster to Read (free) - A phonics adventure game for early readers.
2. Read Theory (free) - AI-driven comprehension games tailored to individual reading levels.
3. Epic! (free plan for teachers called Epic School) - Digital books with interactive quizzes and challenges.
4. Wordwall (offers a free plan) - Customisable vocabulary and comprehension games.
5. Storybird (free access to limited amount of content) - Interactive storytelling challenges that encourage creative writing.

8 Audiobooks

> Audiobooks are a versatile and powerful tool for enhancing primary literacy. They provide an accessible way for pupils to engage with stories, improve listening skills, and develop a love for literature. This chapter explores how teachers can use audiobooks in the classroom, offering practical strategies and ideas to support reading fluency, comprehension, and enjoyment.

Why Use Audiobooks?

Audiobooks offer numerous benefits for primary pupils including fluency development. As skilled narrators read aloud this helps pupils understand pacing, expression and pronunciation. The expressive narration and sound effects bring the stories to life, which can capture pupils' attention and imagination. Pupils can listen to audiobooks while following along with the text, reinforcing word recognition and comprehension.

Audiobooks also provide an alternative way to access stories for struggling readers or those with learning difficulties. They can allow pupils to focus on understanding the story without the added challenge of decoding text.

How to Use Audiobooks in the Classroom

1. Independent Listening Stations

Set up a listening station in your classroom where pupils can enjoy audiobooks independently or in small groups.

- **Headphones and Devices:** Provide headphones and tablets or MP3 players loaded with audiobooks. This can be especially useful for wet playtimes or even to offer children a "time out" if they require one.
- **Activity Sheets:** Create worksheets with questions or activities related to the audiobook, such as drawing a scene or writing a summary. These can be created using ChatGPT or DeepSeek etc.
- **Choice and Variety:** Offer a range of audiobooks to cater to different interests and reading levels.

DOI: 10.4324/9781003621379-9

2. Audiobooks for Struggling Readers

Audiobooks are particularly beneficial for pupils who find reading challenging. They provide a way to access age-appropriate content without the frustration of decoding difficult text.

- **Paired Reading:** Pair an audiobook with a physical copy of the book. Pupils can listen while following the text, building confidence and fluency.
- **Vocabulary Support:** Use audiobooks to introduce new vocabulary in context. Pause the recording to discuss the meaning of unfamiliar words.
- **Confidence Building:** Allow struggling readers to listen to a story multiple times before reading it independently.

3. Audiobooks for Home Learning

Encourage pupils to listen to audiobooks at home as part of their reading routine.

- **Family Listening:** Suggest audiobooks that the whole family can enjoy together. You could send a "listening list" home of recommended audiobooks using the platforms suggested at the end of this chapter.
- **Reading Logs:** Ask pupils to keep a log of the audiobooks they listen to, including the title, author and their thoughts about the story.
- **Discussion Prompts:** Provide questions for pupils to discuss with their families, such as "What was your favourite part of the story?" or "Would you recommend this book to a friend?"

4. Create a Class Audiobook

Encourage pupils to record their own audiobook version of a favourite story or class text:

1. Assign roles for narration and character voices.
2. Practise fluency, expression and pronunciation.
3. Record using free audio software (e.g. Audacity, Voice Recorder apps).
4. Share the final audiobook with the class, another class in school, or their families.

Building Comprehension with Audiobooks

Audiobooks can be used to develop comprehension skills in a fun and engaging way.

- **Predictions:** Pause the audiobook at key moments and ask pupils to predict what will happen next.
- **Character Analysis:** Discuss the characters' traits, motivations, and actions. Ask pupils to compare themselves to a character or describe how they would react in a similar situation.
- **Setting and Plot:** Use audiobooks to explore the setting and plot. Ask pupils to draw a map of the story's world or create a timeline of events.
- **Compare Text vs. Audio:** Discuss differences between reading the book and hearing it aloud.

Using Audiobooks to Model Expressive Reading

Audiobooks are an excellent way to model fluent and expressive reading.

- **Read-Aloud Practice:** Play an audiobook and ask pupils to mimic the narrator's tone, pace and expression.
- **Role-Playing:** Assign pupils roles from the story and have them read their lines with the same expression as the audiobook narrator.
- **Recording Comparisons:** Record pupils reading a passage from a book and compare it to the audiobook version. Discuss how they can improve their fluency and expression.

Integrating Audiobooks with Writing

Audiobooks can inspire creative writing activities.

- **Story Extensions:** Ask pupils to write a new chapter or alternative ending for the story they listened to.
- **Character Diaries:** Have pupils write a diary entry from the perspective of a character in the audiobook.
- **Book Reviews:** Encourage pupils to write a review of the audiobook, including what they liked, disliked, and would recommend to others.

Example Prompt: "After listening to *The Twits* by Roald Dahl, ask pupils to write a diary entry from Mrs. Twit's perspective, describing her plans to play a trick on Mr. Twit."

Caution and Consideration

While audiobooks are a valuable resource, it's important to:

- Balance Formats: Use audiobooks alongside physical books to ensure pupils continue to develop their reading skills.
- Monitor Content: Choose age-appropriate audiobooks that align with your pupils' interests and reading levels.
- Encourage Active Listening: Provide activities and discussions to ensure pupils are engaged and comprehending the story.

Recommended Tools

1. Librivox (free) – Volunteer-read audiobooks of classic literature.
2. Audible Stories (free for kids' books) – Offers a selection of free audiobooks.
3. BBC Sounds (free) – Includes educational material and fictional stories.
4. Project Gutenberg Audiobooks (free) – Features audio versions of public-domain books.
5. Google Play Books (freemium) – AI-generated text-to-speech audiobook features.

9 Simplifying and Extending Texts

Simplifying and extending texts is a practical way to make literacy more accessible and inclusive for every pupil in the classroom. Whether a child needs support with reading or craves additional challenge, AI tools allow teachers to quickly adapt the same core material to suit a wide range of abilities. This chapter explores how to use AI to simplify or enrich texts, offering structured activities, classroom examples, and UK-based story references to ensure your literacy lessons remain rigorous, inclusive and engaging.

What Does It Mean to Simplify or Extend?

Simplifying a text means reducing the complexity of sentence structures and vocabulary while retaining the original meaning. This helps pupils who may struggle with comprehension, EAL learners or those working below age-related expectations.

Extending a text means enriching it, adding more vivid vocabulary, figurative language or detail. It supports higher-attaining pupils by giving them more challenging versions of the same material.

By simplifying or extending a shared class text, you can differentiate without having to plan separate activities for each reading group.

Benefits of Using AI for Text Adaptation

- Provides instant differentiation for guided reading groups.
- Supports inclusive classrooms by making core texts accessible to all.
- Encourages pupils to analyse author style and vocabulary.
- Offers opportunities for challenge and creative writing extension.
- Saves significant teacher time in adapting materials manually.

Using AI to Simplify Texts

Here's an example using *The Boy at the Back of the Class* by Onjali Q. Raúf:

> Original Text: "There used to be an empty chair at the back of my class, but now a new boy called Ahmet is sitting in it."

DOI: 10.4324/9781003621379-10

Prompt: "Rewrite this sentence in a simpler version suitable for a Year 2 pupil."
Simplified Version: "A new boy called Ahmet is sitting in the chair at the back of the class."

This keeps the core message while simplifying vocabulary and sentence structure.

Using AI to Extend Texts

Now, let's take a simple sentence and ask AI to elaborate it for greater-depth learners.

Original Sentence: "The owl flew through the trees."
Prompt: "Extend this sentence with vivid detail and figurative language for a Year 6 pupil."
Extended Version: "The owl swooped silently through the shadowy trees, its wings gliding on the cold night air like a whisper in the dark."

This richer version introduces mood, simile and descriptive vocabulary.

Teaching Strategies

1. Before and After Comparison

Use an extract from a well-known class text like *Fantastic Mr Fox*: "Mr Fox had a plan. A clever plan."
We can create three versions using AI:

- Original
- Simplified for Year 2
- Extended for Year 6

Response:

Original (KS2 - general use): "Mr Fox had a plan. A clever plan."

Short, punchy, and typical of Roald Dahl's voice; rhythmic and intriguing.

Simplified for Year 2: "Mr Fox had an idea. It was a good idea."

Vocabulary simplified: "plan" → "idea," "clever" → "good." Short, clear sentences retain meaning and suspense without challenging language.

Extended for Year 6: "Mr Fox had come up with a brilliant plan - one so daring and clever that even he grinned at the thought of it. He knew it could outsmart the farmers if everything went just right."

Adds complexity with a compound sentence. Introduces expanded vocabulary: *brilliant, daring, outsmart*. Creates anticipation and elaborates on Mr Fox's character

We could then ask pupils to look at the changes in vocabulary and tone and discuss which version best suits which reader. They can then try writing their own simplified or extended versions. This encourages pupils to think critically about writing style and audience.

2. Group Reading Differentiation

Take an excerpt from a text such as *Varjak Paw* by S.F. Said: "Varjak felt the world blur. The wind rushed in his ears as he fell through the darkness."

We can then use AI to produce differentiated versions:

- Group A (simplified, Year 3)

    "Varjak felt dizzy. The wind blew loudly as he fell into the dark."

Vocabulary here is simplified: "blur" → "dizzy," "rushed" → "blew loudly," "through the darkness" → "into the dark." There is a shorter sentence structure too, even though it retains the scene and emotion.

- Group B (original, Year 4) see above.
- Group C (extended, Year 5/6)

    "Varjak's head spun as the world around him melted into swirling shadows. The wind howled in his ears like a storm as he tumbled deeper into the endless dark, not knowing where he would land."

We have richer imagery and figurative language: "melted into swirling shadows," "howled like a storm," "endless dark," plus an extended sentence structure and added emotional tension.

After exploring these different versions, the class can read and discuss the same event from the story, ensuring access while allowing challenge.

3. Simplify for Clarity

We can use an AI tool to help pupils struggling with inference or tricky passages. For example, in *Kensuke's Kingdom* by Michael Morpurgo we have: "I clung to the wreckage, my knuckles white, as the sea tossed me like a rag doll."

> Prompt: "Rewrite this for a Year 3 pupil using simple language."
> Response: "I held onto the broken boat as the sea moved me up and down."

This strategy builds confidence with reading comprehension while allowing all children to engage with class texts.

4. Extend for Writing Challenge

We can provide pupils with a basic plot sentence such as, "Lila went into the cave." Then ask pupils to use AI to generate an extended version for a suspenseful narrative like this:

> Prompt: "Extend this sentence with descriptive language and atmosphere."
> Response: "Lila stepped cautiously into the cave, her torchlight flickering against the damp, jagged walls. Every drop of water echoed like footsteps, and she held her breath, unsure of what lay ahead."

Pupils can then use the AI version to inspire their own descriptive paragraph.

5. Text Level Extension Task

Choose a familiar extract, such as from *The Iron Man* by Ted Hughes: "The Iron Man came to the top of the cliff."

We could then ask higher-attaining pupils to input this line into AI and ask it to rewrite the scene in the style of a myth or legend.

Response:

> Out of the earth he rose, the giant of iron and fire, climbing to the cliff's edge where sky and sea met. The wind sang through his metal limbs as he looked out across the land, searching for the danger foretold in the old stories. The ground trembled beneath his feet, and the birds fell silent – for they knew the guardian had returned.

We can then compare the outputs with the original to identify shifts in tone and vocabulary.

Using AI for Pupil-Led Adaptation

Once pupils are confident, we let them try their own prompts such as:

- "Simplify this for a younger child."
- "Make this sound more exciting."
- "Add more feeling or action."
- "Rewrite this like a scary story."

This empowers them to take control of their reading and writing, encouraging experimentation and creativity.

Caution and Consideration

- Check Accuracy: AI might accidentally change key facts or character details. Always review content before use.
- Maintain Purpose: Simplifying shouldn't mean removing all literary quality. Preserve tone and meaning.
- Avoid Overuse: Not every text needs adapting. Use this tool to support, not replace, rich classroom reading experiences.
- Be Transparent: Show pupils how AI can help, but model critical reading and editing.

Recommended Tools

1. ChatGPT (free/paid) – Ideal for adapting texts with clear prompts.
2. Google Gemini (free) – Great for rewriting in different styles.
3. DeepSeek (free) – Good for summarising and rephrasing content.
4. Rewordify (free) – Specifically for simplifying English text.
5. QuillBot (freemium) – Allows tone and length adjustment.

10 Summarising Texts

> Summarising is a vital skill that helps pupils distil the main ideas of a text, improving their comprehension and retention abilities. It encourages critical thinking, as pupils must identify key points and express them concisely. This chapter explores practical strategies for teaching summarising in the primary classroom, ensuring pupils can confidently and effectively summarise texts of all kinds.

What Is Summarising?

Summarising involves condensing a text into its most important points, leaving out unnecessary details. It requires pupils to identify the main idea or theme. But it also requires the children to recognise supporting details and express the information in their own words, which is excellent for unpacking complex texts. A good summary is concise, clear and captures the essence of the text without adding personal opinions or extra information.

Summarising offers several benefits for primary pupils including improving comprehension as it helps pupils focus on the main ideas and understand the text more deeply. It develops critical thinking as it encourages pupils to analyse and prioritise information. It can also enhance writing skills as it can model how to write clearly and concisely. Summaries can also serve as useful study tools for reviewing key concepts so help with revision in the future.

How to Teach Summarising

1. Start with Short Texts

You should begin with short, simple texts such as paragraphs or short stories. This makes it easier for pupils to identify the main idea and supporting details. For example:

> Text: "The sun was shining brightly, and the birds were singing. Amy decided to go for a walk in the park. She saw flowers, played on the swings, and had a picnic with her friends."
> Summary: "Amy enjoyed a sunny day in the park with her friends."

2. Use the "Who, What, Where, When, Why, and How" Framework

We can encourage pupils to ask these questions to identify key information:

- **Who** is the text about?
- **What** happened?
- **Where** did it happen?
- **When** did it happen?
- **Why** did it happen?
- **How** did it happen?

For example:

> Text: "Last weekend, Tom visited the zoo with his family. They saw lions, elephants, and monkeys. Tom's favourite part was feeding the giraffes."
>
> Summary: "Tom and his family visited the zoo last weekend. They saw many animals, and Tom enjoyed feeding the giraffes."

3. Teach the "Somebody-Wanted-But-So-Then" Strategy

This strategy helps pupils summarise narratives by focusing on the story's structure:

- **Somebody:** Who is the main character?
- **Wanted:** What did they want?
- **But:** What was the problem?
- **So:** How did they try to solve it?
- **Then:** What was the outcome?

For example:

> Text: "Cinderella wanted to go to the ball, but her stepmother wouldn't let her. So, her fairy godmother helped her, and then she danced with the prince."
>
> Summary: "Cinderella wanted to go to the ball, but her stepmother said no. Her fairy godmother helped her, and she danced with the prince."

4. Model Summarising

We can demonstrate how to summarise a text step by step. We should model thinking aloud as we identify the main idea and supporting details thus showing how to condense the information. For example:

> Text: "The Arctic is a cold, icy place. Polar bears live there, and they hunt seals for food. The ice is melting because of climate change, which makes it harder for polar bears to survive."
>
> Modelled Oral Summary: "The Arctic is home to polar bears, but melting ice due to climate change is threatening their survival."

5. Use Graphic Organisers

Graphic organisers, such as story maps or summary frames, can help children to visually organise information. For example:

Main Idea and Details Chart

> Main Idea: Polar bears are struggling because of melting ice.
> Detail 1: The Arctic is their home.
> Detail 2: They hunt seals for food.
> Detail 3: Climate change is causing the ice to melt.

6. Practise Paraphrasing

We can also teach pupils to paraphrase by rewriting sentences in their own words. We could start with simple sentences and gradually move to longer passages. For example:

> Original: "The cat sat on the mat, purring softly."
> Paraphrased: "The cat rested on the mat and made a quiet purring sound."

Using AI to Support Summarising

AI tools like ChatGPT or DeepSeek can be valuable for teaching summarising. For example:

Generating Summaries

Ask the AI to create a summary of a text, then compare it with the pupils' summaries.

> Prompt: "Summarise this short paragraph: 'The rainforest is home to many animals, including monkeys, parrots and jaguars. It rains almost every day and the trees are very tall. Unfortunately, people are cutting down the trees, which is harming the animals."
> Response: "The rainforest has many animals and tall trees, but deforestation is harming them."

Creating Practice Texts

We could also use the AI to generate short texts for pupils to summarise. For example:

> Prompt: "Write a short paragraph about a dog playing in the park."
> Response: "Max the dog ran through the park, chasing a bright red ball. He jumped over logs and splashed in puddles, wagging his tail happily."

Practical Classroom Strategies

1. Summarising Stations

Set up stations around the classroom with different texts (a narrative story, a news article, a poem, etc). Pupils can then rotate through the stations, summarising each text in a few sentences.

2. Peer Summarising

Pair pupils and ask them to summarise a text together. They can compare their summaries and discuss any differences.

3. Summarising Challenges

We can turn summarising into a game by challenging pupils to summarise a text in 10 words or less. This encourages creativity and precision.

4. Summarising Journals

Ask pupils to keep a summarising journal. After reading a text, they write a brief summary and reflect on what they learned.

5. One-Sentence Summary Activity

After reading a passage, challenge pupils to summarise it in just one sentence. You could also encourage them to refine their sentences to include only the most essential details.

6. Scaffolded Summarising

Some pupils may struggle with summarisation so we can provide structured support, like this:

- **Beginner Level:** Provide a sentence starter (e.g. *This story is about...*).
- **Intermediate Level:** Ask pupils to use a template like "Somebody Wanted But So Then."
- **Advanced Level:** Have pupils create their own summaries without prompts.

Caution and Consideration

While teaching summarising, it's important to:

- Avoid Over-Simplifying: Ensure summaries still capture the essence of the text.
- Encourage Originality: Teach pupils to use their own words rather than copying directly from the text.
- Provide Feedback: Offer constructive feedback to help pupils improve their summaries.

Recommended Tools

1. ChatGPT (free/paid) - Uses AI to generate summaries or create practice texts.
2. DeepSeek (free) - Also uses AI to generate summaries or create practice texts.
3. Summarising Apps - Tools like SummarizeThis or SMMRY can help pupils practise summarising.
4. Graphic Organiser Templates - Use printable or digital templates to help pupils organise their thoughts.
5. Reading Comprehension Websites - Platforms like ReadWorks or CommonLit offer texts with built-in summarising activities.
6. SummarizeBot (free/paid) - AI-based summarisation for articles and documents.
7. TLDR This (freemium) - Shortens online articles into key points.
8. Google Bard (free) - AI-powered text simplification and summarisation.
9. QuillBot (freemium) - Provides summary suggestions for complex texts.

PART 2
Comprehension Skills

This section delves into how AI can strengthen comprehension through engaging, enquiry-led learning. From automated quizzes and vocabulary-building tools to avatar-based reading aloud sessions and emotion analysis, each chapter offers a new way to explore texts deeply. Teachers will find ideas for using AI to help pupils predict, clarify and question while reading. Activities like "Guess the Ending" and "Clarify the Confusion" challenge pupils to engage with text structure and narrative development. The section also emphasises the importance of book discussions and introduces creative uses of flashcards, reading challenges, and thematic tasks that AI can help generate and personalise. These tools enhance pupil interaction with both fiction and non-fiction, fostering deeper understanding and retention. With adaptable suggestions for whole-class, group and individual work, this section supports critical thinking, metacognition and independent reading, making comprehension a vibrant and reflective process.

11 Quizzes

> Quizzes are a versatile and engaging way to assess and reinforce comprehension skills in the primary classroom. They provide immediate feedback, encourage active participation and can be tailored to suit different learning styles and abilities. This chapter explores how to use quizzes effectively to support reading comprehension, offering practical strategies and ideas for teachers.

What Are Comprehension Quizzes and Why Should We Use Them?

Comprehension quizzes are short assessments designed to test pupils' understanding of a text. They can include a variety of question types, such as multiple-choice, true/false, short answer or matching. Quizzes can be conducted orally, on paper or digitally, making them a flexible tool for the classroom.

Quizzes offer several benefits for teaching comprehension, including immediate feedback as pupils can quickly see what they've understood and where they need improvement. Quizzes also add an element of fun and competition, motivating pupils to participate and engage. They can also be used for assessment as they provide valuable insights into pupils' comprehension skills, helping us to quickly identify areas for further support. Regularly revisiting key ideas through quizzes helps reinforce learning and improve retention.

How to Use Quizzes in the Classroom

1. Pre-Reading Quizzes

Use quizzes to activate prior knowledge and set a purpose for reading. For example, before reading a text about the rainforest, ask your chosen AI platform to "generate a pre topic quiz of 5 questions about rainforests to assess prior knowledge for a Year 5 class." I did this and ChatGPT replied with:

1 **What is a rainforest?**
   a) A hot, dry area with very few trees
   b) A dense forest with high rainfall and lots of plants and animals

c) A forest that only exists in cold, snowy regions
   d) A place where only cacti and small bushes grow
2 **Where are most rainforests found?**
   a) Near the North and South Poles
   b) In desert regions
   c) Near the Equator in places like South America, Africa, and Asia
   d) Only in Australia
3 **Why are rainforests important to the Earth?**
   a) They provide homes for many animals and plants
   b) They help produce oxygen and clean the air
   c) They help regulate the climate
   d) All of the above
4 **Which of these animals is most likely to live in a rainforest?**
   a) Penguin
   b) Jaguar
   c) Polar Bear
   d) Camel
5 **What is the name of the biggest rainforest in the world?**
   a) The Congo Rainforest
   b) The Amazon Rainforest
   c) The Daintree Rainforest
   d) The Black Forest

Answers:

1 B) A dense forest with high rainfall and lots of plants and animals
2 C) Near the Equator in places like South America, Africa, and Asia
3 D) All of the above
4 B) Jaguar
5 B) The Amazon Rainforest

This type of quiz can help pupils connect new information to what they already know.

2. During-Reading Quizzes

Pause at key points in the text to ask comprehension questions. This encourages active reading and helps pupils monitor their understanding. For example, I generated these questions using DeepSeek:

1 **What just happened in the story?**
   o This helps pupils recall key events and ensures they are following the plot.
2 **Why do you think the character did that?**
   o Encourages pupils to consider characters' motivations and actions.
3 **What do you think will happen next?**
   o Promotes prediction skills and keeps pupils curious about the story's progression.

4 **How do you think the character is feeling right now? Why?**
   o   Helps pupils develop empathy and understand emotions within the story.
5 **Can you explain why [specific event] happened?**
   o   Encourages pupils to make connections between cause and effect in the story.

3. Post-Reading Quizzes

After reading, you can use quizzes to assess overall understanding. Include questions that cover the main idea, supporting details, vocabulary and inference. Here are three examples from ChatGPT:

- What was the main problem in the story?
- How did the character solve the problem?
- What does the word "brave" mean in this context?

Types of Quiz Questions

You can ask your chosen AI platform to create all kinds of questions such as multiple-choice, true or false, short answers, matching questions or inference questions.

Here are some examples of questions I generated on ChatGPT (you can adapt these for your topic/text/age group, etc.).

Question: What did the fox find in the forest?

a)   A treasure chest
b)   A hidden path
c)   A friendly bear
d)   A lost puppy

Question: The fox was afraid of the bear. (True/False)
Question: Why did the fox decide to help the bear?
Question: Match the character to their action.

1   Fox a) Built a bridge
2   Bear b) Found the treasure
3   Rabbit c) Shared the food

Question: How do you think the fox felt when he found the treasure? Why?

Using AI to Create Quizzes

AI tools like ChatGPT can help you create quizzes quickly and easily. For example:

Generate More Specific Questions

Ask the AI to create comprehension questions for a specific text.
Prompt: "Write five multiple-choice questions about this story: 'The fox found a treasure chest in the forest. He decided to share it with his friends.'"

Response:

1. What did the fox find in the forest?
    a) A treasure chest
    b) A lost puppy
    c) A hidden path
    d) A friendly bear
2. What did the fox decide to do with the treasure?
    a) Keep it for himself
    b) Share it with his friends
    c) Hide it in the forest
    d) Sell it at the market
3. Etc.

Practical Classroom Strategies

1. Quiz Games

You could turn quizzes into a game to make them more engaging. For example:

Kahoot!: Create a live quiz that pupils can answer on their devices.

Quiz Bowl: Divide the class into teams and have them compete to answer questions correctly.

2. Peer Quizzes

Perhaps you can ask pupils to create their own quizzes based on a text, then swap with a partner to answer each other's questions.

3. Daily Quick Quizzes

Start each lesson with a short quiz to review the previous day's reading. This helps reinforce learning and keeps pupils focused.

4. Quiz Journals

Ask pupils to keep a quiz journal where they record their answers and reflect on their understanding. For example:

- What did I get right?
- What did I get wrong?
- What do I need to work on?

Caution and Consideration

While quizzes are a valuable tool, it's important to:

- Avoid Over-Testing: Use quizzes as part of a balanced approach to assessment, not as the sole method.

- Provide Support: Ensure all pupils can access the quiz, offering additional support or alternative formats if needed.
- Encourage Reflection: Use quizzes as an opportunity for pupils to reflect on their learning and set goals for improvement.

Recommended Tools

1. Kahoot! (freemium) - Interactive, game-based quizzes.
2. Quizlet (freemium) - Customisable flashcards and quizzes.
3. Google Forms (free) - Self-marking multiple-choice and short-answer quizzes.
4. Socrative (freemium) - Real-time quiz assessments.
5. ChatGPT (free/paid) - AI-generated quizzes tailored to any book or text.
6. DeepSeek (free) - Create your own quizzes and answers.

12 Key Moments

Key moments in a story are the pivotal points that drive the plot forward, reveal character development or convey important themes. Teaching pupils to identify and analyse these moments is essential for deepening their comprehension and helping them engage more meaningfully with texts. This chapter explores strategies for teaching pupils to recognise and reflect on key moments, fostering critical thinking and a deeper understanding of storytelling.

What Are Key Moments and Why Focus on Them?

Key moments are the most significant events or turning points in a story. They often include:

The Introduction: Where characters, setting, and the main problem are introduced.
The Climax: The most exciting or tense part of the story, where the main problem reaches its peak.
The Resolution: Where the problem is solved, and the story concludes.
Character Decisions: Moments where characters make important choices that affect the plot.
Revelations: Scenes where important information is revealed, changing the direction of the story.

By identifying these moments, pupils can better understand the structure of a story and the author's intentions. Therefore, focusing on key moments helps pupils:

Understand Story Structure: Recognising key moments helps pupils see how a story is built and how events connect.
Develop Critical Thinking: Analysing why certain moments are important encourages deeper engagement with the text.
Improve Comprehension: Identifying key moments helps pupils remember and retell stories more effectively.
Build Empathy: Reflecting on characters' decisions and emotions during key moments fosters emotional connection and understanding.

DOI: 10.4324/9781003621379-14

Using AI to Explore Key Moments

AI tools like ChatGPT can help pupils identify and analyse key moments. They can, for example, generate discussion prompts. You can ask the AI to create questions about key moments in a story. Here's an example I made about *The Three Little Pigs*:

Prompt: "What are three key moments in the story?"
Response:

1. The three pigs build homes – one from straw, one from sticks, and one from sturdy bricks.
2. The wolf huffs and puffs, easily destroying the straw and stick houses. The two pigs flee to the brick house.
3. The wolf's strongest blows can't move the brick house. He climbs the chimney but falls into a pot of boiling water and runs away for good.

You can then use AI to summarise the key moments in the story further:

1. The pigs build their houses.
2. The wolf blows down the first two houses.
3. The wolf fails to blow down the brick house.

Breaking Down Key Moments

You can teach AI to use the "Somebody-Wanted-But-So-Then' strategy. This framework helps pupils to understand how to break down key moments by identifying the main character's motivation and challenges:

- Somebody (Who is involved?)
- Wanted (What did they want?)
- But (What was the problem?)
- So (What happened next?)

I asked AI to use this framework for *Charlotte's Web* by E.B. White. The response was:

> In Charlotte's Web, Wilbur wanted to stay alive, but he was a farm pig, so Charlotte spun words in her web to save him.

This summary shows the plot of the book by identifying the key moments for the two main characters.

How to Teach Key Moments

1. Key Moments Sorting Activity with AI

Use AI to generate a list of events from the story, then ask pupils to sort them into "key moments" and "less important events." For example:

Prompt for AI: "List six events from Harry Potter and the Philosopher's Stone and mark which are key moments."

AI Response:

1. Harry discovers he is a wizard. (Key Moment)
2. Harry buys his school supplies in Diagon Alley. (Less Important)
3. Harry, Ron, and Hermione defeat the troll. (Key Moment)
4. Harry receives his Nimbus 2000. (Less Important)
5. Harry discovers the Mirror of Erised. (Key Moment)
6. Harry confronts Quirrell and Voldemort. (Key Moment)

Pupils can discuss their choices and compare them to the AI's suggestions.

2. Story Mountain with AI Assistance

Use AI to help pupils plot key moments on a story mountain. For example:

Prompt for AI: "Help me label a story mountain for Harry Potter and the Philosopher's Stone."

AI Response:

- Beginning: Harry discovers he is a wizard and goes to Hogwarts.
- Build-Up: Harry, Ron, and Hermione uncover the mystery of the Philosopher's Stone.
- Climax: Harry confronts Quirrell and Voldemort.
- Resolution: Harry saves the Stone and defeats Voldemort.
- Ending: Harry returns to the Dursleys, knowing he has a place in the magical world.

Pupils can use this as a guide to create their own story mountains.

3. Key Moments Debate with AI-Generated Scenarios

Use AI to create debate topics based on key moments. For example:

Prompt for AI: "Write a debate question about the key moment when Harry discovers he is a wizard."

AI Response:

Debate Question: "Was it better for Harry to find out he was a wizard at age 11, or should he have been told earlier? Why or why not?"

Pupils can work in groups to prepare arguments and present their ideas to the class.

4. Key Moments Art with AI Inspiration

Use AI to generate descriptions of key moments that pupils can turn into artwork. For example:

Prompt for AI: "Describe the key moment when Harry discovers the Mirror of Erised in vivid detail."

AI Response:

> Harry stands in front of the tall, ornate mirror, his reflection staring back at him. But as he looks closer, he sees not just himself, but his parents smiling and waving at him. His heart swells with a mix of joy and sadness as he realises this is the family he never knew. The room is silent except for the sound of his breathing, and the mirror's golden frame glows softly in the dim light.

Pupils can use this description to create a detailed drawing or collage.

Caution and Consideration

While teaching key moments, it's important to:

- Encourage Multiple Perspectives: Allow pupils to share their interpretations of what makes a moment key.
- Avoid Overwhelming Pupils: Focus on a few key moments rather than every event in the story.
- Link to Themes: Help pupils see how key moments relate to the story's themes or messages.

Recommended Tools

1. ChatGPT (free/paid) – Generates key events and discussion prompts.
2. DeepSeek (free) – Works like ChatGPT.
3. SummarizeBot (freemium) – Highlights key points in texts.
4. Google Bard (free) – Helps summarise significant moments.
5. BookWidgets (freemium) – Allows teachers to create interactive comprehension tasks.
6. CommonLit (free) – Provides guided reading questions and key moment analysis.

---

13 Vocabulary Expansion and Building

> Expanding pupils' vocabulary is a cornerstone of literacy development. A rich vocabulary enhances comprehension, improves writing and boosts confidence in communication. This chapter explores practical strategies for vocabulary building, with a focus on how AI tools can support each step of the process. To illustrate these strategies, we'll use examples from a range of popular children's books from across year groups.

Why Is Vocabulary Expansion Important?

A strong vocabulary helps pupils to understand texts and knowing more words allows them to comprehend complex texts with ease. A wider vocabulary enables children to articulate their thoughts and ideas more clearly. Pupils with a robust vocabulary are more confident and motivated to participate in lessons. Plus, vocabulary is closely linked to overall academic achievement across subjects.

How to Teach Vocabulary Expansion

1. Introduce New Words in Context

Teaching new words within the context of a story or topic helps pupils understand their meaning and usage.

> Example from *The Gruffalo* (Julia Donaldson, 1999): Introduce the word "knobbly" when describing the Gruffalo's knees.
> Sentence: "The Gruffalo had knobbly knees and turned-out toes."

Use AI such as ChatGPT to generate sentences that include new vocabulary words.

> Prompt: "Write a sentence using the word 'knobbly' in the context of The Gruffalo."
> Response: "The Gruffalo stomped through the deep, dark wood, his **knobbly** knees bending as he towered over the little mouse."

Ask the children to then write their own sentences using "knobbly." You could give them AI-generated sentence starters to help such as:

The Gruffalo stomped with his...
Mouse looked up at the Gruffalo and saw...
The Gruffalo sat down with a thud and...

2. Use Visual Aids and Examples

Visual aids like pictures, diagrams or videos can help pupils connect new words to their meanings.

Example from *The Colour Monster*: Show an image of a "scribble" when introducing the word to describe the Colour Monster's mixed-up emotions.
AI Support: Ask ChatGPT to suggest visual aids or create descriptions that can be turned into visuals.
Prompt: "Describe a scene from The Colour Monster that includes the word 'scribble' so I can create a visual aid."
Response: "The Colour Monster's emotions were all mixed up, like a messy scribble of colours on a page."

3. Create Word Banks

Word banks are collections of vocabulary words related to a specific topic or story. They serve as a reference for pupils during reading and writing activities.

Example from *The Nowhere Emporium*: Ask ChatGPT to generate a word bank for this specific story.
Prompt: "Create a word bank for The Nowhere Emporium."
Response:

- Labyrinth
- Enchanted
- Mystery
- Portal
- Illusion
- Curiosity
- Wonder
- Imagination

The word bank can then be displayed and referred to whenever this new vocabulary features when reading the book.

4. Play Vocabulary Games

Games make learning new words fun and engaging. Examples include word bingo, crossword puzzles and charades.

Example from Salamander: Play a game of "Vocabulary Charades" where pupils act out words like "ancient," "mystical," or "artifact."
AI Support: Use AI to create vocabulary games or puzzles.
Prompt: "Create a crossword puzzle using vocabulary words from Salamander."
Response:

- Across:
    1. Very old (Ancient).
    2. A magical object (Artifact).
- Down:
    1. Relating to magic (Mystical).
    2. A type of lizard (Salamander).

5. Encourage Word Usage in Writing

Ask pupils to use new vocabulary words in their writing, such as stories, poems, or journal entries.

Example from *The Colour Monster*: After learning the word "scribble," ask pupils to write a sentence or paragraph using it.
AI Support: Use ChatGPT to provide writing prompts that include new vocabulary.
Prompt: "Write a writing prompt that encourages pupils to use the word 'scribble.'"
Response: "Imagine your emotions were a scribble of colours. Describe what each colour represents and how it makes you feel."

Using AI to Support Vocabulary Expansion

AI tools like ChatGPT can be invaluable for vocabulary building. Here's how.

1. Generate Word Lists

Ask ChatGPT to create lists of vocabulary words related to a specific topic or story.

Prompt: "List 10 advanced vocabulary words from The Iron Man."
Response:

1. Enormous
2. Metallic
3. Gleaming
4. Gigantic
5. Mysterious
6. Mechanical
7. Towering
8. Rusted
9. Colossal
10. Formidable

The children could then create a character description of the Iron Man using these adjectives. The same can be done with verbs and adverbs too.

2. Provide Definitions and Examples

Use AI to explain the meaning of new words in texts and provide examples of how they are used.

Prompt: "Explain the word 'labyrinth' and use it in a sentence."
Response:

- Definition: A complicated network of passages or paths.
- Sentence: "The Nowhere Emporium was like a labyrinth, full of twisting corridors and hidden rooms."

3. Create Vocabulary Activities

Ask AI to design activities like fill-in-the-blank exercises or matching games.

Prompt: "Create a fill-in-the-blank exercise using vocabulary words from The Gruffalo."
Response:

- The Gruffalo had ____ knees and turned-out toes. (knobbly)
- The mouse walked through the ____ forest. (deep, dark)
- The Gruffalo's eyes were ____. (orange)

4. Generate Synonyms and Antonyms

Use AI to explore synonyms and antonyms for new words.

Prompt: "What are some synonyms and antonyms for the word 'mysterious'?"
Response:

- Synonyms: Enigmatic, puzzling, cryptic.
- Antonyms: Clear, obvious, straightforward.

Practical Classroom Strategies

1. Vocabulary Journals

Ask pupils to keep a vocabulary journal where they record new words, their meanings and example sentences.

2. Word of the Day

Introduce a "Word of the Day" using AI and challenge pupils to use it in a talking homework or in their writing. This could be a quick "Morning Task."

3. Interactive Word Walls

Create a word wall in the classroom where pupils can add new words they've learned, along with definitions and illustrations. You could perhaps have an A4-sized sheet for each letter of the alphabet. The children add A words, B words, etc.

4. Peer Teaching

Pair pupils up and ask them to teach each other new vocabulary words, using definitions, examples and illustrations. Or set this as a homework activity.

Caution and Consideration

While using AI to support vocabulary building, it's important to:

- Ensure Age-Appropriate Content: Choose words and examples that are suitable for your pupils' age and reading level.
- Balance AI and Human Input: Use AI as a supplement, not a replacement, for teacher-led instruction and discussion.
- Encourage Active Engagement: Ensure pupils are actively using new words in speaking, reading, and writing, rather than just memorising definitions.

Recommended Tools

1. ChatGPT (free/paid) – Generate word lists, definitions, examples, and activities.
2. Quizlet (free/paid) – Create flashcards and games for vocabulary practice.
3. Vocabulary.com (free/paid) – Offers interactive vocabulary exercises and quizzes.
4. Word Banks and Visual Aids – Use tools like Canva or Google Slides to create engaging visuals.

14 Emotion Analysis

Understanding emotions in a story is a crucial part of comprehension. It helps pupils connect with characters, empathise with their experiences and deepens their engagement with the text. Emotion analysis involves identifying and interpreting characters' feelings, exploring why they feel that way and reflecting on how those emotions drive the story forward. This chapter explores strategies for teaching emotion analysis, with examples from a variety of primary school texts, including *Charlotte's Web*, *The Boy at the Back of the Class*, *The Day the Crayons Quit*, *Varjak Paw* and *The Explorer*.

Why Is Emotion Analysis Important?

Analysing emotions helps pupils to develop empathy. As they begin to understand characters' feelings this then fosters emotional intelligence and compassion. Also, emotions often drive characters' actions and decisions, so analysing them improves children's understanding of the plot. This connection with characters' emotions makes reading more meaningful and enjoyable. Since reading and writing are so closely connected, this then means that pupils can use their understanding of emotions to create more nuanced and relatable characters in their own writing. After all, reading is like breathing in and writing is like breathing out: you cannot have one without the other.

How to Teach Emotion Analysis

1. Identify Emotions in the Text

We can teach pupils to recognise emotions by looking for clues in the text, such as:

- **Descriptive Language:** Words like "angry," "excited," or "heartbroken."
- **Character Actions:** What a character does (e.g. crying, shouting, smiling).
- **Dialogue:** What a character says and how they say it.
- **Illustrations:** Visual clues in picture books.

We can ask AI to help us to spot these clues. Here's an example from *The Day the Crayons Quit*:

- Emotion: Frustration.
- Clues (How do we know?): Red Crayon writes, "I work harder than any of your other crayons!" and lists all the holidays he has to colour.

We can then ask AI to generate examples of emotional language by giving a prompt and asking for a response:

Prompt: "Write a sentence showing a character feeling nervous."

Response: "Her hands trembled as she opened the letter, her heart pounding in her chest."

This writing of "Show and Not Tell' is how children can find their own written voice.

2. Explore Why Characters Feel That Way

We can help pupils understand the reasons behind characters' emotions by asking questions such as:

What happened to make the character feel this way?
How would you feel in this situation?
What does this emotion tell us about the character?

Here's an example from *Charlotte's Web*:

Emotion: Sadness.
Why: Charlotte is dying, and Wilbur is losing his best friend.
Discussion: "Why do you think Wilbur feels so sad? How would you feel if you were in his place?"

We can use AI to generate discussion prompts like these:

Prompt: "Write a question to help pupils explore why a character feels sad."

Response: "Why do you think Wilbur feels so lonely after Charlotte's death? How does this show the importance of friendship?"

3. Analyse How Emotions Drive the Story

As mentioned previously, emotions often influence characters' decisions and actions, shaping the plot. Encourage pupils to think about how emotions move the story forward.

Example from *Varjak Paw*:

Emotion: Fear.
Impact: Varjak is afraid of the unknown but decides to leave his home to save his family. His fear motivates him to be brave.
Discussion: "How does Varjak's fear help him grow as a character? What does he learn from facing his fears?"

AI can create cause-and-effect activities to highlight this:

Prompt: "Create a cause-and-effect chart for Varjak Paw's emotions and actions."
Response:

- Cause: Varjak feels afraid of the outside world.
- Effect: He decides to leave his home and seek help.
- Cause: He feels determined to save his family.
- Effect: He learns new skills and becomes a hero.

By analysing these emotions using AI responses, children can begin to spot patterns like this in other texts they read.

4. Use Visual Aids and Role-Play

Visual aids, like emotion wheels or facial expression charts, can help pupils identify and describe emotions. Role-playing allows them to experience these emotions firsthand. For example, in *The Boy at the Back of the Class* loneliness is a common theme. We can use an emotion wheel to discuss how Ahmet might feel as a refugee in a new school. Then, role-play a scene where a classmate tries to befriend him.

With AI support we can generate role-play scenarios like this:

Prompt: "Write a short role-play scenario about a character feeling lonely and another character trying to cheer them up."
Response:

Character 1: "I don't think anyone likes me. I feel so alone."
Character 2: "I like you! Let's play together at break time."

The children can then act out these scenarios, which can prompt useful discussions that develop comprehension skills

5. Reflect on Personal Connections

We can encourage pupils to connect characters' emotions to their own experiences. This helps them relate to the story and understand emotions on a deeper level. For example, in *The Explorer* we see characters experience fear. We can ask the children if they have ever felt scared like Fred when he was lost in the jungle. We can then ask what helped to make them feel better.

We can then use AI support to generate reflection prompts:

Prompt: "Write a reflection prompt about fear for pupils to connect to The Explorer."
Response: "Think about a time when you felt scared like Fred. What did you do to overcome your fear? How did it change you?"

Using AI to Support Emotion Analysis

AI tools can enhance emotion analysis in several ways, such as:

1. Generate Emotion-Based Questions

Ask ChatGPT or similar to create questions that help pupils analyse emotions like this:

Prompt: "Write three questions to help pupils analyse emotions in Charlotte's Web."
Response:

1. How does Wilbur feel when he first meets Charlotte? Why?
2. Why does Charlotte feel proud when she spins her web?
3. How does Fern's sadness about Wilbur's fate show her love for him?

2. Create Emotion Charts

We can also use AI to generate lists of emotions and their causes like this:

Prompt: "Create a chart showing emotions and their causes in The Boy at the Back of the Class."
Response:

- Emotion: Loneliness.
    - Cause: Ahmet is new to the school and doesn't speak the language.
- Emotion: Kindness.
    - Cause: A classmate offers to share their lunch with Ahmet.

3. Develop Role-Play Scripts

We could ask AI to write scripts for role-playing emotional scenes such as this one:

Prompt: "Write a role-play script about a character feeling nervous and another character comforting them."
Response:

Character 1: "I'm so nervous about the school play. What if I forget my lines?"
Character 2: "You'll be great! Just take a deep breath and remember how hard you've practised."

Practical Classroom Activities

1. Emotion Graphs

- Pupils track a character's emotions across a story, mapping out highs and lows.
- Example: Plop in *The Owl Who Was Afraid of the Dark* starts fearful, becomes curious, and ends confident.

2. Emotion Freeze Frames

- Pupils act out key moments in a story using facial expressions and body language to represent emotions.
- Example: Acting out Leon's excitement in *Leon and the Place Between*.

3. Rewrite the Emotion

- Give pupils a passage and ask them to change the emotion using different adjectives, dialogue, or actions.
- Example: Rewrite a scene in *The Lighthouse Keeper's Lunch* so that Mr Grinling is amused rather than frustrated.

Caution and Consideration

While teaching emotion analysis, it's important to:

- Be Sensitive: Ensure discussions about emotions are respectful and inclusive.
- Encourage Empathy: Help pupils understand that everyone experiences emotions differently.
- Avoid Overwhelming Pupils: Focus on a few key emotions at a time to avoid confusion.

Recommended Tools

1. ChatGPT (free/paid) - Generates questions, charts and role-play scripts.
2. DeepSeek (free) - Generates discussion questions and identifies emotional language.
3. Quizlet (freemium) - Creates emotion-based vocabulary flashcards.
4. Kahoot! (freemium) - Interactive quizzes for emotion analysis.
5. Google Bard (free) - Explains emotional shifts in a passage.
6. CommonLit (free) - Provides emotion-focused reading activities.

15 Book Discussions

Book discussions are a powerful way to develop comprehension skills, encourage critical thinking and foster a love of reading. Through guided conversations, pupils can explore themes, analyse characters and share their interpretations of a text. This chapter explores strategies for facilitating effective book discussions, with examples from a variety of primary school texts, including *The Wild Robot*, *The Girl Who Stole an Elephant*, *The Boy Who Grew Dragons*, *Pax* and *The Last Bear*.

Why Are Book Discussions Important?

Book discussions help pupils deepen their understanding of texts. By talking about a text this helps pupils process and retain information, which develops their critical thinking. In doing that, children will be able to analyse themes, characters and plot points, which encourages higher-order thinking. Also, discussing books improves listening, speaking and debating skills. We can foster a reading community in the classroom by sharing ideas and perspectives about books, which creates a sense of connection and collaboration.

How to Facilitate Book Discussions

1. Prepare Thought-Provoking Questions

Effective book discussions start with open-ended questions that encourage pupils to think deeply and share their ideas. We can ask AI to give us sample questions which will then lead to discussion.

Here's an example using the text *The Wild Robot* with AI-generated questions and discussion prompts:

Question: "How does Roz's relationship with the animals change throughout the story? What does this tell us about her character?"
Discussion: Encourage pupils to explore how Roz's actions and decisions reflect her growth and adaptability.
Prompt: "Write three open-ended questions for a book discussion about The Wild Robot."

Response:
1. How does Roz's environment shape her behaviour and personality?
2. What lessons can we learn from Roz's interactions with the animals?
3. Do you think Roz is more like a machine or a living creature by the end of the story? Why?

2. Encourage Evidence-Based Responses

We can teach pupils to support their opinions with evidence from the text. This helps them develop analytical skills and engage more deeply with the story. Here are more AI-generated prompts and responses linked to *The Girl Who Stole an Elephant*:

Question: "Why do you think Chaya decided to steal the queen's jewels? Was it the right decision?"
Evidence-Based Response: "Chaya says she stole the jewels to help her friend, but it caused a lot of problems. I think she was brave but maybe didn't think about the consequences."
Prompt: "Create an activity where pupils find evidence to support their opinions about The Girl Who Stole an Elephant."
Response:
Activity: "Choose a decision Chaya makes in the story. Find three pieces of evidence from the text that show why she made that decision. Do you agree with her choice? Why or why not?"

3. Explore Themes and Messages

Book discussions are an excellent opportunity to explore the deeper themes and messages in a story. Using *Pax* as a class text, here is some AI support:

Prompt: "What is the theme in Pax by Sara Pennypacker?"
Response: "Friendship and loyalty."
Prompt: "Create a discussion based upon this."
Response: "How does the relationship between Pax and Peter change throughout the story? What does it teach us about friendship and loyalty?"
Prompt: "Write a discussion prompt about the theme of friendship in Pax."
Response: "How does Peter's journey to find Pax show the strength of their friendship? What sacrifices does he make, and what does this tell us about loyalty?"

4. Use Role-Playing and Hot Seating

We can use role-playing and hot seating (where a pupil takes on the role of a character and answers questions) to make discussions more interactive and engaging. For example, using *The Boy Who Grew Dragons*, I asked AI to "Hot seat Tomas as he explains how he feels about growing dragons."

Response: "How did you feel when the first dragon fruit appeared? What's the hardest part about looking after dragons?"
Prompt: "Write a hot seating script for Tomas from The Boy Who Grew Dragons."
Response:
Pupil (as Tomas): "I was so excited when the first dragon fruit appeared, but I didn't know how much work it would be! The hardest part is keeping them out of trouble."

5. Encourage Personal Connections

We can help pupils connect stories to their own lives, making discussions more meaningful and relatable. For example, using *The Last Bear* by Hannah Gold, I asked AI:

> Question: "How do you think April felt when she discovered the polar bear? Have you ever felt a strong connection to an animal or place?"
>
> Discussion: Encourage pupils to share their own experiences of feeling connected to nature or animals.
>
> Prompt: "Write a reflection prompt for pupils to connect The Last Bear to their own lives."
>
> Response: "Think about a time when you felt a strong connection to nature or an animal. How did it make you feel? What did you learn from that experience?"

Using AI to Support Book Discussions

We can use AI tools like ChatGPT to enhance book discussions in several ways, such as:

1. Generate Discussion Questions

Ask your AI platform to create open-ended questions for any book, like this:

> Prompt: "Write five discussion questions for The Last Bear."
> Response:
>
> 1. How does April's relationship with Bear change throughout the story?
> 2. What does the story teach us about the impact of climate change?
> 3. How does April's father's job affect her feelings about the Arctic?
> 4. What would you do if you were in April's situation?
> 5. How does the author use descriptions of the Arctic to create a sense of place?

2. Create Debate Topics

We can also use AI to generate debate topics that encourage critical thinking such as:

> Prompt: "Write a debate topic for The Boy Who Grew Dragons."
> Response: "Is Tomas responsible enough to look after dragons? Why or why not?"

3. Develop Role-Playing Scripts

Ask your chosen AI platform to write scripts for role-playing or hot seating activities.

> Prompt: "Write a role-playing script for April from The Last Bear explaining why she wants to save Bear."
> Response:
> April: "I know Bear is wild, but he's all alone here because of the melting ice. I can't just leave him – I have to help him find a new home."

AI-Suggested Practical Classroom Activities for Book Discussions

1. Think-Pair-Share

- Pupils think about a discussion question, share with a partner, then discuss as a class.
- Example: "What surprised you most about *The Invisible*?"

2. Role-Playing Conversations

- Pupils take on the roles of different characters and discuss events from their perspective.
- Example: Have pupils act as different villagers from *The Storm Whale* and discuss whether Noi should have kept the whale.

3. "Question the Author" Activity

- Pupils write questions they would ask the author about the book's message, characters, or choices.
- Example: "What inspired Alexis Deacon to create the character of Beegu?"

4. AI-Powered Question Generator

- Use AI tools to generate personalised discussion questions.
- Example: "Give me three challenging discussion questions for Year 4 pupils reading A Mouse Called Julian."

Caution and Consideration

While facilitating book discussions, it's important to:

- Encourage Inclusivity: Ensure all pupils feel comfortable sharing their ideas.
- Respect Different Opinions: Teach pupils to listen respectfully and consider different perspectives.
- Balance Structure and Freedom: Provide enough guidance to keep discussions focused, but allow room for spontaneous conversation.

Recommended Tools

1. ChatGPT (free/paid) – Generates discussion questions and debate prompts.
2. DeepSeek (free) – Can generate in a similar way to ChatGPT.
3. Kahoot! (freemium) – Creates interactive book quizzes.
4. Google Bard (free) – Summarises book themes and suggests discussion topics.
5. Padlet (freemium) – Allows pupils to share and respond to book discussion questions online.
6. Book Creator (freemium) – Enables pupils to create digital book discussion journals.

16 Reading Aloud to Avatars

> Reading aloud to avatars is an innovative and engaging way to develop comprehension skills, build fluency and boost confidence in young readers. By using digital tools that feature interactive avatars, pupils can practise reading aloud in a safe, non-judgemental environment. This chapter explores how reading aloud to avatars can enhance literacy skills, with examples from a variety of primary school texts, including *The Miraculous Journey of Edward Tulane*, *The Wolf Wilder*, *The House with Chicken Legs*, *The Polar Bear Explorers' Club* and *The Train to Impossible Places*.

Why Read Aloud to Avatars?

When you read in your head this is useful for silent study, summarising and deeper analytical thinking without the distraction of vocalising. Yet when you read aloud, the "production effect" (saying words out loud) improves memory retention because the brain engages with both seeing and hearing the words. Reading aloud is slower than reading in your head because the brain must coordinate visual decoding, vocalisation and auditory processing. However reading aloud is still enormously beneficial as this skill requires active vocalisation, making the reader more engaged with pronunciation, rhythm and phrasing. The specific action of reading aloud to avatars offers several benefits including building confidence as children can practise reading without fear of judgement, making them more willing to take risks. It can also improve fluency as regular practice helps pupils develop pacing, intonation, and expression. Interactive avatars make reading feel like a game, motivating reluctant readers, therefore encouraging engagement. Some avatar tools offer instant feedback on pronunciation and fluency, helping pupils improve in real time.

How to Use Reading Aloud to Avatars in the Classroom

1. Choose the Right Texts

Select texts that are engaging and appropriate for your pupils' reading levels. Consider using excerpts from longer books or shorter standalone stories. For example, if you were to use

The Miraculous Journey of Edward Tulane by Kate DiCamillo a good excerpt would be: "Once, in a house on Egypt Street, there lived a rabbit who was made almost entirely of china."

This excerpt works because of the rich, descriptive language which is perfect for practising expression and fluency. You can use AI support to generate expanded versions of the excerpt for reading aloud such as:

> Prompt: "Write a short, engaging excerpt from The Miraculous Journey of Edward Tulane for pupils to read aloud."
>
> Response: "Edward Tulane was a proud rabbit, with fine china ears and a tail made of real rabbit fur. He sat on the shelf, staring out at the world with his glassy eyes, waiting for something extraordinary to happen."

2. Introduce the Avatar Tool

Choose a digital tool or app that features interactive avatars, such as Google Read Along, My Storybook or AI-powered platforms like ChatGPT with voice interaction. Explain how the tool works and set clear expectations for its use.

Example from *The Wolf Wilder* by Katherine Rundell:

> Activity: Pupils read aloud a passage where Feo trains the wolves, using an avatar tool to practise their pacing and expression.
>
> Discussion: "How did it feel to read aloud to the avatar? Did it help you focus on your fluency?"

Once the children have practised using the avatar with you then you can ask your AI platform to create guides to help the children use avatar tools independently.

> Prompt: "Write a step-by-step guide for pupils on how to use an avatar tool to practise reading aloud."
>
> Response:

1. Open the avatar tool on your device.
2. Select a story or upload your own text.
3. Press "Start" and begin reading aloud to the avatar.
4. Listen to the feedback and try again if needed.
5. Share your progress with your teacher or classmates.

3. Focus on Fluency and Expression

We can encourage pupils to pay attention to their pacing, tone and expression while reading aloud by providing tips such as pausing at punctuation marks, changing voices for different characters and emphasising key words to convey meaning.

Here's an example using *The House with Chicken Legs* by Sophie Anderson:

> Excerpt: "The house creaked and groaned, its chicken legs stretching as it prepared to move."
>
> Focus recommended by AI: Pupils should practise using a dramatic tone to convey the house's mysterious and magical qualities.

Prompt: "Write three tips for reading aloud with expression."
Response:

1. Use a different voice for each character to make the story come alive.
2. Pause at commas and full stops to give your audience time to absorb the story.
3. Emphasise words in bold or italics to show their importance.

4. Incorporate Comprehension Questions

After reading aloud, ask pupils questions to check their understanding of the text. This ensures they're not just focusing on fluency but also engaging with the content. You can ask AI to create the comprehension questions. Here's an example from *The Polar Bear Explorers' Club* by Alex Bell:

Excerpt: "Stella Starflake Pearl stood at the edge of the ice, her breath forming little clouds in the freezing air."
AI-Generated Comprehension Questions:

1. Where is Stella standing, and how do you know?
2. How does the author describe the weather?
3. What do you think Stella might be feeling in this moment?

Prompt: "Write three more comprehension questions for a passage from The Polar Bear Explorers' Club."
Response:

1. What does Stella's name tell us about her character?
2. How does the author create a sense of cold in this passage?
3. Why do you think Stella is standing at the edge of the ice?

5. Encourage Reflection and Feedback

After reading aloud, ask pupils to reflect on their performance and set goals for improvement. We can use AI to help with this too. After children have read to an avatar you could ask them how it felt to do this, what they felt went well and what they could improve next time. You can then provide constructive feedback, such as their use of great expression but perhaps they need to pause a bit longer at the full stops. We can also ask AI to generate reflection prompts such as:

Prompt: "Write a reflection prompt for pupils after reading aloud to an avatar."
Response: "What part of reading aloud do you find the most challenging? How can you practise to improve this skill?"

Using AI to Support Reading Aloud to Avatars

Free AI tools like ChatGPT can enhance reading aloud activities in several ways:

1. Generate Customised Texts

Ask your AI platform to create or adapt texts for reading aloud, tailored to your pupils' interests and reading levels.

Prompt: "Write a short, engaging passage for Year 4 pupils to read aloud, featuring a magical train."

Response: "The train to Impossible Places whistled as it pulled into the station, its carriages glowing with a soft, golden light. Suzy held her breath as the doors slid open, revealing a world of wonder inside."

2. Provide Real-Time Feedback

Some AI-powered avatar tools can analyse pupils' reading and provide instant feedback on pronunciation, pacing and fluency.

3. Create Interactive Scenarios

Use AI to generate interactive scenarios where pupils read aloud to an avatar and respond to its questions or comments:

Prompt: "Create an interactive scenario where an avatar asks a pupil questions about The Train to Impossible Places by P.G. Bell."

Avatar Response: "Why do you think Suzy decided to board the train? What would you have done in her place?"

Practical Classroom Strategies

1. Avatar Reading Stations

Set up reading stations with tablets or computers where pupils can practise reading aloud to avatars independently or in pairs.

2. Fluency Challenges

Organise a fluency challenge where pupils read aloud to an avatar and compete to improve their scores for pacing, accuracy and expression. For example:

Prompt: "Create a fluency challenge for a Year 3 pupil reading The Bog Baby by Jeanne Willis."

AI Response:

"Read this paragraph twice: once in a whisper, then in a storyteller voice."
"Try using a sad tone when the sisters let the Bog Baby go."

3. Progress Tracking

Use the avatar tool's feedback features to track pupils' progress over time and celebrate their improvements.

Caution and Consideration

While using reading aloud to avatars, it's important to:

- Balance Screen Time: Ensure pupils also have opportunities for traditional reading and discussion.
- Provide Support: Some pupils may need help navigating the technology or understanding feedback.
- Encourage Enjoyment: Keep the focus on fun and engagement to avoid making the activity feel like a test.

Recommended Tools

1. Google Read Along (free) - An app with interactive avatars that provide real-time feedback.
2. My Storybook (free/paid) - Allows pupils to create and read their own stories aloud.
3. AI-Powered Avatar Tools - Platforms like ChatGPT with voice interaction capabilities.
4. Fluency Apps - Tools like Raz-Kids or Reading Eggs offer interactive reading experiences.

17 Reading Challenges

> Reading challenges are a fantastic way to motivate pupils, encourage a love of reading and develop comprehension skills. By setting fun and achievable goals, reading challenges can help pupils explore new genres, improve their fluency and deepen their understanding of texts. This chapter explores how to design and implement reading challenges in the classroom, with examples from a variety of primary school texts.

Why Use Reading Challenges?

Reading challenges can boost children's motivation as they can make reading feel like a game, encouraging reluctant readers to participate. In challenges pupils are encouraged to try new genres, authors and formats. Challenges often include tasks that require deeper engagement with texts so they develop comprehension skills. Also the shared goals and celebrations can create a sense of camaraderie among pupils.

How to Design Reading Challenges

1. Set Clear Goals

Define the purpose of the challenge and set clear, achievable goals. For example, read a certain number of books in a term, explore different genres and complete specific tasks related to reading. Whatever class picture book or novel you are reading you can give tasks related to this with some help from AI. For example, if you were reading Lucy Strange's *The Secret of Nightingale Wood* the challenges could be prompted with, "Write six reading challenge tasks for The Secret of Nightingale Wood."

AI Response:

1. Draw a picture of the mysterious figure Henry sees in the woods.
2. Write a letter from Henry to her mother, explaining her feelings.
3. Research the historical setting of the book and share three interesting facts.
4. Write a diary entry from Henry's perspective.
5. Create a map of the woods based on descriptions in the book.
6. Discuss how the author creates a sense of mystery.

2. Incorporate Variety

It is important to include a mix of activities to cater to different interests and learning styles. For example:

Creative Tasks: Drawing, writing, or role-playing.
Analytical Tasks: Comparing characters, identifying themes, or analysing settings.
Collaborative Tasks: Group discussions or peer reviews.

Here's an example from *The Clockwork Crow* by Catherine Fisher:

Prompt: "After reading The Clockwork Crow give one creative task, one analytical task and one collaborative task for children to do."
Response: "Here are three engaging tasks based on The Clockwork Crow:

Creative Task:

Design Your Own Magical Object
Ask pupils to imagine they have discovered a mysterious object like the Clockwork Crow. They should describe its appearance, its magical abilities, and how it might help or hinder a character. Pupils can draw their object and write a short scene where the protagonist uses it in an adventure.

Analytical Task:

Character Study of Seren
Have pupils analyse how Seren changes throughout the novel. They should focus on her emotions, bravery, and determination, using specific evidence from the text. Encourage them to consider how her past as an orphan influences her actions and relationships with other characters.

Collaborative Task:

Drama: Key Scene Reenactment
In small groups, pupils choose a significant moment from the book (e.g. Seren's discovery of the Clockwork Crow or a confrontation with the Midwinter King). They create a short script and act it out, focusing on how to convey tension and emotion through dialogue and movement.

3. Use Themes and Formats

Themes and formats can make challenges more engaging. For example:

Genre Challenges: Read three books: one a mystery, another a fantasy, followed by a historical fiction book.
Author Challenges: Explore books by a specific author, such as Vashti Hardy or Piers Torday.
Format Challenges: Try a graphic novel, an audiobook or a poetry collection.

Here's an example related to *The Lost Magician* by Piers Torday:

> Prompt: "Create four reading challenges based on the theme of magic for The Lost Magician."
> Response:

- Read The Lost Magician and create a list of magical elements in the story.
- Research a famous magician and write a short biography.
- Compare the magic in the book to magic tricks you've seen or read about.
- Read a non-fiction book about real-life magic tricks and compare the two texts.

4. Track Progress and Celebrate Success

Use charts, badges, or digital tools to track pupils' progress and celebrate their achievements.

For example, after reading *The Great Chocoplot* by Chris Callaghan you could tell your class that they can complete five tasks to earn a "Chocolate Champion" badge.

Five tasks from an AI Response:

1. Write a news report about the chocopocalypse.
2. Create a poster advertising Jelly's plan to save chocolate.
3. Debate whether Jelly made the right decision at the end of the story.
4. Design your own chocolate bar and describe its ingredients.
5. Write a letter to the author, Chris Callaghan, sharing your thoughts on the book.

> Prompt: "Write a list of rewards for completing these tasks based on The Great Chocoplot."
> Response:

- A chocolate-themed certificate.
- A class party with chocolate treats.
- A special mention in the school newsletter.

5. Encourage Reflection

You can ask pupils to reflect on their reading challenge experience, including what they enjoyed, what they learned and what they might do differently next time.

After reading *The Infinite Lives of Maisie Day* by Christopher Edge you can review learning by using this prompt:

> Reflection Prompt suggested by AI: "What did you learn about science and time from reading The Infinite Lives of Maisie Day? How did the challenge help you understand the story better?"
> Further Reflection Prompt: "Write a reflection prompt for pupils after completing a reading challenge."
> Response: "What was your favourite part of the reading challenge? Did you discover any new genres or authors that you'd like to explore further?"

Using AI to Further Support Reading Challenges

AI tools like ChatGPT can enhance reading challenges in several ways:

1. Generate Challenge Ideas

Ask your chosen AI platform to create reading challenge tasks or themes.

Prompt: "Write five reading challenge tasks for The Infinite Lives of Maisie Day."
Response:

1. Research the concept of parallel universes and share three interesting facts.
2. Write a diary entry from Maisie's perspective on her birthday.
3. Create a timeline of events in the story.
4. Compare Maisie's world to our own: what's similar and what's different?
5. Design a poster explaining the science behind Maisie's experiences.

2. Create Customised Challenges

You can also use AI to tailor challenges to individual pupils' interests or reading levels.

Prompt: "Create a personalised reading challenge for a pupil who loves science and adventure."
Response:

- Read The Infinite Lives of Maisie Day and write a short story about a scientific discovery.
- Research a famous scientist and present your findings to the class.
- Create a comic strip showing Maisie's adventures in parallel universes.

3. Themed Reading Challenges

Encourage pupils to explore books based on a specific theme. For example:

The Wild Robot by Peter Brown – A survival and nature-themed challenge where pupils read books about animals, nature, or adventure.
AI Support:

- Ask ChatGPT to generate a list of books on a chosen theme.
- Use CommonLit (free) to find comprehension activities linked to the theme.

4. The "Read Around the World" Challenge

Pupils read books set in different countries or written by authors from various cultures. For example:

Anna Hibiscus by Atinuke – A challenge to read stories set in different parts of the world.
AI Support:

- Use Book Creator (freemium) to create a digital passport where pupils document their reading journey.
- Ask AI to suggest diverse books for each continent.

5. The Character Exploration Challenge

Pupils select a character from a book and read other books with similar protagonists. For example:

Claude in the City by Alex T. Smith – Pupils read about other adventurous animal characters like Paddington Bear or Varjak Paw.
AI Support:

- Use Google Bard (free) to suggest books with similar characters.
- Generate discussion questions comparing different protagonists.

6. The 20-Minute-a-Day Challenge

Pupils commit to reading for 20 minutes each day for a month. For example:

The Nothing to See Here Hotel by Steven Butler – A funny, engaging book that encourages daily reading.
AI Support:

- Use Epic! (freemium for teachers) to track daily reading streaks.
- Ask AI to summarise the daily reading session to reinforce comprehension.

7. The "Book in a Week" Challenge

Pupils read a short book within a week and complete a reflection task. For example:

The Hodgeheg by Dick King-Smith – A great choice for developing readers who need a manageable challenge.
AI Support:

- Use Kahoot! (freemium) to create a quiz about the book.
- AI can generate comprehension prompts for reflection tasks.

8. Provide Feedback and Encouragement

We can also use AI to generate positive feedback or motivational messages for pupils completing challenges.

Prompt: "Write a motivational message for a pupil who has just completed a reading challenge."
Response: "Well done on completing your reading challenge! You've explored new worlds, discovered amazing stories, and grown as a reader. Keep up the fantastic work!"

You can then ask for more responses and state that you want each one to be different in order for each child to receive a personalised response that doesn't take you a lot of time.

Caution and Consideration

While using reading challenges, it's important to:

- Ensure Accessibility: Choose challenges that are inclusive and achievable for all pupils.
- Avoid Overwhelming Pupils: Keep challenges fun and manageable to prevent stress or burnout.
- Celebrate Effort: Recognise and reward effort as well as achievement to encourage a growth mindset.

> **Recommended Tools**
>
> 1. ChatGPT (free/paid) – Generates challenge ideas, tasks, and feedback.
> 2. Reading Logs – Uses printable or digital logs to track progress.
> 3. Badge-Making Tools – Websites like Canva allow you to design customised badges or certificates.
> 4. Online Platforms – Tools like Goodreads or Reading Rockets offer reading challenge templates and ideas.
> 5. Epic! (freemium for teachers) – Tracks reading progress and suggests books.
> 6. CommonLit (free) – Provides comprehension resources linked to books.
> 7. Kahoot! (freemium) – Creates quizzes to test knowledge of books.
> 8. Book Creator (freemium) – Allows pupils to document their reading challenges creatively.

18 Flashcards

Flashcards are a simple yet powerful tool for reinforcing comprehension skills, building vocabulary, and supporting memory retention. Whether used in independent study, peer activities, or whole-class games, they help pupils actively engage with texts in a fun and interactive way. AI can enhance flashcard use by generating personalised content, adapting to pupils' progress, and providing immediate feedback.

Why Use Flashcards for Comprehension?

Flashcards can help pupils to strengthen their recall and retention of key story elements. They can improve vocabulary development by reinforcing new words. They also enhance critical thinking through question-and-answer activities. Plus, they support active engagement with texts in a dynamic way. By incorporating flashcards into literacy lessons, teachers can make learning more interactive and accessible for all reading levels.

Types of Flashcards for Comprehension

Flashcards can be adapted to suit different reading abilities and learning objectives. Below are some ways they can be used effectively in the classroom as suggested by AI (you could ask whichever platform you use to give you more suggestions but these are a few examples).

1. Character and Setting Flashcards

Pupils can create flashcards with character names, descriptions, or settings from a book. These can be used for matching activities, discussions, or creative storytelling exercises.
   For example, with *The Twits* by Roald Dahl you could have:

- Front: Mr Twit.
- Back: A mean and mischievous man with a scruffy beard full of food.
- Activity: Match character flashcards with their descriptions or key actions in the story.

AI Support:

Use ChatGPT to generate concise character descriptions for flashcards.
Use Quizlet (freemium) to create digital flashcards with images and definitions.

2. Key Vocabulary Flashcards

New or challenging words from a text can be placed on flashcards with definitions and example sentences.

For example, using *The Darkest Dark* by Chris Hadfield:

- Front: Astronaut.
- Back: A person trained to travel and work in space.
- Activity: Pupils act out or use the word in their own sentence.

AI Support:

Use Rewordify (free) to simplify difficult vocabulary.
Use Google Bard (free) to generate synonyms and example sentences.

3. Comprehension Question Flashcards

Flashcards with comprehension questions encourage pupils to think critically about the story.

Here's an example for *The Great Kapok Tree* by Lynne Cherry:

- Front: Why does the man stop cutting down the tree?
- Back: He listens to the animals and realises the forest is important.
- Activity: Pupils take turns drawing question flashcards and answering them aloud.

AI Support:

Ask ChatGPT to generate comprehension questions at different difficulty levels.
Use Quizlet to create interactive question-and-answer sets.

4. Sequence and Plot Flashcards

Pupils can arrange flashcards in the correct order to practise sequencing skills.
For example, *Where the Wild Things Are* by Maurice Sendak:

- Card 1: Max is sent to his room for misbehaving.
- Card 2: He sails to the land of the Wild Things.
- Card 3: He becomes king but decides to return home.
- Activity: Pupils put events in order or retell the story in their own words.

AI Support:

Use CommonLit (free) to find summarised versions of books to create flashcards.
Ask AI to generate key plot points from a story.

5. True or False Flashcards

Flashcards with statements about the book test comprehension in a quick, engaging way.
    For example, *The Tiger Who Came to Tea* by Judith Kerr:

- Front: True or False? The tiger drinks all the water in the sink.
- Back: False - he drinks all the tea instead!
- Activity: Pupils hold up "True" or "False" cards in response.

AI Support:

Ask AI to generate true/false questions for any book.
Use Kahoot! (freemium) for interactive true/false quizzes.

Using AI to Personalise Flashcards

AI tools can make flashcard learning more effective by:

Generating flashcard content for different books.
Providing tailored practice based on individual pupil needs.
Creating digital flashcards for online learning.

1. AI-Generated Flashcards

Prompt: "Create five flashcards for The Darkest Dark with key vocabulary and definitions."
AI Response:

1. Moon - The large round object that orbits the Earth.
2. Brave - Facing something scary without giving up.
3. Spacesuit - A special suit astronauts wear in space.
4. Launch - The moment a rocket takes off.
5. Darkness - The absence of light.

2. Customised Flashcard Sets

Prompt: "Generate five comprehension questions for The Twits."
AI Response:

1. Why do Mr and Mrs Twit play mean tricks on each other?
2. How do the monkeys escape from their cage?
3. What does the Roly-Poly Bird warn the other animals about?
4. What happens at the end of the book?
5. How would you describe the Twits' personalities?

3. AI-Powered Interactive Flashcards

You can use Quizlet to create AI-generated flashcard sets and you can also use Brainscape (freemium) for adaptive flashcard learning.

Caution and Consideration

When using flashcards, consider:

- Balancing memorisation with comprehension: Ensure pupils understand concepts, not just recall words.
- Keeping activities engaging: Vary flashcard formats to maintain interest.
- Supporting all learners: Provide visual aids for struggling readers.

Recommended Tools

1. Quizlet (freemium) - Digital flashcards with audio and games.
2. Brainscape (freemium) - Adaptive learning flashcards.
3. Kahoot! (freemium) - Interactive quizzes with flashcard modes.
4. Rewordify (free) - Simplifies vocabulary for flashcards.
5. Google Bard (free) - Generates flashcard content for comprehension.

19 Guess the Ending

Predicting how a story will end is an engaging way to develop pupils' comprehension skills, critical thinking and creativity. Encouraging pupils to make predictions based on clues within the text allows them to actively engage with narratives and strengthens their ability to infer meaning from plot development, character behaviour and themes. AI tools can enhance this activity by generating discussion prompts, personalised predictions and creative alternative endings, which we will explore in this chapter.

Why Teach Prediction Skills?

Guessing the ending of a book helps pupils to develop inference skills by using textual evidence to support their ideas. It also enhances engagement by creating curiosity and excitement about the story. Plus, it can encourage creativity by imagining different possible outcomes. Comprehension can also be improved by analysing character motives and plot structure. By making predictions before finishing a book, children become active participants in their reading, thinking critically about how events will unfold.

How to Use "Guess the Ending" in the Classroom

We can implement this strategy at different stages of reading. Here are some ideas for you to use with your class as generated by AI:

1. Mid-Story Predictions

Before finishing a book, stop at a key moment and ask pupils to predict what will happen next. For example, with *Claude in the City* by Alex T. Smith:

- Pause when Claude and Sir Bobblysock arrive in the city.
- Ask the children: What adventure do you think they will have next? Will they get into trouble?

2. Character-Based Predictions

We can encourage pupils to consider how a character's personality and past actions influence future events. With *Leon and the Place Between* by Angela McAllister we could:

Stop when Leon steps into the magical world.
Ask if the children think Leon will find his way back, or will he choose to stay?

3. Thematic Predictions

We could have pupils make predictions based on the book's themes and messages. For example, with *The Tin Forest* by Helen Ward we could:

Stop when the old man is surrounded by rubbish.
Then ask: How might the old man change his surroundings? What lesson will he learn?

4. Alternative Endings

After finishing a book, we can ask pupils to rewrite the ending. So with *The Owl Who Was Afraid of the Dark* by Jill Tomlinson we could ask pupils to imagine an ending where Plop remains afraid of the dark. Then discuss how this would change the story's message.

Using AI to Support "Guess the Ending" Activities

AI-powered tools can enhance prediction activities by:

Generating discussion prompts to help pupils think critically about possible endings.
Providing alternative endings for pupils to evaluate and compare.
Offering personalised writing prompts to help pupils create their own endings.

1. AI-Generated Prediction Prompts

Prompt: "Generate three prediction questions for Leon and the Place Between."
AI Response:

1. Will Leon find his way home, or will he stay in the magical world?
2. How will the magician react when Leon arrives?
3. What do you think is really inside the magician's box?

2. AI-Suggested Alternative Endings

Prompt: "Provide an alternative ending for The Tin Forest."
AI Response: "Instead of the old man's dream coming true, he decides to leave the wasteland and find a new home, only to return years later to find nature reclaiming the land."

3. Personalised Story Predictions

Prompt: "Suggest an ending to Claude in the City that is funny and unexpected."
AI Response: "Claude accidentally becomes the mayor for a day and makes Sir Bobblysock the official city mascot."

Practical Classroom Activities for Guessing the Ending

1. Prediction Pairs

Pupils can work in pairs to read a book up to a set point. Each pupil then writes a different possible ending. They then read each other's predictions and discuss which is more likely.

2. "End It Your Way" Challenge

Pupils read a book without the final chapter. They then write their own ending and compare it with the author's. For example, with *Leon and the Place Between* pupils could write their own version of Leon's fate.

3. AI vs. Pupil Predictions

Pupils could write their own prediction for a book's ending. Meanwhile, generate an AI prediction for the same book. Show this to the class so that pupils can compare and vote on the most convincing ending.

4. Class Debate: Best Ending

Pupils read different alternative endings. They debate which ending best fits the story's themes. For example, should Plop stay afraid or overcome his fear in *The Owl Who Was Afraid of the Dark*?

Encouraging Independent Prediction Skills

Pupils can:

Keep a **prediction journal** where they write and reflect on their guesses.
Use AI tools to generate discussion prompts for books they read at home.
Read multiple books by the same author and predict common themes in their endings.

Caution and Consideration

When using prediction activities, consider:

- Encouraging open-ended thinking: Pupils should justify multiple possibilities, not just guess "correctly."
- Avoiding spoilers: Choose stopping points carefully so the ending isn't obvious.
- Balancing AI with creativity: AI should enhance, not replace, pupil-led predictions.

Recommended Tools

1. ChatGPT (free/paid) - Generates personalised prediction questions.
2. DeepSeek (free) - Generates prediction questions too.
3. Kahoot! (freemium) - Creates interactive prediction quizzes.
4. Google Bard (free) - Suggests alternative endings for stories.
5. Book Creator (freemium) - Allows pupils to write and illustrate their own endings.
6. StoryJumper (freemium) - Helps pupils create digital books with different endings.

20 Clarify the Confusion

> Reading comprehension is not just about understanding words on a page. It's also about making sense of the ideas, themes and deeper meanings within a text. Pupils often encounter moments of confusion when reading, whether due to unfamiliar vocabulary, complex sentence structures or abstract concepts. Teaching strategies to clarify confusion helps build confident, independent readers. AI tools can support this process by offering instant definitions, context-based explanations and interactive discussion prompts, which we will explore in this chapter.

Why Teach Clarification Skills?

Clarifying helps pupils to improve comprehension by breaking down difficult sections of text. It also develops problem-solving skills by using strategies to find meaning and builds vocabulary by understanding words in different contexts. It also enhances confidence by encouraging children to ask questions and seek answers, which is what we strive for children to do. By fostering a classroom environment where it's okay to be confused, we can encourage our pupils to engage more deeply with texts and take ownership of their learning.

Common Sources of Confusion in Texts

Confusion can arise from various elements within a story. Here are some common challenges, and strategies to overcome them:

1. Unfamiliar Vocabulary

Pupils may struggle with new or complex words. For example, in *The Girl Who Speaks Bear* by Sophie Anderson:

- Difficult word: Ethereal
- Strategy: Break the word into parts, use AI tools like Google Bard to define it and relate it to context.

2. Figurative Language and Metaphors

Literary devices can sometimes make comprehension more challenging. Here's an example for *The Boy at the Back of the Class* by Onjali Q. Raúf:

> Confusing phrase: "His heart sank."
> Strategy: Use AI to generate examples of metaphors, personification and other figurative language to see their meanings in different contexts.

3. Complex Sentence Structures

Long or intricate sentences can make it difficult for pupils to track meaning. For example, in *The Miraculous Journey of Edward Tulane* by Kate DiCamillo we see:

> Challenging passage: "Edward had no understanding of love. He neither loved nor cared to be loved."
> Strategy: Break the sentence into smaller parts, rephrase using AI tools, and discuss the character's emotions.

4. Shifts in Time and Perspective

Books that use flashbacks or multiple narrators can be confusing for young readers too, as in *The Skylarks' War* by Hilary McKay:

> Confusing shift: Moving between World War I events and personal family memories.
> Strategy: Create a timeline with AI assistance or summarise key moments to track narrative shifts.

5. Abstract or Symbolic Ideas

Some books explore deep themes that are hard for children to grasp too, like *The Island* by Armin Greder:

> Confusing theme: Social exclusion and prejudice.
> Strategy: Use AI to generate discussion questions that connect themes to real-world issues.

Using AI to Clarify Confusion

AI tools can enhance clarification activities by generating simplified explanations for difficult passages, providing word definitions and examples to expand vocabulary and suggesting comprehension questions to check understanding.

1. AI-Generated Word Definitions

> Prompt: Define "ethereal" and provide an example sentence.
> AI Response:
> - Definition: "Extremely delicate and light in a way that seems too perfect for this world."
> - Example: "The morning mist made the forest look ethereal, as if it belonged in a fairy tale."

2. Simplified Explanations

Prompt: Simplify this sentence: "Edward had no understanding of love. He neither loved nor cared to be loved."

AI Response: "Edward didn't know what love was. He didn't love anyone, and he didn't care if anyone loved him."

3. AI-Powered Discussion Prompts

Prompt: "Create three discussion questions for The Island."
AI Response:

1. "Why do you think the people on the island were afraid of the stranger?"
2. "How does the artwork in the book help tell the story?"
3. "What lessons can we learn from this story about how we treat others?"

Practical Classroom Activities for Clarifying Confusion

1. "Ask the AI" Activity

Pupils write down confusing parts of a book and ask AI for clarification as to what the author means. For example, in *The Skylarks' War*: "Why does Clarry feel invisible in her family?" AI can generate responses based on the themes and the character development.

2. Sentence Surgery

Pupils take a complex sentence and rewrite it in simpler terms. For example, in *The Miraculous Journey of Edward Tulane* we can ask AI to break down any challenging sentences into short, clear phrases.

3. Word Detective Challenge

When pupils find unfamiliar words in a book, we can use AI to define these words to help children create independent sentences. In *The Girl Who Speaks Bear* we could identify and explore folklore-related vocabulary such as "Yaga" (a reference to Baba Yaga, a character from Slavic folklore known as a wise, sometimes fearsome witch) and "Domovoi" (a household spirit in Slavic folklore, often depicted as a small, bearded creature protecting the home).

4. Timeline Creation

Pupils could create a visual timeline to track time jumps in a story. So, in *The Skylarks' War* the children can map key events in historical context.

5. AI-Generated Summaries

Pupils summarise a passage and compare it with an AI-generated summary to check clarity. They could even summarise the message of the story in one sentence. Here's an AI summary of *The Island*: "A powerful exploration of fear, prejudice, and exclusion, showing how societies can reject outsiders and the consequences of intolerance."

Caution and Consideration

When using AI to clarify confusion, consider:

- Encouraging critical thinking: Pupils should evaluate AI explanations rather than accepting them without question.
- Balancing AI with discussion: Peer- and teacher-led clarification is still essential.
- Ensuring content appropriateness: AI-generated responses should always be reviewed for accuracy.

Recommended Tools

1. Google Bard (free) - Provides word definitions and text simplifications.
2. ChatGPT (free/paid) - Generates explanations and discussion prompts.
3. DeepSeek (free) - as above.
4. Rewordify (free) - Simplifies complex sentences for easier understanding.
5. Kahoot! (freemium) - Creates quizzes to reinforce comprehension of tricky concepts.
6. Book Creator (freemium) - Allows pupils to record and track confusing moments in their reading journey.

PART 3
Character Descriptions

In this section, AI becomes a partner in developing rich, nuanced character writing. Teachers will discover how AI tools can assist pupils in analysing characters from books and crafting their own, using prompts that guide exploration of appearance, personality, actions and development over time. The section includes ideas for comparing characters, using emotive language effectively and experimenting with dialogue writing. It provides classroom-ready tools for sentence starters, opposites and contrasts and contextual exploration in order to help pupils move from basic observations to sophisticated interpretations. With AI's support, pupils can generate fresh character profiles, receive feedback and edit creatively. This part is especially valuable for developing empathy, inference and expressive writing skills. Whether your pupils are analysing a protagonist from a class novel or inventing someone entirely new, this section offers frameworks that build writing fluency and confidence.

21 Checking Book Character Descriptions

> Visualising characters is an essential part of reading comprehension, helping pupils to engage more deeply with the text. AI-powered image generation tools offer an exciting way for pupils to bring book characters to life by converting descriptive text into digital artwork. These tools can help children understand the power of detailed descriptions and the importance of artistic interpretation in storytelling.

Why Use AI to Generate Character Images?

Using AI image generation platforms, pupils can enhance comprehension by visualising characters based on textual descriptions, and also develop descriptive writing skills by seeing how specific words affect an image's outcome. This encourages creativity through exploration of different artistic styles. We can also encourage children to compare different interpretations of the same character description. By engaging with AI tools, pupils not only refine their reading skills but also deepen their understanding of how different artistic choices influence visual representation.

How Text-to-Image Tools Work

AI-powered image generation platforms allow users to input descriptive phrases, which are then transformed into unique images. The results vary in style, ranging from photorealistic representations to cartoon-like illustrations or paintings. The level of detail provided in the description directly influences the image generated.

For example, typing "a gorilla in a retro colourful suit" or "a 3D abstract candy tiered cake" into an AI tool will produce vastly different results depending on the level of detail and artistic settings selected. Some platforms offer watercolour effects, while others mimic oil painting or digital sketching styles.

We can encourage pupils to experiment with these tools by entering different levels of detail in their descriptions. A vague description like "a cat sitting in a field" will generate a simple image, whereas a more detailed phrase such as "a cat with rainbow-coloured fur sitting under a purple sky" will produce a richer and more specific visual outcome. This activity helps children understand the impact of descriptive writing and the importance of precise word choices.

Applying AI to Book Character Descriptions

Once pupils are familiar with AI-generated imagery, connect this activity to a class text. Select a character description from a book and input it into a text-to-image generator. For example, in *Skellig* by David Almond, the mysterious character is described as:

> Sitting with his legs stretched out and his head tipped back against the wall. He was covered in dust and webs like everything else, and his face was thin and pale. Dead bluebottles were scattered on his hair and shoulders. I shined the flashlight on his white face and his black suit.

After generating an AI image based on this description, ask pupils to compare the digital result with their personal mental image of Skellig. Did the AI-generated image match their expectations? In what ways did it differ? Encourage discussion about how individual interpretation influences reading experiences and how personal imagination shapes our perception of characters.

Similarly, if reading *The Gruffalo* by Julia Donaldson, input the description: "He has terrible tusks and terrible claws and terrible teeth in his terrible jaws."

Compare the AI-generated Gruffalo with the famous Axel Scheffler illustrations. How does the AI interpretation differ from the original artwork? This discussion reinforces how artistic choices, whether human-made or AI-generated, shape our understanding of a character.

Classroom Activities Using AI Character Visualisation

1. Visualising Characters through AI

- Pupils select a character description from a book and input it into an AI tool.
- Compare the AI-generated image with their own drawing or mental image.
- Discuss how the description influenced the final image.

2. Comparing Interpretations

- Compare AI-generated images with published book illustrations.
- Discuss the differences in artistic interpretation and visual style.
- Reflect on how different descriptions of the same character may result in varying images.

3. Writing and Illustrating Original Descriptions

- Pupils write their own descriptive passages for a character they imagine.
- Use AI to generate an image based on their writing.
- Swap descriptions with a partner and see how different interpretations emerge.

Encouraging Independent Exploration

Pupils can then go on to experiment with AI-generated images at home using book descriptions. They can also create their own story characters and bring them to life visually. Then they can compare multiple AI-generated results to see how wording affects imagery.

Caution and Consideration

When using AI-generated images, consider:

- Accuracy: AI may not always interpret descriptions exactly as intended.
- Creativity vs. AI Output: Encourage pupils to rely on their own imagination as well.
- Ethical Use: Discuss how AI creates images and the importance of responsible use.

Recommended Tools

1. Deep Dream Generator (freemium) - Generates artistic interpretations of text descriptions.
2. Runway ML (freemium) - Allows for AI-powered character generation and customisation.
3. Craiyon (free) - Text-to-image tool for quick and creative visualisations.
4. Dream by Wombo (free/paid) - Generates stylised artwork based on text input.
5. ChatGPT (free/paid) - Can refine character descriptions before generating images.
6. Adobe Firefly (free/paid) - You get a set number of image generations a month.

22 Character Analysis

Understanding and analysing characters is a key component of reading comprehension. When pupils engage in character analysis, they learn to interpret motivations, relationships, and changes that occur throughout a story. We want all of the children we work with to be empathic human beings and the close examination of characters in books can help with this enormously. But studying character analysis also develops critical thinking skills and a deeper appreciation for storytelling. AI tools can enhance character analysis by helping pupils track character development, generating discussion prompts and providing personalised insights into literary figures, as we shall explore in this chapter.

Why Teach Character Analysis?

Character analysis helps pupils to identify personality traits based on actions, dialogue and descriptions. It also helps children to understand motivations behind a character's decisions, track character development from the beginning to the end of a story and explore relationships between different characters. Children will also be given opportunities to make predictions about a character's future behaviour. By focusing on these aspects, pupils gain a more nuanced understanding of a story's themes and messages.

How to Teach Character Analysis

1. Identify Character Traits

We can teach pupils to identify and describe characters' traits using evidence from the text. Here's an example from *The Boy at the Back of the Class* by Onjali Q. Raúf:

Use your chosen AI platform to generate character trait lists.
Prompt: "List three traits for Ahmet from The Boy at the Back of the Class and provide evidence from the text."
Response:

1. Brave: Ahmet stands up to bullies who tease him about his background.
2. Resilient: He adapts to a new school and culture despite the difficulties.
3. Kind: He shares his lunch with a classmate, showing his generosity.

2. Explore Character Motivations

We can help pupils understand why characters act the way they do by examining their motivations. For example Chaya from *The Girl Who Stole an Elephant* by Nizrana Farook steals the queen's jewels. We can use AI to explore her motivations with our children.

> Prompt: "Write a discussion prompt about Chaya's motivations in The Girl Who Stole an Elephant."
> Response: "Chaya steals the jewels to help her friend, but her actions cause a lot of problems. Do you think she was right to do this? What would you have done in her place?"

3. Analyse Character Development

We can also examine how characters change and grow throughout the story. In *The Boy Who Grew Dragons* by Andy Shepherd, Tomas's character evolves as the story unfolds. We can use AI to create character development charts like this one:

> Prompt: "Create a character development chart for Tomas from The Boy Who Grew Dragons."
> Response:
> - Beginning: Tomas is nervous and overwhelmed by the dragons.
> - Middle: He starts to understand their needs and behaviours.
> - End: Tomas becomes a confident and caring dragon owner.

4. Compare and Contrast Characters

We can encourage pupils to compare characters to understand their roles and relationships better. In *The House with Chicken Legs* by Sophie Anderson we can compare Marinka and her grandmother, Baba Yaga, using AI.

> Prompt: "Write a comparison activity for Marinka and Baba Yaga from The House with Chicken Legs."
> Response: "Create a Venn diagram comparing Marinka and Baba Yaga. Focus on their desires, responsibilities and how they change throughout the story."

5. Create Character Profiles

We can ask pupils to create detailed profiles for characters, including traits, motivations and key moments. For example in Christopher Edge's *The Infinite Lives of Maisie Day* we can ask AI to create a profile on Maisie like this:

> Prompt: "Create a character profile template for The Infinite Lives of Maisie Day."
> Response:
> - Name: Maisie Day.
> - Traits: Curious, determined, resilient.

- Motivations: To understand the science behind her experiences.
- Key Moments: Discovering parallel universes, solving the mystery of her existence.

Using AI to Further Support Character Analysis

AI can enhance character analysis by generating discussion prompts about a character's actions and decisions, providing comparative analysis of characters from different books and summarising character arcs to help pupils track development.

1. AI-Generated Character Questions

Prompt: "Create three discussion questions about Roz in The Wild Robot."
AI Response:

1. "How does Roz adapt to living in the wild, and what does this say about her character?"
2. "What challenges does Roz face, and how does she overcome them?"
3. "How does Roz's relationship with the animals change throughout the book?"

2. Comparing Characters with AI

Prompt: "Compare Fred from The Explorer and Leo from The Lion Above the Door."
AI Response:

- Fred is resourceful and determined to survive in the Amazon, while Leo must find courage to embrace his identity.
- Both characters grow in confidence, but Fred's challenges are physical, while Leo's are emotional and social.

Encouraging Independent Character Analysis

Pupils can:

- Keep a Character Journal tracking how a character evolves throughout a book.
- Use AI tools to generate character discussion questions to deepen their understanding.
- Draw character mind maps showing relationships and key influences.

Caution and Consideration

When analysing characters, consider:

- Encouraging multiple interpretations: Characters can be understood in different ways.
- Avoiding stereotyping: Encourage pupils to look beyond surface traits.
- Using AI as a support tool: Pupils should still form their own opinions about characters.

Recommended Tools

1. ChatGPT (free/paid) – Generates discussion questions and character summaries.
2. DeepSeek – as above.
3. Google Bard (free) – Provides comparative analysis of characters.
4. Book Creator (freemium) – Allows pupils to create digital character profiles.
5. Kahoot! (freemium) – Creates quizzes on character traits and development.
6. CommonLit (free) – Offers character study guides with comprehension questions.

23 Context of Characters

Understanding the context of a character helps pupils develop a richer appreciation of their actions, motivations and development within a story. Context includes historical settings, cultural backgrounds, personal experiences and societal expectations, all of which shape how a character thinks and behaves. By examining these factors, pupils can engage more deeply with literature and gain insight into perspectives different from their own. The AI tools suggested here can enhance character context analysis by offering background information, generating discussion prompts and facilitating historical or cultural research.

Why Teach Character Context?

Exploring the context of characters helps pupils to understand motivations by linking personal background to actions. Children will also be able to make connections between historical events and characters' experiences and develop empathy by considering different social and cultural perspectives. This can also enhance their comprehension by recognising the influence of time and place on character development. By incorporating context into character analysis, pupils build a broader understanding of the world and how literature reflects different societies and historical moments.

Key Aspects of Character Context

Context can be explored in several ways, each contributing to a well-rounded understanding of a character's role in a story, as we shall explore in these four activities using AI for support:

1. Historical Context

We can use AI tools to provide historical background on specific time periods to help pupils understand characters' experiences. AI-generated timelines or summaries can give pupils a clearer picture of historical events that shape a character's journey. A character's experiences are often shaped by the time period in which they live. For example, in *Goodnight*

Mister Tom by Michelle Magorian we see the character of Willie Beech who is an evacuee sent to live in the countryside to escape the bombings in London in World War II.

We can use AI to help research World War II evacuees and discuss how real-life experiences might compare to Willie's journey.

2. Social and Cultural Context

A character's culture, traditions, and societal norms influence their actions and worldview.

In *Planet Omar: Accidental Trouble Magnet* by Zanib Mian the character Omar is a British Muslim boy navigating school life and friendships while facing misconceptions about his background. The story explores themes of identity, acceptance, and community.

We can use AI tools to generate cultural background summaries to help pupils understand unfamiliar traditions for this text and other books.

3. Personal Background

AI can generate summaries on specific conditions, such as OCD, helping pupils understand how these challenges affect daily life. AI-powered discussion prompts can also encourage deeper exploration of a character's personal struggles and growth. A character's upbringing, family situation, and personal experiences shape their decisions and growth.

For example, *The Goldfish Boy* by Lisa Thompson shows how Matthew suffers from OCD, which affects his interactions and perceptions of the world. His anxiety and compulsions create challenges, but he gradually overcomes personal struggles through friendships and problem-solving.

> Activity: Use AI to create prompts for discussion on how Matthew's condition affects his choices and how other characters respond to him.

4. Environmental and Geographical Context

The setting in which a character lives influences their lifestyle, challenges and opportunities.

In *Sky Song* by Abi Elphinstone, Eska lives in the snowy landscapes of Erkenwald, a mystical and harsh environment. Her survival skills and connection to nature are essential for her journey and identity.

We can use AI-generated setting descriptions to compare Eska's world with real-life Arctic conditions. We can also compare these descriptions with our own environments.

Using AI to Support Context Analysis

AI can enhance understanding of character context by providing historical and cultural overviews to support reading comprehension, generating discussion prompts to encourage critical thinking and suggesting real-world parallels to deepen pupils' connections to the text.

1. AI-Generated Historical Summaries

Prompt: "Provide a short explanation of evacuees during World War II."

AI Response: "During World War II, many children in Britain were evacuated from cities to the countryside to escape bombings. They lived with host families and had to adapt to a new way of life. Some had positive experiences, while others struggled with homesickness and mistreatment."

2. Discussion Prompts from AI

Prompt: "Generate three discussion questions about Omar's cultural background in Planet Omar."

AI Response:

1   "How does Omar's cultural background influence his experiences at school?"
2   "What challenges does Omar face because of misunderstandings about his faith?"
3   "How does Omar's family support him in staying true to his identity?"

3. AI-Powered Comparative Analysis

Prompt: "Compare the settings in Sky Song and The Goldfish Boy."
AI Response:

> Sky Song is set in a magical, frozen landscape where survival depends on resilience and bravery, while The Goldfish Boy takes place in a modern suburban setting where internal struggles define the protagonist's journey. Both characters face challenges in their environments, but Eska's are physical while Matthew's are psychological.

This response might be too complex for your class but can be easily simplified:

Prompt: "Could you simplify to simple sentences to include a relative clause or a subordinate clause using but, or, and, because, then or so?"
Simplified Response:

> Sky Song is set in a cold, magical land **where** people need to be brave **because** it is hard to survive. The Goldfish Boy is set in a modern town, **and** the main character has to deal with his feelings. Eska faces physical problems, **but** Matthew's problems are in his mind.

Practical Classroom Activities for Context Analysis

1. Historical Role-Playing

Use AI to generate historically accurate scenarios based on different time periods. AI can also suggest realistic dialogue for pupils to use in their role-playing activity, helping them to engage more deeply with the historical context.

- Pupils take on the roles of characters from different historical settings and act out how they might respond to events in their time period.
- Example: Act out a day in the life of Willie Beech as an evacuee in *Goodnight Mister Tom*.

2. Compare and Contrast Contexts

AI can generate comparison charts summarising character backgrounds and experiences. Pupils can input two character names and receive a structured table outlining key similarities and differences, helping them to articulate their comparisons more effectively. Pupils could compare two characters from different backgrounds. For example, they could compare Matthew's experiences in *The Goldfish Boy* with Eska's in *Sky Song*.

3. Research and Reflect

AI can also generate brief summaries of different cultures, historical events or traditions to support pupils' research. AI-generated discussion questions can also help guide pupils in analysing how these real-life elements are reflected in the text. Pupils could research a real-life cultural or historical context related to their book and present their findings. For example, they could research British Muslim traditions and compare them with Omar's experiences in *Planet Omar*.

4. AI-Assisted Context Exploration

Pupils can use AI to generate setting descriptions and historical insights to deepen their understanding. For example, they could ask AI to summarise wartime evacuee experiences to help analyse *Goodnight Mister Tom*.

Encouraging Independent Exploration

To independently explore the AI platforms of your choice, your pupils could keep a context journal where they record notes on how setting and background shape characters, use AI tools to research historical or cultural elements in books they read or/and discuss how real-world parallels can be drawn from fictional characters.

Caution and Consideration

When exploring context, consider:

- Avoiding assumptions: Encourage pupils to base interpretations on textual evidence.
- Providing accurate information: AI-generated insights should be fact-checked.
- Ensuring inclusivity: Approach discussions on culture and history with sensitivity.

Recommended Tools

1. ChatGPT (free/paid) - Generates historical and cultural summaries.
2. Google Bard (free) - Provides detailed setting and context descriptions.
3. Book Creator (freemium) - Allows pupils to document their context analysis.
4. CommonLit (free) - Offers historical and cultural background readings.
5. Kahoot! (freemium) - Creates quizzes to test knowledge on book contexts.

24 Appearance and Personality

Describing a character's appearance and personality is essential for bringing them to life in a story. By analysing how authors create vivid characters through physical descriptions and personality traits, pupils can deepen their understanding of literature and develop their creative writing skills. AI tools can support this process by helping pupils identify descriptive techniques, generate new characters and refine their own descriptions.

Why Teach Character Appearance and Personality?

Understanding and describing character traits helps pupils to recognise descriptive techniques used by authors to bring characters to life and to distinguish between appearance and personality, identifying how both contribute to character development. Pupils will also develop empathy by considering how a character's traits influence their actions. We will explore here how to create original characters by using AI-powered prompts and suggestions.

By focusing on these aspects, pupils enhance their comprehension skills and writing abilities, making their own characters more engaging and believable.

Analysing Character Appearance and Personality

Character descriptions involve both physical features and personality traits, both of which contribute to how a reader visualises and understands a character.

1. Describing Physical Appearance

Authors often use vivid details to help readers picture a character. For example, in *The Twits* by Roald Dahl, Mr. Twit is described as being "Hairy-faced, with bits of old food caught in his beard," which creates an image of an unkempt, unpleasant character who lacks hygiene.

Use an AI tool like ChatGPT to generate descriptions of characters based on given traits. For example, ask: "Describe a villain with a mysterious and eerie appearance." AI can then provide varied responses, helping pupils understand different descriptive styles.

2. Exploring Personality Traits

Personality traits define how a character thinks, feels, and behaves. *Matilda* by Roald Dahl features Miss Honey who is kind, patient and gentle. Her warmth contrasts sharply with Miss Trunchbull's cruelty.

Pupils can list adjectives describing a chosen character's personality and use AI to generate new synonyms or alternative phrases.

3. Linking Appearance to Personality

Sometimes, an author's description of appearance reflects a character's nature. In *The Lion, the Witch and the Wardrobe* by C.S. Lewis, the White Witch is described as "tall and cold, her skin as white as snow" and her icy appearance symbolises her cold and unfeeling nature.

Pupils can ask AI to provide further examples of characters where appearance reflects personality. Pupils can compare AI-generated examples with their own interpretations too.

Creating New Characters with AI

AI tools can help pupils develop original characters by generating detailed descriptions based on prompts, which we will explore here.

1. Generating Character Descriptions

Prompt: "Create a character who is adventurous and mischievous, with a striking physical appearance."
AI Response:

- Name: Felix Stormrunner
- Appearance: A wiry boy with unruly red hair, bright green eyes, and a scar on his left eyebrow. Always dressed in a patched-up leather jacket.
- Personality: Fearless, playful, and quick-witted. Loves to explore hidden places and play harmless pranks.

Pupils can then refine the AI-generated character by adding their own unique details.

2. Expanding Character Backstories

Prompt: "Write a short backstory for a character who is quiet but incredibly brave."
AI Response:

- "Nina was always the quietest in her village, but when a wildfire threatened her home, she was the first to organise an escape plan, guiding the frightened children to safety."

Pupils could use this AI-generated backstory as inspiration to write their own extended backstories.

3. Creating Character Comparison Charts

Pupils can compare an AI-generated character with one from a book they've read. For example, they could compare Felix Stormrunner (AI-generated) with Peter Pan (J.M. Barrie). Both are mischievous, but Peter refuses to grow up, whereas Felix dreams of becoming a famous explorer.

Using AI to Support Character Exploration

AI can enhance character exploration by generating diverse character descriptions based on prompts, providing alternative ways to describe a personality trait and suggesting character arcs to develop a character throughout a story.

1. AI-Generated Descriptive Synonyms

Prompt: "Give me five different ways to say 'brave' in a character description."
AI Response:

1. Fearless
2. Courageous
3. Bold-hearted
4. Tenacious
5. Lionhearted

Pupils could use the AI-generated synonyms to rewrite a description of a new character.

2. AI-Powered Personality Development

Prompt: "Describe how a shy character becomes more confident by the end of a story."
AI Response:

- "At the start, Aria barely spoke above a whisper. But by the final chapter, she stood before her entire class, proudly presenting her science project, her voice strong and unwavering."

Pupils could then take a different personality trait and write their own version of how a character changes over time.

Practical Classroom Activities for Character Exploration

1. Character Sketching

Pupils draw a character based on a written description. For example they could illustrate Felix Stormrunner based on the AI-generated description.

2. Character Interviews

Pupils take turns "interviewing" a character. For example, one pupil plays Miss Honey from *Matilda*, while another asks about her past and feelings. If pupils struggle to come up with interview questions, AI can generate a list of possible questions based on a character's background. For example: "Give me five interview questions for Miss Honey from Matilda."

AI Response:

1. How did your childhood shape the way you teach?
2. What do you admire most about Matilda?
3. How do you feel about Miss Trunchbull's treatment of pupils?
4. What are your hopes for Matilda's future?
5. If you could change one thing about your life, what would it be?

3. Character Development Timelines

Pupils can ask AI to map out how a character's appearance and personality change over time. For example, they could track Edmund's growth in *The Lion, the Witch and the Wardrobe* from selfish to selfless like this:

> Edmund begins *The Lion, the Witch and the Wardrobe* as a selfish and jealous boy who betrays his siblings for personal gain, but through hardship and redemption, he learns the value of loyalty and courage. By the end, he fights bravely for good and is crowned King Edmund the Just, embodying wisdom and selflessness.

4. AI-Assisted Writing Challenge

Pupils input traits into an AI tool and receive a character description. For example, they could say, "Use these traits to create a short character description - 'magical, mysterious, ancient, quiet yet kind'."

Response:

> Eldrin moved through the forest like a whisper, his **ancient** robes trailing over the mossy ground. A **mysterious** glow surrounded him, shimmering in the twilight, hinting at the **magical** power woven into his being. Though his eyes held the weight of centuries, they softened with warmth when he spoke. He was **quiet yet kind**, his voice barely above a murmur, yet each word carried wisdom that lingered long after it was spoken.

The children could then add more to this description or create a narrative scene about the character.

Caution and Consideration

When using AI, consider:

- Avoiding stereotypes: Encourage varied and original character descriptions.
- Balancing AI with creativity: AI should be a tool for inspiration, not a replacement for imagination.
- Ensuring ethical use: Discuss responsible AI use in creative writing.

Recommended Tools

1. ChatGPT (free/paid) – Generates character descriptions and writing prompts.
2. Deep Dream Generator (freemium) – Creates visual representations of characters.
3. Book Creator (freemium) – Allows pupils to design their own character profiles.
4. Kahoot! (freemium) – Creates quizzes on character descriptions.
5. Storybird (freemium) – Helps pupils turn character ideas into illustrated stories.

25 Revealing Character through Actions

> A character's actions are one of the most powerful ways an author reveals their personality, motivations and emotions. Instead of telling the reader what a character is like, actions allow them to show a character's nature in a dynamic and engaging way. Whether it's an act of bravery, a moment of hesitation or a quiet gesture of kindness, actions shape how readers perceive and understand a character. AI tools can support pupils in analysing how authors use actions to reveal character traits, generating creative writing prompts and also helping pupils create their own characters with depth and believability.

Why Teach Character through Actions?

Focusing on actions helps pupils to identify personality traits by examining what characters do rather than what is said about them, and understand motivations behind a character's choices. They can also infer emotions by interpreting gestures, expressions and movement while developing their own richer writing by using action-based descriptions instead of direct statements. We can help children create believable characters by ensuring actions match a character's personality. By analysing and creating action-based descriptions, pupils deepen their comprehension and strengthen their narrative writing skills.

How Actions Reveal Character

Authors use a character's physical movements, choices and habits to reveal their traits. Instead of saying a character is brave, an author may show it through how they respond to danger. Instead of stating that someone is selfish, their actions, such as refusing to share, reveal it organically.

1. Small Gestures Reveal Personality

Sometimes, the tiniest action can speak volumes about a character. For example, in *The Boy at the Back of the Class* by Onjali Q. Raúf, Ahmet keeps his head down and stays quiet in class, which reveals that he is shy and possibly scared, showing his struggle as a refugee adjusting to a new school.

Pupils can use AI to generate examples of small gestures that reveal personality. For example, using the prompt, "Give me five different ways a nervous character might act in a classroom," the response was:

1. Biting their nails under the desk.
2. Avoiding eye contact and fidgeting with their sleeves.
3. Whispering answers instead of speaking confidently.
4. Hesitating before writing anything down.
5. Jumping slightly at sudden noises.

Pupils can apply these AI-generated examples to their own characters.

2. Reactions to Challenges Show Growth

A character's response to a challenge can highlight their development or reinforce a trait. In *The Last Bear* by Hannah Gold, April carefully approaches the polar bear instead of running away in fear, which reveals she is compassionate and brave, willing to help an animal in need.

AI can generate prompts for pupils to explore how characters react in different situations. We can ask AI:

"How might a cautious character react to discovering a hidden door?"
"Describe how a determined child would respond to failing a test."

Pupils can then compare AI responses with book characters or use them to inspire their own writing.

3. Contradictions in Actions and Words

Sometimes, a character's words do not match their actions, revealing hidden traits. For example, in *The Secret Garden* by Frances Hodgson Burnett, Mary Lennox insists she doesn't care about the garden, but she secretly tends to it every day. This reveals that she is learning to care about something beyond herself, even if she won't admit it yet.

AI can help generate examples of contradictory behaviour to spark discussion.

Prompt: "Give me three examples of a character who says one thing but does another."
Response:

- A character who claims they aren't afraid of the dark but always leaves the lights on.
- A character who says they don't like animals but feeds stray cats every night.
- A child who insists they don't want to be part of a team but always helps their friends succeed.

Pupils can analyse similar contradictions in texts they read, or create their own.

Creating New Characters through Actions

AI can assist pupils in creating original characters whose traits are revealed through actions instead of direct statements.

1. Generating Action-Based Character Introductions

Instead of stating a character's traits, AI can help pupils show them through movement and behaviour.

> Prompt: "Create a character who is curious but cautious. Describe them entering a mysterious house."
> Response: "Lena stepped onto the dusty porch, her fingers twitching at the edge of her coat. She hesitated at the door, peeking through the keyhole before slowly turning the handle, heart pounding with both fear and excitement."

This response might be too complex for your class but can be easily simplified:

> Prompt: "Could you simplify to simple sentences to include a relative clause or a subordinate clause using coordinating or subordinating conjunctions?"
> Response: "Lena stepped onto the dusty porch and held her coat. She stopped at the door because she felt a little scared. She looked through the keyhole and then turned the handle slowly. Her heart was beating fast because she was scared and excited."

Pupils can refine AI responses, adding personal details or changing the setting.

2. Expanding Character Development with AI

Pupils can ask AI to generate:

- A list of small actions that show nervousness, excitement or anger.
- How a character's actions might change throughout a story.
- Unexpected actions that reveal hidden personality traits.

For example, children could prompt AI with "How does a quiet child's actions change after they gain confidence?"

> AI Reponse: "A quiet child's actions shift from avoiding eye contact and hesitating to speak to actively participating in discussions and engaging with peers. As their confidence grows, they move from observing to contributing, using open body language, initiating conversations, and even taking on leadership roles."
> Simplified Response: "A quiet child is someone who does not look at others and finds it hard to speak. They often wait and watch because they feel shy. Then they start to join in and talk with friends. They speak more and use open body language. They may even lead a group because they feel more confident."

Children can use the response to track character growth of their own character in a narrative they are writing.

Practical Classroom Activities for Character Exploration

1. Action-Driven Story Starters

When pupils receive an AI-generated character action they can expand it into a short scene. For example:

> AI-Generated Action: "Kai clutched the crumpled note, his fingers shaking as he stepped toward the teacher's desk."

The children can then go on to describe the character further from this starter prompt.

2. Character Observation Journals

Pupils can note the actions of book characters and infer their personality traits. For example:

> Prompt: "What do Lyra's actions in *Northern Lights* by Philip Pullman tell us about her courage?"
>
> Response:

> "Defying Authority: Lyra consistently challenges authority figures, such as when she deceives the Master of Jordan College and later stands up to Mrs. Coulter, showing her bravery in questioning power and making independent decisions.
>
> Rescuing Others: Her determination to save kidnapped children from Bolvangar, despite the danger, highlights her willingness to risk her own safety for others, proving her selfless and fearless nature.
>
> Facing the Unknown: Whether venturing into the frozen North, navigating treacherous situations with Iorek Byrnison, or confronting the mysteries of Dust, Lyra's actions demonstrate her courage in embracing the unknown without hesitation."

This analysis can be used as a model to help children to analyse other book characters in the same way.

3. AI-Powered "What Happens Next?"

We could provide pupils with an AI-generated action and let them predict what the character will do next. For example: "Mina glanced at the locked diary, her hand hovering over the key. She took a deep breath and…"

They could then write what Mina does and what occurs from this action.

Caution and Consideration

When using AI, consider:

- Encouraging originality: Pupils should use AI-generated ideas as inspiration rather than copying responses.
- Fact-checking: AI can occasionally produce inconsistent character traits.
- Balancing AI with creativity: AI should support, not replace, pupils' own analysis and writing.

Recommended Tools

1. ChatGPT (free/paid) – Generates action-based character descriptions.
2. Deep Dream Generator (freemium) – Creates visual interpretations of characters.
3. Book Creator (freemium) – Allows pupils to design interactive character profiles.
4. Kahoot! (freemium) – Creates quizzes on character traits.
5. Storybird (freemium) – Helps pupils develop narratives using action-driven characterisation.

26 Character Development

Character development is the process of how a character changes and grows throughout a story. Strong, well-developed characters engage readers and make narratives feel real and compelling. By tracking character changes over time, pupils can better understand storytelling and how an author builds complexity into a character's journey. AI can support this learning by analysing character arcs, generating development prompts and assisting pupils in creating their own evolving characters.

Why Teach Character Development?

Focusing on character development can help pupils to recognise changes in personality, motivation, and emotions over the course of a story. Plus, they'll get to understand cause and effect by linking events to character growth and analysing how challenges shape a character's actions and decisions. But they can also create their own characters with depth and realistic progression. By using AI tools to track, analyse and generate evolving character arcs, children can explore how characters change, thus gaining a deeper appreciation of narrative structure and storytelling techniques.

Tracking Character Development

Characters evolve through their experiences, relationships and challenges. Pupils can analyse this transformation, using AI to assist, by focusing on these elements:

1. Internal vs. External Change

Internal Change is how a character's thoughts, beliefs, and emotions shift. Whereas External Change is how a character's physical circumstances or relationships change. For example in *The Wild Robot* by Peter Brown, Roz the Robot is programmed for survival but lacks understanding of emotions and nature. She then learns how to care for animals and becomes a protector of the island. Finally, she sacrifices her own safety to protect those she loves, showing her transformation from machine to caregiver.

Pupils can use AI to generate a character transformation chart, prompting AI with: "Describe how a robot character could change from cold and logical to caring and protective."

> Response: "A robot initially follows strict programming, making cold, logical decisions without emotion, but after forming an unexpected bond with a human or another being, it begins to understand empathy, leading it to make protective and selfless choices. Over time, its mechanical actions soften – hesitating before making calculated decisions, shielding others from danger, and even breaking its programming to prioritise compassion over efficiency."
>
> Simplified Response: "A robot is a machine that follows rules and makes choices without feelings. It does what is logical and does not care about others. But one day, it makes a new friend. Because of this, it starts to feel something new – kindness. Then it begins to help others and tries to keep them safe. It even breaks the rules because it wants to care instead of just being right."

AI-generated responses can help pupils map out stages of character growth for their own characters by following the same transformation story arc.

2. Challenges That Drive Change

Characters often change as a result of the struggles they face. In *The Highland Falcon Thief* by M.G. Leonard and Sam Sedgman, Harrison Beck is uninterested in trains and reluctant to travel. But he is then challenged to solve a theft mystery aboard the Highland Falcon train. After this challenge, Harrison develops a love for adventure and detective work, showing greater confidence and independence.

With pupils, we can ask AI to generate character challenges that drive growth. For example: "Give me three challenges that could make a shy character more confident."

> Response:
>
> 1. Public Speaking Opportunity – The character is unexpectedly asked to present something in front of the class. At first, they feel anxious, but with practice and encouragement, they gain confidence in their ability to speak up.
> 2. Making a New Friend – The character is paired with a friendly and outgoing classmate for a project. Through teamwork and shared experiences, they learn to communicate more openly and develop stronger social skills.
> 3. Taking on a Leadership Role – When an unexpected situation arises, such as leading a group during a school trip or helping organise a class event, the character steps up. Despite initial hesitation, they realise their abilities and grow more self-assured.

AI can generate other tailored prompts to inspire creative writing and literary analysis.

Building a Strong Character Arc

A well-developed character arc follows a structure:

1. Introduction – Who they are at the beginning.
2. Conflict and Growth – The challenges they face and lessons learned.
3. Transformation – How they have changed by the end.

For example, in *A Kind of Spark* by Elle McNicoll, Addie struggles with being understood as an autistic girl. She faces challenges at school but learns to stand up for herself. She then transforms to becomes a strong advocate for herself and others, embracing her identity.

Pupils can use AI to expand a character arc by asking, "How would a character with low confidence change throughout a story?"

> Response: "A character with low confidence may start off avoiding challenges and staying in the background, but through facing personal struggles or unexpected opportunities, they gradually learn to trust themselves, speak up, and take risks. By the end of the story, they are more assertive, comfortable in their abilities, and willing to take on leadership roles or new challenges with self-assurance."

AI-generated outlines can help pupils brainstorm realistic growth paths.

Creating New Characters with Development in Mind

AI can support pupils in designing original characters that grow and change over time.

AI-Generated Character Growth Prompts

Pupils can use AI to generate development prompts such as:

- "Describe a character who starts out selfish but learns to be kind."
- "How would a lonely child change after making a new friend?"
- "Give me an example of a character who overcomes a great fear."

Responses:

- Beginning: James avoids social interactions, preferring to be alone.
- Middle: He is paired with a talkative friend for a school project.
- End: Learns to enjoy companionship and grows more confident in speaking up.

Pupils can refine AI responses by adding personal touches and unique details.

Practical Classroom Activities for Character Development

1. Character Change Journals

Pupils can track a character's changes over time, noting key events that influence growth. For example, Lyra's development in *Northern Lights* by Philip Pullman from rebellious child to courageous heroine.

> Prompt: "Summarise Lyra's character growth in Northern Lights in three sentences."
>
> Response: "Lyra begins 'Northern Lights' as a rebellious and impulsive child, driven by curiosity and a desire for adventure. Through her journey, she faces moral dilemmas, betrayal, and loss, which force her to grow in wisdom, resilience, and empathy. By the end, she is no longer just a mischievous girl but a courageous leader, willing to make great sacrifices for those she loves."

2. Role-Playing Growth Scenarios

Pupils can also act out character challenges and discuss how their actions might change. For example, how would Auggie from *Wonder* by R.J. Palacio respond to a bullying situation at the start versus the end of the book?

Prompt: "Write a dialogue where Auggie stands up for himself after gaining confidence."
Response:

Bully:	"Still hiding behind your desk, Auggie? Afraid to show your face?"
Auggie (standing up):	"No, I'm not afraid anymore. My face doesn't define who I am, but my actions do. Maybe it's time you stop judging and start listening."
Bully (awkwardly):	"Uh... whatever."
Friend:	"That was amazing, Auggie. You didn't let him get to you."
Auggie (smiling):	"I've spent too long worrying about what people think. I know who I am, and that's enough."

AI-generated dialogues help pupils visualise emotional growth through speech and actions.

3. AI-Assisted "Before and After" Writing

Pupils write a short scene of a character at the beginning of a story and use AI to suggest how they might change by the end.

Prompt: "Describe a character who is afraid of water. How might they overcome their fear?"

Response: "Lena feared water ever since she slipped into a deep pond as a child, avoiding it at all costs. But after befriending a patient swimming instructor, she slowly built her confidence, first dipping her toes, then floating, until one day she swam across the lake with joy instead of fear."

All of these responses have been made deliberately short but you can create more detailed responses if you choose to.

Caution and Consideration

When using AI, consider:

- Avoiding simplistic character arcs: Pupils should refine AI-generated ideas to ensure depth and originality.
- Ensuring character growth is realistic: AI responses may need human adjustments for believability.
- Balancing AI with creative input: AI should serve as a support tool, not a replacement for pupil-led ideas.

Recommended Tools

1. ChatGPT (free/paid) - Generates character growth ideas and development charts.
2. Deep Dream Generator (freemium) - Creates visual representations of characters at different stages of growth.
3. Book Creator (freemium) - Allows pupils to document character arcs interactively.
4. Kahoot! (freemium) - Builds quizzes on character development analysis.
5. Storybird (freemium) - Helps pupils create illustrated narratives showing character change.

27 Sentence Starters

Sentence starters are a powerful tool in character descriptions, helping pupils craft engaging and vivid portrayals of fictional individuals. By providing structured openings, pupils can develop confidence in their writing, explore different narrative styles and experiment with the depth of their descriptions. AI can support this process by generating, refining and expanding sentence starters, ensuring pupils have a strong foundation for character writing.

Why Use Sentence Starters for Character Descriptions?

Sentence starters help pupils by providing structure to assist pupils to begin their writing with confidence, and encouraging variety in sentence structures and vocabulary choices. They can also enhance creativity by guiding pupils towards more imaginative descriptions. Sentence starters can also support differentiation so that all pupils, regardless of ability, can engage with character writing. In this chapter we will be using AI tools to generate personalised sentence starters and refine character descriptions for your pupils.

Types of Sentence Starters

1. Appearance-Based Sentence Starters

Pupils can use sentence starters to create detailed visual descriptions of a character's appearance. For example, in *The Iron Man* by Ted Hughes we could ask AI to give us sentence starters that describe the Iron Man's appearance, such as:

AI Prompts:

- "His massive, shadowy frame towered over the fields…"
- "Glowing eyes peered through the darkness, scanning the horizon…"

2. Personality-Based Sentence Starters

Sentence starters can reveal aspects of a character's personality, showing how they think, feel, and interact with the world. So, in *Matilda* by Roald Dahl the protagonist is described as:

- "Matilda had always been quietly determined, her mind buzzing with ideas…"
- "Despite her small size, an unstoppable fire burned within her…"

Pupils can input personality traits, like these, into an AI tool and generate sentence starters.

> Prompt: "Create three sentence starters that show a character who is both shy and clever."
> Response:

1. With her eyes fixed on the floor, she hesitated before answering, but when she spoke, her words were…
2. He shrank back from the group's chatter, yet his quiet mind was thinking of…
3. She fidgeted with the hem of her sleeve, barely whispering her idea – until the teacher wrote it on the board, which said…

3. Action-Based Sentence Starters

Actions often reveal more about a character than direct description. These sentence starters place the character in motion, showcasing their personality through their behaviour. In *The Explorer* by Katherine Rundell, the author says, "Fred grasped the vines tightly, his breath quickening as he climbed higher…" and "With careful precision, he examined the broken compass, hoping for a clue…"

AI can suggest action-based sentence starters suited to different genres or themes.

> Prompt: "Generate three action-based sentence starters for a brave explorer."
> Response:

1. With steady hands, he pushed aside the vines, revealing the hidden temple.
2. She leapt across the crumbling bridge, her heart pounding.
3. Dodging falling rocks, he raced toward the treasure's glow.

4. Emotion-Based Sentence Starters

Characters' emotions drive their actions and decisions. Sentence starters focusing on emotions help pupils connect to a character's internal world. In *Wonder*, R.J. Palacio says, "Auggie clenched his fists, willing himself to stay strong…" and "A wave of nerves washed over him as he stepped into the classroom…"

Pupils can use AI to generate emotion-driven sentence starters by providing key feelings.

> Prompt: "Create three sentence starters for a nervous but determined character."
> Response:

1. Her hands trembled, but she took a deep breath and stepped forward.
2. He swallowed hard, forcing himself to meet their gaze.
3. Despite the fear twisting in her stomach, she refused to turn back.

Using Sentence Starters to Create New Characters

AI can also help pupils build original characters by generating structured sentence openings that lead into unique descriptions.

AI-Generated Character Introductions

Pupils input a character type into AI (e.g. "a mischievous fox who loves riddles"). AI then generates three possible sentence starters. Your pupils select one and continue writing their own full description.

Example AI Output:

- "The sly fox tiptoed through the moonlit forest, a knowing glint in his eyes…"
- "With a flick of his bushy tail, the fox darted between the trees, whispering a riddle to the wind…"
- "Perched on a fallen log, the fox grinned, his golden eyes filled with secrets…"

Classroom Activities Using AI and Sentence Starters

1. Sentence Starter Mix and Match

Provide pupils with a list of sentence starters for appearance, personality, action and emotions, such as:

Appearance: His tattered cloak billowed in the wind, revealing a silver pendant beneath.
Personality: Her kindness was quiet but constant, like a steady flame in the darkness.
Action: They edged closer to the mysterious door, their fingers hovering over the ancient key.
Emotion: Her stomach churned as she stepped onto the stage, her hands clammy with nerves.

Pupils can mix and match starters to create varied character descriptions. AI can also generate more customised sentence starters for specific genres or themes.

2. Expanding Sentence Starters with AI

Your pupils select a short sentence starter. They then input it into AI and ask for an expanded version. For example:

- Pupil's Starter: "She walked into the room, her heart pounding."
- AI Expansion: "She walked into the room, her heart pounding like a drum, each step echoing in the silence as all eyes turned toward her."

3. AI-Prompted Writing Challenges

Pupils can input different character traits and let AI generate unique sentence starters. For example:

Prompt: "Create three very different sentence starters for a pirate who has lost their treasure."

Response:

1. Captain Blacktooth stomped across the deck, his fists clenched. Someone would pay for this betrayal.
2. He stared at the empty chest in disbelief, the salty wind whipping through his tangled beard.
3. With a heavy sigh, she scanned the endless ocean, knowing the treasure was out there... somewhere.

Pupils can then build a full paragraph based on a chosen AI-generated starter.

Caution and Consideration

When using AI, consider:

- Ensuring variety: AI may generate repetitive sentence structures – encourage pupils to refine them.
- Keeping creativity at the centre: AI should support, not replace, a pupil's unique ideas.
- Checking appropriateness: Always review AI-generated content before sharing with pupils.

Recommended Tools

1. ChatGPT (free/paid) – Generates personalised sentence starters based on prompts.
2. DeepL Write (free) – Helps refine and enhance descriptive sentence structures.
3. Book Creator (freemium) – Allows pupils to compile their descriptions into interactive digital books.
4. Wordtune (freemium) – Suggests ways to improve and extend sentence starters.
5. Storybird (freemium) – Provides illustrated prompts and sentence starters for storytelling.

28 Opposites and Comparisons

> Using opposites and comparisons in character descriptions helps pupils create more vivid, engaging portrayals of their characters. By contrasting personalities, appearances and actions, pupils can highlight key traits and make their characters more dynamic. AI can support this process by generating comparative descriptions, suggesting opposite character traits and helping children to refine their writing.

Why Use Opposites and Comparisons in Character Descriptions?

Opposites and comparisons can help pupils enhance descriptions by emphasising contrasts between characters and develop deeper characterisation by showing how differences impact relationships. They can also create conflict and balance by pairing characters with contrasting traits. In this chapter we will use AI tools to generate comparisons and explore different character dynamics.

Using Comparisons to Build Stronger Characters

Comparisons help define a character by relating them to another person, an animal, an object, or even a force of nature as a simile.

1. Comparing Characters to Objects or Nature

In *The Firework-Maker's Daughter*, Philip Pullman says, "Lila's courage burned like a firework, fierce and unstoppable" and "Her father was as steady as the mountains, unshaken by fear."

We can help pupils to use AI to generate similar similes using prompts and giving examples:

Prompts:

"Describe a brave character using a comparison to nature."
"Create a simile comparing a wise old man to an object."

AI Examples:

"Her courage was like a roaring wildfire, unstoppable and fierce, lighting the way for others."
"The old man's wisdom was like an ancient oak tree; rooted deep in experience, standing tall through every storm."

DOI: 10.4324/9781003621379-31

2. Comparing Characters to Each Other

Comparing characters to one another can highlight their differences and similarities, making their personalities stand out. In *Charlotte's Web*, E.B. White says, "Wilbur was nervous and excitable, while Charlotte was calm and wise." Plus "Templeton the rat was selfish and sneaky, whereas Wilbur was kind-hearted and trusting."

We can challenge our pupils to create their own paired descriptions with AI-generated prompts as examples:

Prompt:

"Compare a timid character with a confident one."
"Describe two best friends who are complete opposites."

Response:

"Ella shuffled her feet, hesitant to speak, while her twin brother Max strode into the room, greeting everyone with a booming voice."
"Lena was always neat and organised, planning everything to the last detail, while her best friend Jake lived in a whirlwind of last-minute ideas and messy notebooks."

Using Opposites to Show Contrast

Opposites make character descriptions stronger by creating a clear contrast in traits, behaviours or appearances.

1. Opposing Personality Traits

In *The Lion, the Witch and the Wardrobe*, C.S. Lewis describes Edmund as "selfish and deceitful," while Lucy was "kind and honest."

Lewis goes on to say, "The White Witch ruled with cruelty, but Aslan led with wisdom and compassion."

Pupils can input two opposite traits into AI and generate a description with a prompt like, "Describe a character who is both cold and ruthless, and another who is warm and forgiving."

Response:

> Commander Vex moved through the battlefield like an unyielding storm, his icy gaze scanning for weakness. Mercy was a word he had long erased from his vocabulary and every decision he made was calculated, efficient, and without hesitation.
>
> Mira's laughter was like a gentle breeze after a storm, carrying comfort wherever she went. Even when betrayed, she found kindness in her heart, believing that every mistake held the chance for redemption.

Simplified Response:

> Commander Vex moved across the battlefield like a strong storm. He had cold eyes that looked for weakness. He did not believe in mercy because he had forgotten the word long ago. Every choice he made was quick and planned. He never stopped to think twice.

Mira's laugh was soft and made people feel calm. It was like a breeze after a storm. She stayed kind even when others were not. She believed mistakes could be fixed because everyone deserves a second chance.

2. *Opposing Appearances*

Characters' physical descriptions can also use contrasts to make them more distinctive.

Roald Dahl describes the BFG as, "enormous but gentle, while the other giants were even bigger and terrifying." And Sophie as, "Sophie was tiny and frail, but her bravery made her feel ten feet tall."

Pupils can use AI to generate contrasting descriptions by prompting:

"Describe two siblings who look completely different."
"Write a contrast between a towering villain and a small but fierce hero."

Response:

"Lena had golden curls that bounced with every step, while her brother Felix had straight black hair that never seemed to move."
"The villain loomed over the battlefield, his shadow stretching like a storm cloud, while the tiny warrior stood firm, her blade gleaming in the dim light."

Creating New Characters with Opposites and Comparisons

AI can help pupils design original characters by using contrasts and comparisons. Pupils input a character type into AI, such as "a mischievous boy and his serious best friend."

AI generates descriptions for both characters and then pupils refine the descriptions and use them in their writing.

Example AI Output:

"Jack's grin was always wide, his pockets full of tricks, while Oliver walked with a frown, his books neatly tucked under his arm."
"Where Jack saw adventure, Oliver saw danger; where Jack laughed, Oliver sighed."

Classroom Activities Using AI and Opposites in Character Descriptions

1. *Opposite Pairs Writing Exercise*

Pupils pick two opposite traits such as loud/quiet, reckless/cautious, etc. and describe a character for each. AI can suggest descriptions of opposite traits based on these prompts such as:

Loud/Quiet: "Jake's voice boomed through the hall, drawing every eye, while Sam shrank into the corner, speaking only when necessary."
Reckless/Cautious: "Eva raced ahead without a plan, leaping before she looked, while Leo carefully mapped every step, calculating the safest path forward."
Brave/Fearful: "Mila stood tall, facing the beast without hesitation, while her brother clutched her arm, his knees trembling beneath him."

2. Expanding Contrasts with AI

Pupils can write a short character comparison then input it into AI and ask for an expanded version. For example:

Pupil's Starter: "She was quick and clever, while he was slow and thoughtful."

AI Expansion: "She darted from idea to idea like a hummingbird, always chasing the next adventure, while he moved carefully, considering every possibility before speaking."

3. AI-Prompted Writing Challenges

Pupils can also input different character pairs and let AI generate descriptions.

Example Prompt: "Create a short comparison between a fearless knight and a nervous squire."

Response: "The knight strode forward without hesitation, his sword gleaming under the sunlight, while the squire lingered behind, clutching his shield with trembling hands, eyes darting for an escape."

Pupils can then use the AI-generated descriptions to write a short scene or describe the characters further.

Caution and Consideration

When using AI, consider:

- Encouraging original thinking: AI should inspire, not replace, pupil creativity.
- Ensuring balance: Not all characters need extreme opposites – subtle contrasts can be effective too.
- Checking AI accuracy: AI-generated descriptions should be reviewed for relevance and appropriateness.

Recommended Tools

1. ChatGPT (free/paid) – Generates comparisons and opposite character traits.
2. DeepL Write (free) – Helps refine contrasting descriptions.
3. Book Creator (freemium) – Allows pupils to document character comparisons interactively.
4. Kahoot! (freemium) – Builds quizzes comparing character traits.
5. Storybird (freemium) – Provides illustrated prompts for developing opposite characters.

29 Emotive Language

> Emotive language plays a crucial role in character descriptions, allowing readers to connect with characters on a deeper level by conveying their thoughts, feelings and experiences. By choosing words carefully, writers can shape how a character is perceived and evoke an emotional response. AI can support this process by generating descriptive phrases, refining word choices and suggesting variations in tone and intensity.

Why Use Emotive Language in Character Descriptions?

Emotive language helps pupils to develop empathy by understanding a character's emotions and reactions. It also enhances storytelling by making characters more believable and engaging. It can improve vocabulary by introducing powerful adjectives, verbs and figurative language. In this chapter we will use AI tools to explore different levels of emotion and refine descriptions for children.

Emotive Language in Character Descriptions

1. Describing a Character's Feelings

Emotive language allows readers to experience what a character is going through rather than just being told. In *The Boy at the Back of the Class*, Onjali Q. Raúf says, "Ahmet sat alone, his eyes fixed on the floor, his hands twisting the frayed edge of his jumper. He was lost in silence, a sadness clinging to him like a shadow."

Pupils can use AI to generate emotion-driven sentences by prompting: "Describe a character feeling nervous before speaking in front of a crowd."

- AI Response: "Her heartbeat drummed in her ears, and her hands clutched the paper so tightly that the edges curled under the pressure."
- Further Prompt: "Write a sentence showing excitement without using the word 'excited.'"
- AI Response: "His feet bounced against the floor, his fingers tapping a wild rhythm on the desk as he waited for his name to be called."

Children can use these responses as models to then create their own sentences to describe a character's feelings.

2. Using Emotive Verbs and Adjectives

Strong verbs and adjectives can enhance emotional depth in writing. In *The Last Bear*, Hannah Gold does this. She says, "April's chest ached as she watched the bear disappear into the distance, swallowed by the endless stretch of ice and loneliness."

Pupils can input a neutral sentence and ask AI to enhance it with emotive words such as:

Neutral Sentence: "The child walked into the room."
AI Response: "The child crept into the room, her small hands trembling as she peeked around the doorway."

Once this model has been explored, then children can have a go at writing their own independent sentences in the same style.

Building Emotional Contrast in Characters

1. Expressing Opposing Emotions

Characters often experience a range of emotions throughout a story. Contrasting these emotions can highlight character development. *The Goldfish Boy* by Lisa Thompson has this sentence we can use as an example:

> At first, Matthew recoiled from the thought of stepping outside, his stomach twisting in fear. But as he took one shaky step forward, a flicker of pride warmed his chest.

Pupils can prompt AI to generate opposing emotions within the same character such as:

Prompt: "Describe a character feeling scared, then gradually becoming braver."
AI Response: "She hesitated at the edge of the diving board, her toes curling over the rough surface. But then, with a deep breath and a surge of determination, she leapt, slicing through the water like a fearless arrow."

We can give children a scaffold like this to help them create their own sentences:

> "She hesitated at the _____, her fingers _____. But then, with a deep breath and a _____, she _____ like a _____."

After practice, the children can then create their own sentences.

2. Creating New Characters with Emotive Language

AI can help pupils design emotionally rich characters by providing structured prompts and detailed responses. Pupils begin by inputting a basic character type into AI, such as "a lonely scientist."

Response: "Dr. Lorne sat alone in his cluttered lab, his fingers hovering over the half-finished blueprint. His chest tightened as he realised – no one was waiting for him at home tonight, just as no one had the night before."

Once AI has generated emotionally descriptive sentences then pupils can refine the descriptions to enhance depth.

Classroom Activities Using AI and Emotive Language

1. Emotion Swap Writing Exercise

Pupils write a sentence showing a strong emotion such as anger and input it into AI. They can ask for the emotion to be changed to perhaps sadness or joy. For example:

> Original: "She slammed the door, her fists clenched." (Anger)
> AI Response: "She pressed the door closed gently, her fingers tracing the wood as a single tear slipped down her cheek." (Sadness)

Children can then do this, using AI as a prompt, for other emotions before independently creating their own sentences.

2. Expanding Emotional Depth with AI

Pupils can then write a simple sentence and input it into AI for expansion, for example:

> Pupil's Starter: "He was sad."
> AI Expansion: "His shoulders sagged as he stared at the empty chair, the ghost of a smile lingering in his memory."

After practice, children can then create their own descriptions.

3. AI-Prompted Writing Challenges

Pupils can go on to inputting different emotional states into AI and letting it generate descriptions. For example:

> Prompt: "Describe a character feeling hopeful after a long struggle."
> Response: "The weight of the past months lifted from her chest as she saw the sunrise, golden rays stretching across the horizon, whispering promises of a new beginning."

After being given a few examples, encourage children to write their own in the same style.

Caution and Consideration

When using AI, consider:

- Encouraging pupils to revise AI suggestions to ensure their writing remains personal and meaningful.
- Discussing emotional sensitivity when exploring strong emotions in character descriptions.
- Balancing AI-generated ideas with personal creativity to maintain originality.

Recommended Tools

1. ChatGPT (free/paid) - Generates emotionally descriptive sentences and vocabulary.
2. DeepL Write (free) - Enhances emotional tone and clarity in writing.
3. Book Creator (freemium) - Allows pupils to compile their emotive writing into digital stories.
4. Wordtune (freemium) - Suggests alternative words and phrasings for stronger emotional impact.
5. QuillBot (freemium) - Helps refine sentence structures for more expressive descriptions.

30 Dialogue

Dialogue is a powerful tool in character descriptions, revealing personality, emotions and relationships through speech. Well-crafted dialogue makes characters more engaging and helps readers connect with them. AI can support the development of dialogue by generating examples, refining speech patterns and helping pupils explore character voices.

Why Use Dialogue in Character Descriptions?

Dialogue helps pupils show, not tell, by revealing emotions and traits through spoken words. It can also develop unique character voices to distinguish personalities and shows how to build relationships between characters, highlighting interactions and conflict. In this chapter we will use AI tools to generate, refine, and experiment with different dialogue styles.

Using Dialogue to Reveal Character

1. Expressing Personality through Speech

When we write dialogue with our pupils, we should model that characters should speak in ways that reflect their traits. Dialogue can show confidence, hesitation, excitement or sadness without explicitly stating these emotions. In *The Worst Witch* by Jill Murphy we see this dialogue:

> "I'm sure I'll get it right next time," Mildred muttered, gripping her broomstick nervously. "Next time?" scoffed Ethel. "If you survive this time!"

After discussing this model, pupils can use AI to generate dialogue that reflects different emotions.

> Prompt: "Write a line of dialogue for a shy character asking a question."
> AI Response: "Um... excuse me, but... do you think I could maybe... borrow that book? If it's not too much trouble?"
> Prompt: "Write a line of dialogue for a confident character making an announcement."
> Response: "Ladies and gentlemen, the wait is over – our greatest adventure begins now!"

Ask the children to write more lines of dialogue that shows the personality of characters who are aggressive, resilient, curious or compassionate.

2. Developing Distinct Character Voices

Each character should have a unique way of speaking. Factors like word choice, sentence length and tone create differentiation. In *The Gruffalo* by Julia Donaldson, the fox asks, "Where are you going to, little brown mouse?" and the mouse replies, "I'm off to have tea with a Gruffalo."

We can ask pupils to generate contrasting voices using AI.

Prompt: "Create dialogue for an old, wise character and a reckless young adventurer."
AI Response:

- Wise Character: "Patience, young one. A journey is measured in lessons, not just steps."
- Reckless Adventurer: "Lessons? I don't have time for lessons! I just want to go!"

Ask the children to use contrasting characters and create dialogue between them. There could be opposite characters such as:

Curious vs. indifferent.
Brave vs. fearful.
Logical vs. emotional.
Optimistic vs. pessimistic.
Independent vs. dependent.

Using Dialogue to Build Relationships

1. Showing Conflict and Tension

Dialogue can also highlight differences between characters and create conflict. In *Harry Potter and the Philosopher's Stone* by J.K. Rowling, Hagrid says, "You're a wizard, Harry."
And Harry replies, "I - I'm a what?"
We can encourage pupils to ask AI to create dialogue showing tension between characters, like this:

Prompt: "Write a conversation between two best friends arguing about a secret."
AI Response:
"You promised you wouldn't tell!"
"I didn't mean to! It just slipped out!"

Ask the children to use this model to create conversations between friends who find something exciting, are scared of something or are planning a trip somewhere.

2. Creating New Characters through Dialogue

AI can help pupils explore new character voices and interactions by prompting creative exchanges. If we ask our pupils to input a character type into AI, such as a grumpy shopkeeper, then AI can generate the dialogue matching that personality. For example:

"Hmph! If you're not buying anything, don't touch the merchandise!"

Or, a kind teacher:

"Take your time, dear. Mistakes mean you're learning, and that's the most important part."

After discussing this model, children can then have a go at writing lines of dialogue for an excitable inventor, a wise grandparent, a mischievous trickster or a mysterious stranger.

Classroom Activities Using AI and Dialogue

1. Voice Swap Exercise

We can ask pupils to write a piece of dialogue for one character, then ask AI to respond with an opposite character. For example, a dialogue between an excitable person and an anxious person:

Original: "I can't wait for the trip! It's going to be amazing!"
AI Response: "I just hope everything goes smoothly. Trips can be unpredictable."

After modelling this a few times, children can then create their own dialogue with opposite characters.

2. Expanding Dialogue with AI

If pupils write a short dialogue exchange then we can show them how to input it into AI and ask for expansion. For example:

Pupil's Starter: "I don't trust him."
AI Expansion: "I don't trust him. There's something about the way he avoids looking me in the eye. Like he's hiding something."

3. AI-Prompted Role-Play Scenarios

Pupils can also input different character types and let AI generate dialogue, like this:

Prompt: "Create a conversation between a lost traveller and a mysterious stranger."
Response: "Are you lost, traveller? The forest doesn't take kindly to strangers."
"I - uh - I was just looking for the village. Could you help me?"

Children can then create their own role-play scenarios. Here are five scenarios suggested by AI to do this:

- The Lost Traveller and the Mysterious Stranger – A traveller is lost in the woods when a cloaked figure appears. Are they friend or foe?
- The Nervous Student and the Encouraging Teacher – A pupil is afraid to perform in the school play, and their teacher tries to boost their confidence.
- The Best Friends' Big Argument – Two best friends argue over a secret that was accidentally revealed. Will they forgive each other?
- The Brave Knight and the Cowardly Squire – A knight prepares for battle, but their squire is terrified. How does the knight reassure them?
- The Shopkeeper and the Trickster – A mischievous customer tries to haggle for an item, but the grumpy shopkeeper isn't having it.

Caution and Consideration

When using AI, consider:

- Ensuring authenticity: Pupils should refine AI-generated dialogue to suit their story.
- Encouraging creativity: AI should inspire, not replace, pupils' original ideas.
- Maintaining character consistency: Dialogue should match the character's personality and context.

Recommended Tools

1. ChatGPT (free/paid) – Generates character-specific dialogue.
2. DeepL Write (free) – Helps refine tone and speech patterns.
3. Book Creator (freemium) – Allows pupils to create illustrated dialogue scenes.
4. QuillBot (freemium) – Suggests alternative ways to phrase conversations.
5. Kahoot! (freemium) – Can be used for interactive dialogue games.

PART 4
Setting Descriptions

This section focuses on how AI can support children in crafting vivid and imaginative setting descriptions, enhancing both creative and descriptive writing. Through the use of AI-generated imagery, sensory vocabulary banks, and scaffolded prompts, pupils can explore how to convey atmosphere, time and place with precision and flair. Chapters include tools that generate settings based on different genres including mystery, adventure and historical. Plus, ideas for using AI to visualise scenes, brainstorm sensory details and explore similes and metaphors. These chapters look at how pupils can use AI to revise and enhance their writing, analysing tone, vocabulary variety and sentence structure. Whether describing a magical forest, a bustling market or a Stone Age cave, pupils are encouraged to write with clarity and creativity. These approaches help deepen understanding of how setting shapes narrative and mood, while offering practical support to develop expressive, ambitious writing across the curriculum.

31 Example Texts

> A well-crafted setting description immerses readers in a story, painting vivid images of landscapes, buildings and atmospheres. By exploring example texts from literature and using AI-generated descriptions, pupils can develop their own rich and detailed settings that bring stories to life.

Why Use Example Texts for Setting Descriptions?

When we use example texts these help pupils to observe how authors create atmosphere through descriptive techniques and to learn from established literary styles and apply them in their own writing. In this chapter we will use AI tools to generate or refine setting descriptions, plus compare different settings to analyse how mood and tone are established.

Exploring Setting Descriptions in Literature

1. Creating Mood and Atmosphere

Most authors use sensory details, figurative language and carefully chosen vocabulary to evoke a setting's mood. For example, in *The Hobbit* by J.R.R. Tolkien, he says, "It was a hobbit-hole, and that means comfort. It had a perfectly round door like a porthole, painted green, with a shiny yellow brass knob in the exact middle."

We can encourage pupils to ask AI to rewrite setting descriptions in different moods, like this:

Prompt: "Make this setting feel eerie instead of cosy."
AI Response: "The round door loomed in the hillside, its once-bright green paint peeling, the brass knob dull and lifeless. A cold draught whispered through the cracks, carrying the scent of damp earth and something long forgotten."

Or we can write our own description and ask AI to change it, like this:

Prompt: "Rewrite this description of a house to make it a haunted house: As I walked towards the house I could see its beautiful red roof tiles shining in the shimmering sun.

The yellow walls were like gold suggesting that it held treasure within. Cherry blossom trees snuggled the house with comforting wafts of perfume."

Response: "As I walked towards the house, its once-red roof tiles lay cracked and crumbling, dull under the grey, brooding sky. The faded yellow walls, streaked with grime, loomed like a forgotten relic, whispering secrets of those who had once lived within. Gnarled, twisted trees clawed at the rotting wood, their bare branches rattling in the wind, releasing the scent of damp decay that curled through the air like an unspoken warning."

By examining this rewrite, children could then rewrite their original passage and make it a castle, a Roman barracks, a house of the future, etc.

2. Using Sensory Details

Vivid descriptions engage multiple senses to create a fully immersive setting. In *Kensuke's Kingdom* by Michael Morpurgo, we have this setting description:

"The sand was soft and white, the sea as blue as I had ever seen it, stretching away into the distance to meet a cloudless sky. The only sounds were the rhythmic crash of waves and the distant cries of seabirds."

Pupils can use AI to expand this description with extra sensory details.

Prompt: "Add more sensory details to this description [insert description]."

Response: "The sand was soft and warm beneath my toes, each step sinking slightly into its silky grains. A salty breeze curled around me, carrying the tang of the ocean and the faint scent of sun-baked driftwood. The sea shimmered under the golden light, its deep blue waters rippling gently before surging into frothy white waves that tumbled onto the shore. The rhythmic crash of the surf filled the air, punctuated by the distant cries of seabirds gliding overhead, their wings slicing through the endless stretch of cloudless sky."

Children can then try to rewrite other setting descriptions from texts, adding their own details in this way.

3. Varying Sentence Structure for Impact

Short, sharp sentences can create tension, while longer, flowing sentences build calm or grandeur. In *The Nowhere Emporium* by Ross MacKenzie, we have: "The shop appeared overnight. Word spread quickly. No one knew where it had come from."

Pupils can input descriptions into AI and request different sentence structures. For example:

Prompt: "Rewrite this setting description using 3 different sentence structures such as longer, descriptive sentences or short, tension filled sentences."

Response:

1. Longer, descriptive sentence: "Out of nowhere, a peculiar little shop materialised on the empty street, its crooked wooden sign swaying gently in the cold night breeze, as if it had been there forever – yet no one could recall ever seeing it before."

2   Short, tension-filled sentences: "The shop wasn't there yesterday. Now it stood, silent and waiting. No one had seen it arrive. No one dared go inside."
3   Balanced structure with a mix of both: "The shop appeared overnight, its dark windows reflecting nothing but shadows. By morning, whispers spread through the town, each story more fantastical than the last. No one had seen who built it. No one knew why it was there."

Ask the children to rewrite other passages of setting descriptions in different ways after discussing these examples.

Creating New Setting Descriptions Using AI

AI can assist pupils in generating their own setting descriptions by providing structured prompts and variations based on themes. Pupils can input a basic setting such as a mysterious forest and AI can expand this with descriptive elements. Then pupils can refine and personalise the AI-generated text.

Example AI Output: "The trees stood impossibly tall, their ancient branches weaving a tangled canopy that blocked out the sun. Strange whispers rustled through the undergrowth, the air thick with the scent of damp moss and something unknown, something watching."

Classroom Activities Using AI and Example Texts

1. Mood Transformation Exercise

Pupils take a setting description and rewrite it in a different mood (e.g. make a bright meadow feel sinister).

AI Support: AI provides suggestions for tone shifts.

2. Expanding Settings with AI

Pupils write a simple setting sentence and input it into AI for expansion. For example:

Pupil's Starter: "The castle stood on the hill."
AI Expansion: "The towering castle loomed over the valley, its weathered stone walls bathed in the golden glow of the setting sun, turrets casting jagged shadows across the rugged landscape."

3. AI-Prompted Writing Challenges

Pupils input different themes (e.g. futuristic city, haunted house) and generate setting descriptions using the five senses.

Example Prompt: "Describe a setting using only sound and smell."
AI Response: "The air was thick with the scent of damp wood and rusting metal. Distant echoes of dripping water mixed with the muffled shuffle of unseen footsteps."

Caution and Consideration

When using AI, consider:

- Encouraging originality: AI should enhance, not replace, pupils' creativity.
- Discussing mood and style choices: Ensure AI-generated descriptions align with the story's tone.
- Refining AI outputs: Pupils should revise and personalise AI-generated settings.

Recommended Tools

1. ChatGPT (free/paid) - Generates setting descriptions based on prompts.
2. DeepL Write (free) - Helps refine sentence structure and tone.
3. Book Creator (freemium) - Allows pupils to compile setting descriptions into interactive books.
4. QuillBot (freemium) - Suggests alternative phrasings for setting descriptions.
5. Night Zookeeper (freemium) - Encourages creative writing through interactive setting prompts.

32 Change the Timeline

The way a setting is described can change drastically depending on the time period in which it is set. By altering the timeline, pupils can explore how settings evolve over time, how historical context shapes descriptions, and how futuristic settings can be imagined. AI can support this process by generating historically accurate descriptions, transforming modern settings into historical or futuristic ones, and helping pupils compare different time periods.

Why Change the Timeline in Setting Descriptions?

Exploring different time periods helps pupils to understand historical context by imagining how a place might have looked in different eras and develops creativity by transforming settings into the past or future. We can help children to enhance descriptive writing by adapting language and sensory details to suit a specific time period. In this chapter we will demonstrate how to use AI tools to generate historically accurate or futuristic setting descriptions.

Transforming Settings by Changing the Timeline

1. Rewriting Modern Settings in Historical Contexts

A setting can take on a completely new atmosphere when rewritten in a different historical period. For example: a busy market.

- Modern-day description: "The high street bustled with shoppers, the scent of freshly brewed coffee and warm pastries wafting from the bakery. Neon signs flickered as people hurried past, chatting on their mobile phones."
- Prompt: "Rewrite this setting as if it were in Viking times."
- AI Response: "The air carried the briny scent of the sea as Viking traders gathered at the wooden stalls, exchanging silver coins for barrels of mead and freshly caught fish. Crows cawed from the rooftops as warriors sharpened their axes under the dim glow of a setting sun."

Children can then use their topic knowledge to add to this description.

DOI: 10.4324/9781003621379-36

2. Moving a Setting into the Future

Imagining how a setting might evolve over time helps pupils think creatively about technological advancements, societal changes and futuristic landscapes. Ask the children to describe their school in the present. They might write something like, "The bell rang loudly and pupils rushed to their next lesson, books clutched in their hands. The walls were covered with colourful posters and the smell of lunch drifted in from the canteen."

> Prompt: "Rewrite this description to be set in the future."
> Response: "The classroom shimmered with holographic displays as pupils adjusted their visors, accessing interactive lessons floating in midair. Small robots hummed as they glided between desks, offering help where needed. Outside, hover-buses zipped past glass-walled towers stretching towards the clouds."
> Prompt: "Add more detail here."
> Response: "In 2124, schools no longer had traditional classrooms. Instead, pupils learned through immersive virtual reality lessons, experiencing history firsthand by stepping into digital reconstructions of the past. AI tutors assisted students, adapting lessons to their individual learning styles."
> Prompt: "Simplify this response for younger children."
> Simplified Response: "In 2124, schools did not have normal classrooms because learning had changed. Pupils learned through virtual reality so they could step into the past and see history for themselves. AI tutors helped them and changed lessons to match how each child learned best."

The children could then use this description to write "a day in the life of a futuristic school."

Exploring Different Historical Timelines

Changing the timeline allows pupils to explore settings within key historical periods.

> ### The Stone Age
>
> The cave walls flickered with shadows from the crackling fire, illuminating paintings of wild bison and deer. The scent of roasting meat filled the air, as hunters prepared for another day of survival in the vast, untamed land.

Pupils can use AI to rewrite a setting in a specific historical period, such as:

> Prompt: "Rewrite this setting as if it were in Ancient Egypt."
> Response: "The sandstone walls of the grand temple flickered with the glow of oil lamps, casting long shadows over intricate hieroglyphs depicting mighty pharaohs and sacred gods. The scent of spiced bread and roasted fish drifted through the bustling marketplace, where traders arranged their wares beneath the golden sun. Beyond the towering pyramids, the Nile flowed steadily, its life-giving waters ensuring the survival of farmers and artisans in the vast, sun-scorched land."

The children could then try to rewrite other passages from different historical settings themselves using an AI example as a model. For example:

The Romans

The grand stone roads stretched for miles, leading to the towering columns of the forum where merchants called out their wares. Fountains trickled under the midday sun, and the scent of freshly baked bread mixed with the distant clang of blacksmiths hammering metal.

Changed to:

The Victorians

Thick fog curled through the narrow streets as the clatter of carriage wheels echoed off soot-covered buildings. Chimney sweeps scurried through the alleyways, their faces streaked with ash, while gas lamps flickered dimly against the night sky.

Classroom Activities Using AI and Changing the Timeline

1. Timeline Transformations

Pupils could also choose a familiar setting such as a park, a school, a city, etc. and write it in two different time periods, such as the Tudor period or Ancient Greek times. AI can generate descriptions based on different eras to use as a model text.

Prompt: "Describe a city in the Tudor period."
Response: "The narrow, cobbled streets of the Tudor city bustled with merchants calling out from wooden market stalls, selling fresh bread, cured meats, and colourful fabrics. Tall, timber-framed houses leaned over the streets, their thatched roofs and small, leaded windows casting long shadows as smoke curled from chimneys. The air carried the mingled scents of roasting meat, open sewers, and the occasional perfume of herbs hung outside apothecary shops to ward off disease."

If you are studying the Ancient Greeks, then ask the children to rewrite the passage in this period.

2. Historical and Futuristic Comparisons

Pupils can compare an old setting description with its modern or futuristic counterpart. For example, a library in Ancient Greece and a library in the year 2150.

AI-Generated Comparison:

Ancient Greek Library

Marble columns towered over rows of wooden shelves filled with carefully rolled scrolls, their papyrus edges curling with age. Scholars in flowing robes debated philosophy in hushed tones, while oil lamps flickered, casting golden light over the stone walls engraved with wisdom from the great thinkers of the time.

Library in the Year 2150

Glass walls shimmered with holographic displays, books replaced by floating digital archives that responded to a mere gesture. AI assistants hovered silently, ready to retrieve any text or translate ancient languages in an instant. The hum of data streams filled the air as visitors explored entire worlds of knowledge through immersive virtual reality chambers.

3. AI-Prompted Writing Challenges

Pupils could input different historical themes (e.g. Ancient Egypt, Tudor England) and generate specific setting descriptions such as a marketplace, a home, a farm, a harbour, a barracks, etc.

Example Prompt: "Describe a marketplace in Ancient Egypt."

Response: "Golden sunlight reflected off towering obelisks as traders shouted over the noise of clanking metal and chattering crowds. The scent of spices and incense curled through the hot air as merchants unrolled bolts of fine linen for wealthy buyers."

Children can then use this brief description to write a diary about the life of someone who lived or worked in this setting.

Caution and Consideration

When using AI, consider:

- Encouraging historical accuracy: Pupils should fact-check AI-generated historical descriptions.
- Refining AI outputs: Pupils should personalise and refine AI-generated descriptions.
- Maintaining creativity: AI should inspire, but not replace, pupil-generated ideas.

Recommended Tools

1. ChatGPT (free/paid) - Generates setting descriptions in different time periods.
2. DeepL Write (free) - Helps refine historical and futuristic writing.
3. Book Creator (freemium) - Allows pupils to document timeline transformations interactively.
4. Night Zookeeper (freemium) - Encourages creative writing through historical and futuristic prompts.
5. Kahoot! (freemium) - Can be used for historical setting quizzes and comparisons.

33 Adding Sensory Detail

Sensory details are essential for bringing settings to life, making them immersive and memorable for readers. By engaging the five senses - sight, sound, smell, taste, and touch - pupils can create vivid descriptions that draw their audience into the world of their stories. AI can support this process by generating rich sensory descriptions, helping pupils refine their language, and offering alternative ways to enhance their writing.

Why Use Sensory Detail in Setting Descriptions?

Sensory details help pupils to create immersive settings that feel real and engaging. They can also evoke emotions and atmosphere through descriptive language and improve writing clarity by showing instead of telling. In this chapter we will use AI tools to expand and refine sensory details in pupils' descriptions.

Exploring Sensory Details in Literature

1. Sight - Painting a Picture with Words

Sight descriptions help readers visualise a setting by focusing on colour, light, movement and detail. For example, in *The Explorer* by Katherine Rundell, the author says, "The jungle was green, but not just green - every shade of green that could possibly exist. Emerald green, lime green, the dark green of the moss on trees, and the bright green of parrots flashing their wings through the canopy."

Pupils can use AI to generate varied visual descriptions in the same style as Rundell, such as:

Prompt: "Describe a futuristic city using vivid visual details."
Response: "Towering skyscrapers shimmered with neon lights, their glass surfaces reflecting the endless stream of flying vehicles. Above, digital billboards pulsed with holographic images, casting multicoloured glows onto the sleek, metallic streets below."

Children can then expand this by adding more visual description.

DOI: 10.4324/9781003621379-37

2. Sound – Bringing a Setting to Life

Sounds can add atmosphere, making a setting feel busy, eerie or peaceful. In *Stig of the Dump* by Clive King, we have, "There was a crash and a rattle and a lump of chalk landed at Barney's feet. Then there was silence again, except for the rustling of the ivy in the wind."

Pupils can use AI to expand on sound descriptions, like this:

> Prompt: "Describe a bustling medieval marketplace focusing on sound."
> Response: "The air buzzed with the chatter of merchants bargaining, the clatter of hooves on cobbled streets, and the rhythmic clang of a blacksmith's hammer shaping iron over roaring flames."
> Prompt: "Create a list of other sounds that would be heard in a medieval marketplace."
> Response:
>
> "Shouts of traders calling out their goods: 'Fresh bread! Juicy apples! Fine silk!'
> The bleating of goats and sheep being herded through the stalls.
> The bubbling and sizzling of food stalls cooking meats and spiced stews.
> The distant tolling of a church bell, marking the hour.
> The creaking of wooden carts being pulled over uneven cobbles."

Children could then turn the suggested sounds into a paragraph of description. Younger pupils could turn a phrase into a sentence.

3. Smell – Evoking Memories and Atmosphere

Scents can make settings feel real and add emotional depth. In Michelle Magorian's *Goodnight Mister Tom*, the author says, "The room was filled with the scent of damp wood and coal dust, mixed with the faint sweetness of apples stored in the corner."

Pupils can use AI to generate unique smell-based descriptions.

> Prompt: "Describe the smell of a Victorian bakery."
> Response: "The air was thick with the rich aroma of warm bread, caramelised sugar, and spiced cinnamon buns fresh from the oven, mingling with the faint scent of wood smoke from the brick-fired stove."

Children could ask AI to generate a list of smells for their chosen setting and expand these into a description themselves after seeing this model.

4. Taste – Adding Unexpected Depth

Taste descriptions help create sensory immersion, even in settings that don't seem to involve food. For example, in *The Lion, the Witch and the Wardrobe* by C.S. Lewis, we have, "Each piece was sweet and light to the very centre and Edmund had never tasted anything more delicious."

Pupils can generate food-related setting descriptions with AI such as:

> Prompt: "Describe the taste of fruit in an enchanted forest."
> Response: "The golden fruit melted on the tongue, a perfect blend of honeyed sweetness and the sharp zing of citrus, leaving a warm, tingling sensation that spread through the body like magic."

Ask the children to describe the dinner hall at school using the same structure as the sentence above:

"The _____ melted on the tongue, a perfect blend of _____ and _____, leaving a warm, tingling sensation that spread through the body like magic."

5. Touch - Enhancing the Physical World

Touch descriptions help readers feel connected to the setting through texture, temperature and movement. In *Skellig* by David Almond, we have, "His skin was dry and rough like paper, his bones fragile beneath my fingertips."

Pupils can use AI to generate tactile descriptions like this:

Prompt: "Describe the feel of walking through deep snow."
Response: "Each step sank into the soft, powdery snow, the cold seeping through boots and numbing toes. The crisp surface gave way with a satisfying crunch, leaving behind deep, uneven footprints."

Ask the children to rewrite this imagining that they are walking through a desert.

Creating New Sensory-Rich Settings with AI

AI can support pupils in crafting original settings by prompting sensory-based descriptions. Pupils can input a basic setting idea such as a haunted house and ask AI to expand this with sensory-rich details.

Example AI Output: "The house groaned in the wind, its wooden beams creaking like whispered warnings. A musty, damp smell clung to the air, thick with the scent of rotting wood and faded perfume. The floorboards were ice-cold underfoot, dust stirring with each cautious step."

Children could use this example as a model to write a description of a theme park, a swimming pool or a library.

Classroom Activities Using AI and Sensory Detail

1. Five Senses Challenge

Pupils describe a setting using all five senses then ask AI to suggest additional sensory details based on their initial description.

2. Sensory Swap

Pupils write a setting description focused on one sense, then ask AI to rewrite it focusing on another. For example:

Original (sight-focused): "The forest was dark, towering trees blocking the sky."
AI Expansion (sound-focused): "The forest whispered with rustling leaves, the occasional snap of a twig breaking the eerie silence."

3. AI-Prompted Writing Challenges

Pupils input different settings such as a spaceship or a Tudor marketplace and ask AI to generate sensory descriptions.

Example Prompt: "Describe a pirate ship using touch and smell."
AI Response: "The rough, salt-stained wood of the deck burned under the midday sun, while the heavy scent of damp rope and fish lingered in the salty sea breeze."

Caution and Consideration

When using AI, consider:

- Encouraging originality: AI should enhance, not replace, pupils' creativity.
- Ensuring balanced descriptions: Too many sensory details can overwhelm a scene.
- Refining AI outputs: Pupils should revise AI-generated descriptions for personalisation.

Recommended Tools

1. ChatGPT (free/paid) - Generates sensory descriptions based on prompts.
2. DeepL Write (free) - Helps refine detailed writing.
3. Book Creator (freemium) - Allows pupils to compile sensory-rich stories interactively.
4. QuillBot (freemium) - Suggests alternative phrasings for sensory descriptions.
5. Night Zookeeper (freemium) - Encourages creative writing through sensory prompts.

34 Developmental Prompts

> Using developmental prompts is a powerful way to help pupils expand and refine their setting descriptions. Carefully crafted questions and sentence starters guide pupils to think more deeply about place, atmosphere and sensory details, ensuring their writing is vivid and engaging. AI can support this process by generating prompts, expanding pupils' ideas and offering alternative phrasings for descriptions.

Why Use Developmental Prompts in Setting Descriptions?

Developmental prompts help pupils enhance creativity, by encouraging deeper exploration of settings, and strengthen writing structure through guided sentence expansion. Children can also improve sensory detail by prompting descriptions of sights, sounds and textures. In this chapter we will use AI tools to generate and refine setting descriptions interactively.

Using Prompts to Expand Setting Descriptions

Prompts can be used at different stages of writing to help pupils develop their ideas further. Below are some effective prompts, AI-generated responses, and how they can be applied in the classroom.

1. Expanding Basic Descriptions

Starting with a simple setting, prompts can be used to add layers of detail. For example, if we use a familiar setting such as a school playground, we could start with a sentence like, "The playground was empty."

Developmental Prompts:

- What does the playground look like when full of children?
- What sounds would you hear at break time?
- How does the atmosphere change when it starts to rain?

AI Response: "The playground echoed with the joyful shrieks of children, their feet pounding across the worn-out tarmac as swings creaked in the breeze. The scent of damp grass lingered after the morning drizzle, while the faint chime of the school bell signalled the end of playtime."

Ask the children to use this model to describe another familiar setting such as a playpark, the beach or a supermarket.

2. Transforming Settings Based on Mood

The same location can be described in vastly different ways depending on mood and atmosphere. For example, we could ask AI to describe a forest using these developmental prompts:

- How does the forest feel during the day versus at night?
- What emotions does the setting create for the character?
- How do different weather conditions change the atmosphere?

AI-Generated Mood Variations:

- Peaceful: "Sunlight dappled through the thick canopy, birds chirping softly in the still morning air. The scent of pine needles filled the space, as a gentle breeze rustled the emerald leaves."
- Eerie: "The trees loomed like silent sentinels, their twisted branches clawing at the sky. A thick fog curled along the ground, muffling the snap of unseen footsteps in the undergrowth."

Children could then use this as a template to describe a bedroom, a library or a pirate ship.

Using Prompts to Explore Different Types of Settings

1. Natural Settings

Prompt: "What would you hear, see, smell and feel on the beach?"
Response: "The golden sand warmed underfoot, waves whispering gently as they rolled onto the shore. The tang of salt filled the air, mingling with the scent of sun-bleached driftwood."

Ask children to expand this description with their own ideas. If they are struggling, then you can ask AI to give you a list of nouns you might find at this setting.

2. Urban Settings

Prompt: "How does a futuristic city change from day to night?"
Response: "Neon signs flickered against the steel and glass buildings, their lights casting a glow over the endless stream of hover-cars zipping through the sky. In the alleyways below, robotic street sweepers whirred as they tidied the empty pavements."

Ask the children to work in pairs or groups to brainstorm more ideas for a futuristic city at night, then they can independently describe this setting.

3. Mysterious Settings

Prompt: "What small details make an abandoned house feel unsettling?"
Response: "Dust motes swirled in the dim light filtering through cracked shutters. A single chair lay overturned in the corner, its shadow stretching eerily across the peeling wallpaper."

You could ask AI to create an image of this description using Craiyon or Adobe Firefly and then ask the children to describe the scene further with this visual prompt.

Classroom Activities Using AI and Developmental Prompts

1. Sentence Expansion Challenge

Pupils start with a basic setting sentence and expand it using prompts. The AI can generate suggestions to improve descriptions.

Prompt: "Make this setting feel more mysterious: 'The castle stood on the hill.'"
Response: "The ancient castle loomed on the misty hill, its towering spires lost in swirling fog. The scent of damp stone and faded memories clung to the air."

2. Describe a Setting through a Character's Eyes

Pupils describe a place from the perspective of different characters (e.g. an excited child vs. a nervous traveller). AI can rewrite descriptions based on emotional perspective.

Prompt: "Describe a forest from the point of view of someone who is lost."
AI Response: "The trees pressed in on all sides, their knotted roots forming a maze beneath my feet. Every rustling leaf sent a shiver through me, the wind's low howl whispering warnings in my ear."

Caution and Consideration

When using AI, consider:

- Encouraging personalisation: AI should enhance, not replace, original ideas.
- Ensuring clarity: Some AI-generated descriptions may need refinement.
- Discussing word choice: Pupils should select the best phrases to match their intended atmosphere.

Recommended Tools

1. ChatGPT (free/paid) – Generates descriptive expansions based on prompts.
2. DeepL Write (free) – Helps refine detailed writing.
3. Book Creator (freemium) – Allows pupils to compile setting descriptions interactively.
4. Night Zookeeper (freemium) – Encourages creative writing through structured prompts.
5. QuillBot (freemium) – Suggests alternative phrasing for improved descriptions.
6. Adobe Firefly (free/paid) – Generates images based on descriptions.
7. Craiyon (free) – Generates images based on prompts.

---

35 Weather and Other Influences

> Weather and environmental influences play a crucial role in shaping the atmosphere of a setting. Whether a storm foreshadows danger or sunshine brings warmth and hope, these details enhance storytelling and deepen a reader's connection to a scene. Using AI, we can explore different weather effects, experiment with how settings change under different conditions and even generate immersive 3D visualisations through tools like SkyBox AI.

Why Consider Weather and Other Influences in Setting Descriptions?

Weather and environmental influences help pupils set the mood in their writing. For example, a bright morning might symbolise hope, while heavy rain might signal sadness. They can also use this device to create dynamic settings; a forest changes drastically between a summer afternoon and a winter night. We can introduce symbolism and foreshadowing, such as the use of figurative language like pathetic fallacy, which can hint at upcoming events. In this chapter we will explore the use of AI tools like ChatGPT and SkyBox 360 to help pupils generate immersive descriptions.

Exploring Weather in Literature

Many well-known primary school texts use weather effectively. The *Lion, the Witch and the Wardrobe* by C.S. Lewis has Narnia trapped in a never-ending winter, symbolising the White Witch's cold-hearted rule. *Charlotte's Web* by E.B. White uses the changing seasons to reflect life cycles, from birth to death to renewal. The *Storm Whale* by Benji Davies shows how the grey stormy sea mirrors the loneliness of the boy and his father.

AI can help pupils analyse how authors use weather and even generate their own weather-based descriptions, like this:

> Prompt: "Describe a stormy night in a small village."
> Response: "Thunder growled in the distance as jagged lightning slashed across the sky. Rain hammered against the rooftops, turning narrow alleyways into rushing streams. The wind howled through the trees, shaking the shutters of the tiny cottages."

Using this as a model, pupils could write about a sunny day at a playpark or a foggy night sky above a graveyard.

Using Pathetic Fallacy

Pathetic fallacy is a literary device where weather reflects a character's emotions or events in the story. For example, in *The Wreck of the Zanzibar* by Michael Morpurgo, when Laura is facing hardship, the storm at sea mirrors her struggle, and when she finds hope, the weather calms, reflecting her emotions.

> Prompt: "Describe a setting where the weather matches a character's sadness."
> Response: "Grey clouds loomed over the hills, heavy with unfallen rain. The air felt thick and cold, wrapping around the lonely figure who trudged through puddles, his reflection rippling in the dark water."

Pupils can experiment by selecting different emotions and matching them with weather patterns.

Exploring Other Environmental Influences

While weather is important, other environmental influences also shape a setting:

1. Time of Day

A bustling city at midday feels different from a silent one at midnight. For example: "The streetlights flickered on, casting long shadows as the city settled into its quiet nighttime rhythm."

Children can ask AI to help them to generate descriptions of time of day in a variety of settings, such as a deserted island, a rainforest or a school.

2. Seasons

A summer meadow bursting with colour versus a winter meadow buried in snow would have a very different description. For example, if the children had written, "The crisp autumn leaves crunched beneath their boots as they wandered through the golden woods," they could then ask AI to rewrite this for a summer meadow. Or vice versa: the AI writes it first, then the children rewrite the description.

3. Settings in Contrasting Seasons

A countryside setting feels open, fresh and natural, yet it varies vastly depending on what season it is. For example, "In spring, the rolling hills are alive with the scent of fresh blossoms and the chatter of nesting birds, yet in winter, the landscape is hushed under a thick layer of snow, the bare trees standing like silent sentinels against the pale sky."

Within the same sentence, two settings are compared. We can ask AI to help us to do the same thing with other settings:

> Prompt: "Describe the same setting in summer and in winter."
> Response (Summer): "The river glistened under the golden sunlight, dragonflies darting over its shimmering surface as the air buzzed with the hum of bees."

Response (Winter): "Icicles clung to the bare branches, the river frozen solid beneath a sheet of white. The crisp silence was broken only by the crunch of snow underfoot."

Prompt: "Put these two sentences together into one sentence to describe the river in Summer and in Winter."

Response: "In summer, the river glistened under the golden sunlight, dragonflies darting over its shimmering surface as the air buzzed with the hum of bees, while in winter, icicles clung to the bare branches, the river frozen solid beneath a sheet of white, with only the crunch of snow underfoot breaking the crisp silence."

Prompt: "Make a simplified version using simple sentences and basic conjunctions like and, but, so, or, then or because."

Response: "In summer, the river shone in the sunlight **and** dragonflies flew over the water. Bees buzzed in the warm air. **But** in winter, the river turned to ice **and** icicles hung from the trees. Everything was quiet **except** for the crunch of snow underfoot."

Children could try and rewrite the sentence for Spring and Autumn or use it as a model for other settings.

Using SkyBox AI for Immersive Visualisation

SkyBox 360 is an AI-powered tool that allows users to create panoramic 3D environments. Pupils can use it to:

- Visualise different weather conditions – Generate a sunny village or a stormy forest.
- Explore lighting effects – See how time of day changes a setting.
- Enhance setting descriptions – Use AI-generated images as inspiration for writing.

After exploring the website, ask the children to choose a setting from the images provided, such as a castle, a rainforest or a futuristic city. Then in the User Interface (UI) description make changes or edits to generate different versions of the setting. For example, if the UI states: "city square, futuristic whimsical buildings, pastel colours, retro-futurism architecture, glass and plastic buildings, flower boxes and trees, utopia, beautiful dusk sunset swirling clouds," then this could be changed to: "city scene, futuristic metallic buildings, vibrant colours, glowing architecture, metal and glass buildings, bioluminescent plants, beautiful sunrise, shining sun."

On "View" you can then get rid of the UI and select "Autopan" to see the environment created in a 360 degree perspective. Compare how the mood changes with these two images and describe it in writing.

Classroom Activities Using AI and Weather-Based Descriptions

1. Changing Weather Challenge

Pupils choose a setting and rewrite it in different weather conditions. AI generates variations based on prompts.

Prompt: "Describe a marketplace on a bright sunny day, then in a thunderstorm."
Response:

(Sunny): "The sunlit stalls overflowed with vibrant fruits and spices, the air filled with laughter and the scent of fresh bread."

(Stormy): "Rain hammered against the canopies, the once-cheerful market now a tangle of soaked cloth and hurried footsteps splashing through puddles."

2. Mood and Weather Connection

Pupils write a scene where the weather reflects the protagonist's mood. AI can then suggest emotional weather pairings.

Prompt: "What kind of weather matches excitement?"

AI Response: "A bright, breezy day where golden sunlight dances on rippling water."

3. Extreme Environment Writing Task

Pupils describe a setting in an extreme climate (e.g. desert, tundra, deep ocean). AI can then help generate specific details.

Prompt: "Describe what it feels like to stand in the middle of a sandstorm."

Response: "The wind howled like a wild beast, whipping fine grains of sand into every exposed space. Each breath felt dry and sharp, the swirling dust reducing the world to a blur of shifting gold."

Caution and Consideration

When using AI, consider:

- Encouraging personal creativity: Pupils should modify AI responses to match their own style.
- Checking accuracy: AI-generated settings might need refining for historical or scientific accuracy.
- Balancing AI with imagination: AI should be a starting point, not a replacement for thinking deeply about descriptions.

Recommended Tools

1. ChatGPT (free/paid) - Generates weather-based setting descriptions.
2. SkyBox AI (freemium) - Creates immersive 3D visualisations of different settings.
3. DeepL Write (free) - Helps refine descriptive language.
4. Book Creator (freemium) - Allows pupils to compile and illustrate weather-based settings.
5. QuillBot (freemium) - Suggests alternative phrasings for improved descriptions.

36 Colour and Tone

> Colour and tone play a vital role in setting descriptions, shaping mood, atmosphere and reader perception. The way a scene is coloured, through vibrant hues or muted shades, can evoke strong emotions and provide depth to storytelling. Using AI, pupils can explore different colour palettes, generate descriptive passages and refine their use of colour and tone in writing.

Why Use Colour and Tone in Setting Descriptions?

Describing colour and tone helps pupils to create mood, for example a bright blue sky suggests happiness, while a dull grey one can feel gloomy. It can also enhance sensory detail; rich colour descriptions make a setting more immersive. Children can also establish contrast with colour and tone as a once-colourful place that becomes dull can reflect changes in mood or time. In this chapter we will use AI devices like AI-generated descriptions and image tools to help visualise and expand colour choices.

Exploring Colour in Literature

Many primary school texts use colour effectively to set the tone. In *The Snow Queen* by Hans Christian Andersen, the icy blue and white imagery reflects coldness and isolation. In *The Tale of Peter Rabbit* by Beatrix Potter, soft pastels create a warm, comforting tone, despite Peter's mischief. In *The Firework-Maker's Daughter* by Philip Pullman, bright bursts of colour symbolise adventure and transformation.

AI can help pupils analyse how authors use colour and generate their own vibrant descriptions. Here's an AI prompt example: "Describe a forest using warm, autumnal colours."

> Response: "The trees blazed with fiery oranges, deep reds, and golden yellows, their crisp leaves rustling in the cool breeze as the low sun bathed the forest in amber light."

We could then ask the children to describe the same forest using cold, wintery colours or bright, summer colours.

Using Tone to Shape Atmosphere

Tone is the emotional quality of a description. The same setting can feel peaceful, eerie or exciting, depending on the tone used. For example, a castle can be bright and grand: "Golden banners rippled in the breeze, sunlight glinting off towering white stone walls." Or dark and foreboding: "Heavy grey clouds loomed over the towering blackened walls, their crumbling edges lost in the creeping mist."

We can ask AI to help us to do this.

Prompt: "Describe a city street as lively and bustling."
Response: "Neon signs flashed against the glass skyscrapers, the streets humming with laughter and conversation as vendors called out their daily specials and taxis honked impatiently at pedestrians."
Prompt: "Describe the same city street as eerie and abandoned."
Response: "Streetlights flickered weakly, their glow barely reaching the cracked pavements, where the wind carried scraps of forgotten paper between silent, empty buildings."

Children can use this model to describe other settings too.

How Colour and Tone Change with Time and Weather

The same setting can change dramatically based on time of day or weather conditions. For example, when using a meadow as a setting we might write:

Morning: "The meadow glowed with fresh green grasses, dewdrops sparkling like diamonds in the golden sunrise."
Night: "The same meadow lay shrouded in shadow, the long grass whispering under the silver moonlight."
Prompt: "Describe a beach at sunrise and at sunset."
Response:
(Sunrise): "Soft pinks and gentle purples painted the sky, the sea reflecting a golden glow as waves lapped lazily at the shore."
(Sunset): "A fiery orange sun sank behind the horizon, casting deep indigos across the sky as the tide pulled back, leaving glistening shells in its retreat."

Children can then change a setting description using time and weather to alter the colour and tone.

Exploring Colour and Tone through AI Image Tools

Using AI-generated images can help pupils visualise how colour and tone shape a setting. SkyBox 360 allows pupils to create immersive 3D landscapes, changing lighting, colour schemes and tone with a few clicks and description alterations.

The children can choose a setting (e.g. a city, a forest, an enchanted castle), then generate different versions in SkyBox 360 (e.g. daytime vs. nighttime, bright vs. muted colours) and compare how the mood changes and write descriptions based on the visuals.

Classroom Activities Using AI and Colour-Based Descriptions

1. Colour-Based Writing Challenge

Pupils describe a setting using a limited colour palette. AI can suggest new ways to describe colours without using the colour name.

Prompt: "Describe a sunset without using the words 'red' or 'orange.'"
Response: "The sky blazed with the fiery glow of molten gold, melting into deep shades of ripe apricot and burning embers."

2. Tone Transformation Task

Pupils could also rewrite the same setting in two different tones. AI can suggest alternative phrasings to shift tone.

Prompt: "Make this description feel more ominous: 'The cottage sat nestled in the green hills.'"
Response: "The crooked cottage lurked in the misty hills, its sagging roof barely visible through the twisted, grasping branches."

3. Seasonal Shifts Writing Exercise

Pupils could write about the same place in different seasons as well. AI can generate these seasonal transformations.

Prompt: "Describe a garden in summer and in winter."
Response:
(Summer): "Sunflowers stretched towards the sky, their golden heads swaying gently as butterflies flitted between vibrant flowerbeds."
(Winter): "The garden lay silent under a crisp layer of frost, skeletal branches coated in icy lace, glistening under the pale morning light."

Caution and Consideration

When using AI, consider:

- Encouraging personal creativity: Pupils should refine AI descriptions to match their writing style.
- Checking appropriateness: AI-generated content should align with the intended tone and setting.
- Balancing AI with imagination: AI is a tool, but the best writing comes from a mix of inspiration and personal creativity.

Recommended Tools

1. ChatGPT (free/paid) - Generates colour and tone descriptions based on prompts.
2. SkyBox 360 (freemium) - Creates immersive 3D settings with different lighting and colour schemes.
3. DeepL Write (free) - Helps refine descriptive language and tone.
4. Book Creator (freemium) - Allows pupils to compile and illustrate their setting descriptions.
5. QuillBot (freemium) - Suggests alternative phrasing for mood and tone adjustments.

37 Feedback on Descriptions

> Giving and receiving feedback on setting descriptions is a key skill in developing strong, immersive writing. Effective feedback helps pupils refine their use of sensory details, structure and tone to create more vivid settings. AI can support this process by generating alternative descriptions, suggesting improvements and guiding self-assessment.

Why Is Feedback Important?

Feedback helps pupils to improve clarity, ensuring descriptions are detailed but not overwhelming, and strengthen engagement, making settings feel more immersive. But it can also develop revision skills and encourage a growth mindset in writing. We can use AI tools and AI-generated suggestions to provide constructive support and alternatives.

Types of Feedback for Setting Descriptions

1. Peer Feedback

Encouraging pupils to review each other's work helps them develop a critical eye. Using structured peer review prompts ensures feedback remains constructive. For example, we could ask children to ask each other if their description makes you feel like you're in the setting and what words or phrases help create the mood. We can also ask AI to support this too. AI tools like ChatGPT can provide instant feedback on pupils' writing.

> Prompt: "Give feedback on this description of a forest: 'The tall trees swayed in the wind, their leaves rustling like whispers.'"
>
> Response: "This description effectively conveys movement and sound, but you could enhance the sensory detail by adding smells or textures. For example, describing the scent of pine or the feel of rough bark would make the setting even more immersive."

2. Teacher Feedback

Teacher feedback helps guide pupils in refining their work, focusing on descriptive accuracy (are the details vivid and precise?), tone consistency (do the descriptions match the intended mood) and the use of figurative language (are the similes, metaphors and personification effective?). For example, in *The Hobbit* by J.R.R. Tolkien, we have, "It was a perfectly round door like a porthole, painted green, with a shiny yellow brass knob in the exact middle."

We could ask children to enhance the texture of the door, such as how does the brass knob feel under Bilbo's fingers, would it be cold, smooth, or polished? AI can refine our comments, providing structured revision suggestions.

Prompt: "Suggest three ways to improve this setting description: 'The castle stood tall with large towers and stone walls.'"

AI Response:

1. Describe the texture of the stone - was it rough, weathered, or covered in moss?
2. Expand on the towers - did they pierce the sky, cast long shadows, or glisten in the sun?
3. Add sound - was the wind howling through the cracks, or was it eerily silent?

Children can then follow this response in their writing.

3. Self-Assessment

Pupils can learn to critique their own work using structured reflection questions:

- Does my setting description include at least three senses?
- Have I used precise vocabulary to create an image in the reader's mind?
- Is the mood clear and consistent?

We can ask our pupils to highlight words in their descriptions that evoke sensory details. Then they can use an AI tool to suggest additional adjectives or reword sentences for clarity.

Prompt: "Improve this description by making it more immersive: 'The beach was nice and the waves moved.'"

Response: "The golden sand was warm beneath my toes, and the waves rolled gently onto the shore, their salty spray misting the air with a fresh, ocean scent."

Children can then follow this immersive model to create further descriptive setting sentences.

Using AI for Setting Feedback

AI can assist in improving descriptions in real-time. Tools like ChatGPT, Grammarly, DeepSeek and DeepL Write can:

- Highlight weak areas - Identifying vague language.
- Suggest stronger word choices - Replacing overused adjectives.
- Enhance imagery - Offering figurative language alternatives.

Here's an example of an AI feedback session:

Pupil's original sentence: "The sky was pretty with lots of colours."
AI Suggestions:

1. "Try describing the colours in more detail - what shades do you see?"
2. "Could you compare the sky to something familiar, like a painting or a sunset?"
3. "Think about movement - are the colours blending, streaking, or glowing?"

Revised sentence: "The sky burned with streaks of crimson and gold, melting into soft purples as the sun dipped below the horizon."

Classroom Activities Using AI for Feedback

1. Feedback Stations

Pupils could rotate through different feedback stations, including AI-assisted feedback, peer review and self-assessment. For AI support, pupils can input their description into AI and receive suggestions for improvement.

2. Two Versions Challenge

Pupils can write two versions of a setting description: one detailed and one simple. They then use AI to enhance the simple version, as below:

Prompt: "Expand this basic sentence into a vivid setting: 'The mountain was big and snowy.'"
Response: "The towering mountain loomed over the valley, its jagged peaks blanketed in thick, untouched snow that glowed under the pale winter sun."

3. Emotion-Based Descriptions

Pupils can write the same setting in two different tones (e.g. a park as peaceful vs. eerie). The AI can then help to adjust word choice for tone shifts.

Prompt: "Make this description sound eerie instead of peaceful: 'The lake was calm under the moonlight.'"
Response: "The lake lay unnervingly still, its black surface swallowing the moonlight in eerie silence."

Caution and Consideration

When using AI, consider:

- Encouraging original thought: AI should enhance, not replace, pupil creativity.
- Ensuring age-appropriate responses: Review AI-generated feedback before use.
- Using AI as a tool, not a shortcut: Pupils should engage with suggestions critically.

Recommended Tools

1. ChatGPT (free/paid) - Provides instant feedback on descriptions.
2. Grammarly (freemium) - Suggests clarity and word choice improvements.
3. DeepL Write (free) - Helps refine tone and detail in descriptions.
4. Hemingway Editor (free) - Highlights readability issues and sentence complexity.
5. QuillBot (freemium) - Rewords sentences for variety and engagement.

38 Movement

> Movement in setting descriptions brings scenes to life, adding energy and dynamism to a story. A setting that shifts and changes feels immersive and realistic, whether it's the swaying of trees, the bustling of a marketplace, or the rolling waves of a stormy sea. AI tools can help pupils explore movement in their descriptions, offering alternative phrasing, generating dynamic settings, and refining their use of motion in writing.

Why Is Movement Important in Setting Descriptions?

Movement enhances setting descriptions by creating a sense of place. For example, a still forest feels different from one where leaves rustle and animals scurry. But movement also builds atmosphere too, as gentle movement can create calm, while frantic movement can add tension. These are all tools to engage the reader as moving elements keep the description active and interesting. In this chapter we will look at using AI tools and AI-generated descriptions to provide varied ways to describe motion effectively.

Exploring Movement in Literature

Many primary school texts use movement to bring settings to life:

- *The Wind in the Willows* by Kenneth Grahame – The river's current, rippling reeds, and drifting boats create a flowing, ever-changing world.
- *The Iron Man* by Ted Hughes – The way the Iron Man moves, from crashing down a cliff to rebuilding himself, is central to the story's vivid descriptions.
- *The Gruffalo* by Julia Donaldson – The creatures scurry, scamper, and flee, giving the forest a lively, engaging energy.

AI can help pupils analyse how movement is used in these texts and generate new descriptions of dynamic settings. For example:

Prompt: "Describe a stormy ocean with movement."
Response: "Waves crashed against jagged cliffs, sending white foam spraying into the air as the tide surged forward, dragging seaweed and driftwood in its relentless pull."

We can give children ideas to write their own sentences in this same style. We could ask them to describe the wind moving through a forest or tumbleweed over desert sands.

Using Verbs to Show Movement

Strong verbs help describe how a setting moves. Compare:

- Weak Verb Use: "The leaves moved in the wind."
- Strong Verb Use: "The leaves danced and twirled in the restless autumn breeze."

Here's an AI-generated example for using strong verbs in two different ways in a forest:

- Still: "The forest stood silent, its trees towering in endless rows."
- Moving: "Branches swayed in the whispering wind, their shadows shifting across the mossy ground."

> Prompt: "Suggest five verbs to describe movement in a busy city street."
> Response: "Bustling, weaving, darting, clattering, rushing."

We can ask the children to use these five strong verbs to describe a busy street.

Using Movement to Set the Tone

The way things move can change the mood of a scene:

- Calm Movement: "The river meandered gently through the valley, its surface rippling with the lazy drift of leaves."
- Tense Movement: "The river surged over jagged rocks, churning with frothy rage as it tumbled downstream."

The children could choose a calm or tense movement to describe a setting. Here's an example using AI:

> Prompt: "Describe a haunted house with movement to make it feel eerie."
> Response: "The tattered curtains billowed despite the still air, and a slow creak echoed through the empty hallway as the floorboards seemed to shift beneath unseen footsteps."

The children could then expand this description or create their own, describing a chosen setting.

Movement over Time

Settings don't have to stay the same: they evolve and shift. For example, a marketplace changes as the day goes on, as we see in this AI-generated description:

> Morning: "Stalls were set up in the golden dawn, vendors stretching and yawning as they arranged their goods."
> Afternoon: "The market hummed with life, voices overlapping, baskets swinging, and the scent of roasted spices wafting through the crowd."
> Evening: "Canopies flapped in the breeze as traders packed away their wares, the chatter fading to a quiet murmur."

Pupils could describe the same setting at different times of the day using movement in this way. We can ask AI to generate alternative descriptions based on time shifts to use as an example, like this:

> Prompt: "Describe a meadow in the morning and at night."
> Response (Morning): "Bees hovered lazily over dew-speckled petals, while the golden sunlight stretched across rolling hills."
> Response (Night): "Crickets chirped in the long grass, and a gentle breeze sent ripples through the moonlit meadow."

Ask the children to use this as a model to describe a graveyard, a beach or another chosen setting.

Using AI Image Tools for Movement in Setting Descriptions

SkyBox 360 and other AI image-generation platforms can visually represent movement, helping pupils describe it more vividly. Pupils can generate images of a setting such as a forest, city street, ocean, etc. using Craiyon, Adobe Firefly or SkyBox 360. They observe moving elements such as waves crashing or leaves rustling and describe them in writing. They can then compare how different times of day or weather conditions change the movement in their setting.

Classroom Activities Using AI for Movement in Descriptions

1. Action-Based Writing Challenge

Pupils can describe a setting, but every sentence must include movement. AI can support this with suggestions for alternative verbs for more dynamic descriptions.

> Prompt: "Suggest three alternative ways to say 'the wind blew through the trees.'"
> Response: "The wind whispered through the trees, the wind howled past the branches, the wind rushed through the tangled canopy."

Challenge the children to describe a setting in three different ways using movement like this.

2. Movement Transformation Task

Pupils can rewrite a still setting description to make it more active. The AI support here could be that it suggests how to add movement to static descriptions:

> Prompt: "Make this description more dynamic: 'The mountains were tall and snowy.'"
> Response: "The towering mountains loomed over the valley, their snowy peaks catching the golden light as mist curled around their jagged edges."

Ask the children to make these sentences more dynamic in the same way:

- The desert was hot and lonely.
- The ocean was calm and still.
- The city was busy and noisy.

3. Describe a Scene in Motion

Pupils could choose a setting such as a rainforest, a stormy sea or a city at rush hour and describe how it moves. The AI support here is that it generates a descriptive paragraph to provide inspiration.

> Prompt: "Describe a rainforest full of movement."
> Response: "The rainforest pulsed with life. Leaves trembled under the weight of raindrops, sending tiny waterfalls cascading to the forest floor. Vibrant parrots flapped their wings, darting through tangled vines as monkeys leapt effortlessly between branches. The distant roar of a waterfall mingled with the chirps, croaks, and rustling of unseen creatures, while the humid air shimmered with the constant hum of insects. Beneath the towering canopy, a jaguar slinked silently through the undergrowth, its sleek body barely disturbing the carpet of fallen leaves. The rainforest never rested – it breathed, whispered, and danced in an endless rhythm of movement."
> Prompt: "Create a simplified version using short sentences with basic conjunctions like and, but, so, because or then and a few relative/subordinate clauses."
> Response: "The rainforest was full of life. Rain fell on the leaves **and** made tiny waterfalls. Bright parrots flew through the vines **and** monkeys jumped from tree to tree. You could hear a faraway waterfall **and** the sounds of animals in the trees. The air was hot and wet. The insects never stopped buzzing. Under the tall trees, a jaguar moved quietly **so** the leaves did not make a sound. The rainforest never stopped. It moved, it whispered, **and** it was always alive."

The children could use the same structure and some of the same movements but to describe an alternative setting.

Caution and Consideration

When using AI, consider:

- Encouraging originality: AI should be a tool for inspiration, not a substitute for creativity.
- Reviewing AI suggestions: Ensure generated descriptions align with the desired tone and detail.
- Balancing AI with hands-on writing: Let pupils refine and personalise AI-generated ideas.

Recommended Tools

1. ChatGPT (free/paid) – Generates movement-based descriptions and alternative verb choices.
2. SkyBox 360 (freemium) – Creates moving 3D environments for pupils to describe.
3. Craiyon (free) – Creates free images.
4. Adobe Firefly (free/paid) – Creates a limited number of images for free.
5. DeepL Write (free) – Helps refine movement descriptions for clarity and fluency.
6. Book Creator (freemium) – Allows pupils to compile movement-based descriptions into digital books.
7. QuillBot (freemium) – Rewrites descriptions to enhance movement and engagement.

39 Other Worlds

Creating other worlds in stories allows pupils to explore limitless possibilities, where settings can be inspired by reality or entirely original. Whether crafting a magical kingdom, an alien planet, or an underwater civilisation, setting descriptions bring these worlds to life. AI tools can enhance this process by generating ideas, providing descriptive models, and refining pupils' writing to make their otherworldly settings immersive and engaging.

Why Explore Other Worlds in Writing?

Imaginary settings allow pupils to develop creativity, as they can build landscapes that don't exist in reality, and enhance description skills, as writing about new worlds requires strong sensory detail. When pupils engage in world-building, it helps them to understand how different elements interact in a fictional world. In this chapter we will use AI tools to help generate unique locations, sensory descriptions and names for fantastical places.

Exploring Other Worlds in Literature

Many primary school texts feature richly described other worlds:

- *The Lion, the Witch and the Wardrobe* by C.S. Lewis – Narnia's snowy forests, mythical creatures, and enchanted castle create a vivid alternative world.
- *The Wild Robot* by Peter Brown – A futuristic island where technology and nature collide.
- *The Explorer* by Katherine Rundell – A deep Amazonian world filled with uncharted wonders.
- *The Last Bear* by Hannah Gold – A setting that takes readers to the Arctic wilderness, blending realism with emotional depth.

AI can analyse these books to identify key descriptive elements, helping pupils replicate similar techniques in their own writing. For example:

Prompt: "Describe a world where the sky is made of water."
Response: "Above, rippling waves replaced clouds, casting shifting blue light over the floating islands below. Schools of silver fish darted through the sky, their scales flashing as they wove between translucent jellyfish drifting in the air."

We could ask our pupils to use this model to write about a world where the sky is made from cotton candy, lava or Lego.

Building an Otherworldly Setting

1. Geography and Environment

Creating an original world starts with its physical features. We can use AI to give us some ideas for these physical features by using prompts such as:

> Prompt: "Describe a lava planet."
> Response: "The ground cracked with each step, glowing veins of molten rock pulsing beneath a jagged crust. Ash rained down like black snow, and towering cliffs of obsidian shimmered in the intense heat."
> Prompt: "Now describe a frozen planet where the trees are made of ice."
> Response: "Crystal branches stretched towards the sky, their sharp tips glistening like frozen daggers. The ground cracked underfoot, ice splintering with each step as an eerie wind howled through the glassy forest."

With these two example, we could ask children to describe a poisonous gas swamp or upside down planet.

2. Creatures and Inhabitants

Other worlds often feature unique creatures or beings that live within them. For example an underground city might have "bioluminescent vines that snaked through the cavern walls, lighting the city with a soft blue glow. Silent, cloaked figures moved through the streets, their footsteps barely making a sound on the polished stone paths."

> Prompt Example: "Describe an alien species that communicates through colours."
> Response: "The Skelari shifted their iridescent skin in waves of purple and green, their silent language flowing like a dance of light across their bodies."

The children could write a non-chronological report about the Skelari where they describe the creatures' physical appearance, habits, habitat, movement, noises, etc.

3. Weather and Climate

The weather in other worlds can be exaggerated versions of Earth's or something entirely new. For example in a storm world, "The sky boiled with constant lightning, crackling across the darkened clouds like veins of silver fire. Winds howled through the jagged valleys, carrying the scent of electric storms."

> Prompt: "Describe a world where it always rains, but the raindrops are glowing."
> Response: "Soft blue droplets fell from the violet sky, landing with a shimmer before vanishing into the ground, leaving tiny sparks of light where they touched."

The children could then describe hurricane worlds, a world with three suns or a monsoon world.

Using AI to Develop Unique Other Worlds

AI can provide inspiration and help refine world-building by generating:

- Setting descriptions – Unique landscapes, creatures, and climates.
- Name ideas – Unusual names for locations and inhabitants.
- Sensory details – Enhancing world descriptions with rich language.

Pupils input a setting idea into AI such as:

> Prompt: "Describe an underwater city where people live in giant shells."
>
> Response: "Beneath the waves, the underwater city of **Mirellia** shimmered with bioluminescent light. Giant pearlescent shells formed elegant homes, linked by swaying seaweed bridges. Schools of fish wove between coral towers, while residents glided effortlessly, their voices echoing softly. At the city's heart, a vast nautilus palace spiralled into the deep, glowing with flickering sea anemones."

Pupils can expand, refine and personalise this AI-generated description, or even write more about Mirellia.

Bringing Other Worlds to Life

1. Writing Challenges with AI

Children could invent and describe a magical portal that leads to another world.

> Prompt: "Describe a door that leads to a hidden world."
>
> Response: "The door shimmered, shifting between colours as ancient runes pulsed along its frame. A whispering breeze curled through the cracks, carrying the scent of something unknown and exciting."

They could also imagine travelling through the portal to another dimension which is like a familiar setting or an ordinary location but in this dimension is much more fantastical.

> Prompt: "Describe a school where the classrooms float on clouds."
>
> Response: "Desks bobbed gently as the cloud floor swayed beneath them, the sky stretching endlessly in all directions."

The children could then expand these descriptions with their own ideas.

2. Descriptive Maps

Pupils can draw maps of their created worlds and write descriptions for each area. AI can then generate descriptions for different locations on their maps.

> Prompt: "Describe the dark forest in my fantasy world."
>
> Response: "Gnarled trees loomed over narrow, winding paths, their twisted branches forming an unbroken canopy that blocked out the sky. Glowing mushrooms pulsed faintly, casting eerie shadows along the forest floor."

3. Character and Creature Development

Pupils can also create inhabitants for their worlds, detailing their appearance, language and communication and daily life and traditions. AI can help to refine these details.

Prompt: "Describe a peaceful but powerful alien race."

Response: "The Eldari glided through their crystalline cities, their silver robes catching the starlight. Though they never spoke, their thoughts resonated through the air in melodic waves, a silent symphony of understanding."

Caution and Consideration

When using AI, consider:

- Encouraging originality: AI should provide inspiration, but pupils should develop their own voice.
- Reviewing AI responses: Ensure descriptions fit the intended world.
- Balancing AI with hands-on creativity: Combine AI support with drawings, discussions, and group brainstorming.

Recommended Tools

1. ChatGPT (free/paid) - Generates descriptions for fantastical settings.
2. DeepL Write (free) - Helps refine world-building descriptions.
3. SkyBox 360 (freemium) - Creates visual representations of otherworldly locations.
4. Artbreeder (freemium) - Generates character and creature visuals.
5. Book Creator (freemium) - Allows pupils to compile world-building details into interactive books.

40 Contrasting Places

Contrasting places in storytelling create vivid and engaging descriptions, emphasising differences between two settings. Whether comparing bustling cities and quiet villages, lush forests and barren deserts, or magical worlds and reality, these contrasts help shape mood, atmosphere and character experiences. AI tools can support pupils in generating, refining and expanding their descriptions, ensuring their settings feel rich and immersive.

Why Use Contrasting Places in Writing?

Using contrasting places helps pupils to develop descriptive skills as highlighting differences makes settings more vivid. This also creates tension and atmosphere, as opposing environments affect a story's tone. It can be used to enhance character development too as different places challenge and change characters. In this chapter we will use AI tools to generate setting descriptions, refine comparisons and suggest unique contrasts.

Contrasting Places in Literature

Many primary school books use contrasting settings effectively:

- *The Lion, the Witch and the Wardrobe* by C.S. Lewis – The grey, war-torn reality of London contrasts with the snowy, magical world of Narnia.
- *The Secret Garden* by Frances Hodgson Burnett – The dark, lifeless manor house contrasts with the vibrant, hidden garden full of life and colour.
- *The Explorer* by Katherine Rundell – The modern world of school and routine contrasts with the wild, unpredictable Amazon rainforest.
- *Northern Lights* by Philip Pullman – The orderly, strict atmosphere of Jordan College contrasts with the dangerous, icy vastness of the Arctic.

AI can help pupils analyse how these contrasts are built and suggest their own unique setting comparisons, like this:

Prompt: "Describe a gloomy, crowded city and a peaceful countryside."

Response: "The city roared with the honking of cars and the chatter of hurried footsteps, buildings pressing close like silent onlookers. In contrast, the countryside stretched wide, golden fields swaying in the breeze under a sky untouched by smoke."

Children could replicate this technique by describing a gloomy, deserted castle overlooking a vibrant market square.

Building Contrasting Settings

1. Urban vs. Rural

Comparing city and countryside settings is a useful way to show contrast. For example:

City: "Neon signs flickered in the rain as crowds surged forward, weaving between streams of taxis and buses."
Countryside: "The winding dirt path was lined with wildflowers, and the only sound was the distant call of a skylark."
Prompt Example: "Describe a city at rush hour and a village at dawn."
Response: "In the city, sirens wove through the tangled streets, engines growling and people rushing with purposeful strides. In the village, the sky glowed soft pink as the first birds stirred, dewdrops clinging to quiet hedgerows."

The children could then expand these contrasting scenes with their own vocabulary.

2. Natural vs. Industrial

Some contrasts highlight nature's beauty against man-made environments. For example:

Forest: "The trees whispered secrets, their emerald leaves rustling in the cool breeze."
Factory: "Smoke billowed into the sky, the air thick with the scent of oil and metal."
Prompt: "Compare a jungle to a polluted city."
Response: "The jungle pulsed with life, vines curling around ancient trees as parrots flashed between branches. Meanwhile, the city streets lay choked with fumes, concrete towering where trees once stood."

Children could then look at a variety of images of natural and industrial settings and compare them, as the AI model has demonstrated.

3. Real vs. Imaginary Worlds

Fantasy settings often contrast with familiar, real-world locations. For example:

Real World: "The school hall echoed with the chatter of students, chairs scraping against the tiled floor."
Imaginary World: "Crystal towers spiralled into a lavender sky, their surfaces shifting with reflected starlight."
Prompt: "Describe a school in reality and one in a magical world."
Response: "The real school smelled of ink and pencil shavings, lessons ticking along to the steady rhythm of the clock. The magical school shimmered, corridors shifting as if alive, staircases curling to form new paths with each step."

The children could go on to describe the magical school further using their actual school as a stimulus for the fantastical. They could describe the magical school's tables, chairs, playground, dinner hall, etc.

4. Day vs. Night

A single setting can change dramatically between different times of day. For example:

Day: "The marketplace bustled with traders, vibrant fabrics draped over wooden stalls as voices rose in friendly barter."
Night: "Lanterns flickered in the quiet market, shadows stretching long between empty stalls, the once lively square now eerily silent."
Prompt: "Describe a castle at sunrise and at midnight."
Response: "At sunrise, golden light spilled through stained glass windows, painting the stone walls in soft hues. At midnight, the corridors lay in eerie silence, only the distant hoot of an owl breaking the stillness."

The children could replicate this activity for an ice palace, a pirate ship or a fairy village.

Using AI to Enhance Contrasting Settings

AI tools can support pupils in writing richer descriptions by:

- Generating comparisons – AI can create unique setting contrasts.
- Refining word choice – AI can suggest stronger vocabulary for contrast.
- Providing alternative perspectives – AI can offer different angles for the same setting.

Pupils choose two contrasting settings, such as a desert vs. an ocean, a futuristic city vs. a medieval village, etc. They describe one setting, then use AI to generate a contrasting description. For example:

Prompt: "The desert was a barren landscape of golden sand. Tumbleweeds rolled lazily from one dune to another while armoured cacti stood proud and tall. Now describe the ocean using this sentence structure."
Response: "The ocean was a vast expanse of rolling blue waves. Silver fish darted swiftly from one coral reef to another while towering kelp swayed majestically."

Pupils can then refine and expand their descriptions and the AI-generated description.

Bringing Contrasting Places to Life

1. Writing Challenges with AI

Children could create opposite places. They can use AI prompts to help with this:

Prompt: "Describe a peaceful meadow, then turn it into a dangerous wasteland."
Response: "The meadow was a sea of soft grass, dotted with wildflowers swaying in the breeze. But as the storm rolled in, the flowers withered, the air thick with the scent of scorched earth."

Or, the children could transform a setting over time such as how a place changes across centuries.

Prompt: "Describe a forest before and after a magical curse."

Response: "Before, the trees stood tall, their emerald leaves sheltering the creatures below. After the curse, the branches twisted unnaturally, their leaves shrivelled and blackened under a sickly purple sky."

The children can then experiment with creating opposite places or transforming a setting over time.

2. Compare Two Places in a Story

Pupils can also pick two locations in a book and compare how they shape the characters' experiences. For example, in *The Lion, the Witch and the Wardrobe* we have:

- London during wartime: Grey, cold and full of worry.
- Narnia: Bright, snowy and filled with adventure.

Children could then look at other differing locations in books, such as Harry Potter's cupboard under the stairs compared with the hall of Hogwarts, or in *Wild* by Emily Hughes, the city compared with the forest.

AI Suggestions: "Here are some primary school books with contrasting locations within the same story:

1. The Secret Garden by Frances Hodgson Burnett
    - Misselthwaite Manor: Dark, gloomy, and filled with secrets.
    - The Secret Garden: Vibrant, full of life, and a place of healing and discovery.
2. The Explorer by Katherine Rundell
    - The Plane Crash Site: Isolated, dangerous, and unfamiliar.
    - The Amazon Jungle: Wild, unpredictable, but filled with beauty and survival opportunities.
3. Holes by Louis Sachar
    - Camp Green Lake: Dry, desolate, and punishing.
    - The Past (Flashbacks to Green Lake's History): A thriving town with a shimmering lake and bustling community.
4. Journey to the River Sea by Eva Ibbotson
    - Cambridge, England: Cold, strict, and uninspiring.
    - The Amazon Rainforest: Lush, free, and full of adventure.
5. Alice's Adventures in Wonderland by Lewis Carroll
    - The Real World: Logical, ordinary, and structured.
    - Wonderland: Strange, nonsensical, and ever-changing.
6. Skellig by David Almond
    - Michael's New House: Bare, unfamiliar, and unsettling.
    - The Garage: Mysterious, magical, and the home of Skellig.

7. The Wild Way Home by Sophie Kirtley
    - Modern-Day England: Safe, structured, and familiar.
    - The Stone Age: Dangerous, unpredictable, and survival-based.
8. Tom's Midnight Garden by Philippa Pearce
    - Tom's Aunt and Uncle's House: Small, lonely, and confined.
    - The Midnight Garden: Vast, enchanting, and timeless.
9. Varjak Paw by S.F. Said
    - The House: Secure, sheltered, and strict.
    - The City: Dangerous, full of threats, but offering independence.
10. The Last Bear by Hannah Gold
    - England: Structured, familiar, and ordinary.
    - Bear Island: Remote, wild, and full of raw beauty.

Caution and Consideration

When using AI, consider:

- Encouraging originality: AI should inspire, not replace, creative thinking.
- Ensuring balanced contrasts: Not all contrasts need to be extreme.
- Reviewing AI suggestions: Pupils should refine AI responses for clarity and creativity.

Recommended Tools

1. ChatGPT (free/paid) - Generates setting comparisons and alternative descriptions.
2. DeepL Write (free) - Helps refine contrasting details.
3. SkyBox 360 (freemium) - Creates visual representations of different worlds.
4. Book Creator (freemium) - Allows pupils to compile setting descriptions.
5. Storybird (freemium) - Helps develop illustrated setting comparisons.

PART 5
Poetry

In this section, AI is used to unlock creativity, rhythm and wordplay, making poetry an accessible and enjoyable form of expression for all pupils. Teachers will find tools that support structured poetry forms, such as haikus, acrostics and cinquains, as well as free verse and performance poetry. AI can generate model poems, help pupils find rhyming words, explore figurative language, and offer real-time feedback on rhythm and syllable patterns. Chapters suggest ways to use AI for collaborative poetry writing, visual poetry creation and thematic exploration based on class topics or current events. Pupils can experiment with mood, sound and imagery, building confidence to write, edit and perform their work. Whether you are introducing poetry to younger children or supporting more advanced analysis and composition, this section offers flexible strategies to inspire personal voice, imagination and a love of language.

41 Explaining Literary Devices

Poetry is rich with literary devices that enhance rhythm, meaning and emotion. Teaching pupils how to recognise and use these devices deepens their understanding and appreciation of poetry. AI tools can support this process by providing instant examples, analysing patterns and generating creative prompts to help pupils experiment with their own poetry writing.

Why Teach Literary Devices in Poetry?

Understanding literary devices helps pupils to develop comprehension skills by recognising patterns and meanings in poetry. It enhances creative writing by showing them how to use poetic techniques to add depth and style. It can also help to engage children with poetry more deeply by assisting them to appreciate the artistry of language. In this chapter we will use AI to support learning by generating examples, analysing poetic structure and providing feedback on pupils' poems.

Common Literary Devices in Poetry

1. Similes and Metaphors

A simile compares two things using "like" or "as" such as "The storm raged like a lion," while a metaphor states one thing is another without using "like" or "as" such as "The storm was a roaring lion." Both create vivid imagery in poetry. For example, in "The Tyger" by William Blake, the poet says, "Tyger Tyger, burning bright, in the forests of the night." The metaphor here is likening the tiger to fire.

AI can generate similes and metaphors for pupils, such as:

Prompt: "Create a simile about a storm."
Response: "The storm raged like a lion, roaring across the sky."
Prompt: "Write a metaphor about the ocean."
Response: "The ocean was a restless giant, tossing and turning in its sleep."

The children could then try to write similes of their own about a volcano, tsunami or earthquake. Then they could try a metaphor about a forest, desert or mountain.

2. Alliteration

Alliteration is the repetition of initial consonant sounds to create rhythm and emphasis.
   "The Jabberwocky" by Lewis Carroll has lots of nonsense words but also alliteration like, "He took his vorpal sword in hand: long time the manxome foe he sought."
   AI can help pupils generate alliterative lines like this:

   Prompt: "Write an alliterative sentence about the wind."
   Response: "The wild wind whistled through the whispering willows."

Challenge the children to write alliterative sentences. They could write a sentence about silver swords, ghostly ghouls or crazy cats.

3. Personification

Personification gives human qualities to non-human things. In "Who Has Seen the Wind?" Christina Rossetti states, "But when the leaves hang trembling, the wind is passing through."
   AI can create personification examples such as:

   Prompt: "Describe a thunderstorm using personification."
   Response: "The thunder growled angrily as the lightning danced across the sky."

Ask the children to expand what the thunder and lightning did with further personification.

4. Onomatopoeia

Onomatopoeia is the use of words that imitate sounds. "The Sound Collector" by Roger McGough gives this as an example, "The whistling wind, the gurgling drain."
   Ask AI to list onomatopoeic words and to help pupils use them in poetry.

   Prompt: "List five onomatopoeic words for a busy city."
   Response: "Honk, buzz, chatter, clatter, screech."
   Prompt: "Write a poem line about a busy city using onomatopoeia."
   Response: "Horns blared, brakes screeched, and footsteps pattered on the crowded pavement."

Ask the children to continue the poem using "honk, buzz, chatter and clatter."

5. Repetition

Repetition emphasises key words or phrases for effect. In "The Highwayman" by Alfred Noyes, we have "And the highwayman came riding - riding - riding -" which is repeated in the first and final stanzas, reinforcing the image of the highwayman approaching and returning.
   Also, we have "Tlot-tlot; tlot-tlot!" which mimics the sound of the horse's hooves and appears multiple times to build tension.
   "A red-coat troop came marching - marching - marching -" mirrors the earlier phrase about the highwayman but now signals danger.

   Prompt: "Write a poem line with repetition about the moon."
   Response: "The moon was silver, the moon was bright, the moon watched over us all night."

Ask the children to write lines that repeat the same word, like this one, but note that rhyme is not necessarily needed here.

6. Rhyme and Rhythm

Rhyme and rhythm can be explored here though. These devices create musicality and flow in poetry. In "Gran, Can You Rap?" by Jack Ousby, we have "My gran is really groovy, she's hip and she can hop." This demonstrates a simple rhythm to a poem. AI can help us to generate rhyming words and help pupils create rhythmic patterns. For example:

Prompt: "Generate a rhythmic rhyming couplet about a cat."
Response:

"The tabby cat sat on the mat,
watching the mice go this way and that."

Give children some sets of rhyming words like these:

"Night – Light – Sight
Cold – Bold – Gold
Street – Beat – Feet"

Then ask them to write three couplets of poetry, mirroring the style of the cat couplet.

Using AI to Explore Literary Devices

1. AI-Generated Poetry Analysis

AI can analyse famous poems and highlight literary devices. For example, if pupils input "The Owl and the Pussycat" by Edward Lear, they can ask AI to identify its rhyme scheme, repetition and figurative language.

Response:

Rhyme Scheme, Repetition, and Figurative Language in The Owl and the Pussycat

1. Rhyme Scheme:

"The Owl and the Pussycat" by Edward Lear follows a consistent AABCCB rhyme scheme in each stanza.
Example (First Stanza):

The Owl and the Pussy-cat went to sea (A)
In a beautiful pea-green boat, (A)
They took some honey, and plenty of money, (B)
Wrapped up in a five-pound note. (C)
The Owl looked up to the stars above, (C)
And sang to a small guitar. (B)

This pattern is repeated throughout the poem, giving it a musical and rhythmic flow.

2. Repetition:

Repetition is used to enhance rhythm and create a whimsical tone.

- "The Owl and the Pussy-cat" is repeated at the beginning of different stanzas to reinforce the central characters.
- "O lovely Pussy! O Pussy, my love" is repeated for emphasis and to highlight the affectionate relationship between the two characters.
- The phrase "And they danced by the light of the moon, the moon, the moon" in the final stanza is a strong example of repetition, reinforcing the dreamy, magical ending.

3. Figurative Language:

The poem includes various literary devices that make it engaging and imaginative:

- Personification: The owl and the cat act like humans (talking, playing a guitar, getting married).
- Imagery: "By the light of the moon, the moon" creates a vivid, dreamy scene.
- Alliteration: "Bong-tree" and "beautiful pea-green boat" add musicality.
- Metaphor: The "pea-green boat" could symbolize an escape or adventure.

This combination of rhyme, repetition, and figurative language contributes to the playful and lyrical nature of the poem, making it an enduring classic for young readers.

This method of analysing poems can be used for any copyright-free poem (a copyright-free poem is a poem in the public domain, meaning it can be freely used, shared and modified without permission, usually because the author has been deceased for at least 70 years or the work was published before modern copyright laws).

2. AI-Prompted Poetry Challenges

Pupils can generate poetry with AI by choosing a literary device and asking AI to create an example.

Prompt: "Write a short poem using personification about the sun."
Response:

"The sun stretched its golden arms, waking the world from sleep,
It whispered warmth upon the hills and kissed the ocean deep."

Prompt: "Give me three alliterative poem lines about a river."
Response:

"The rushing river ran through rocky ridges,
Whispering water wove through willows wild,
Silver streams sparkled, splashing softly."

Caution and Consideration

When using AI, consider:

- Encouraging originality: AI should inspire, but pupils should personalise their writing.
- Reviewing AI-generated examples: Ensure age-appropriate language and structure.
- Balancing AI with traditional methods: Pupils should also write without AI support to build confidence.

Recommended Tools

1. ChatGPT (free/paid) - Generates poetic examples and literary device exercises.
2. Poem Generator (free) - Helps pupils create poems with guided prompts.
3. DeepL Write (free) - Refines poetic language and enhances descriptions.
4. RhymeZone (free) - Provides rhyming words and synonyms for poetry writing.
5. Book Creator (freemium) - Allows pupils to compile AI-assisted poems into digital collections.

42 More Figurative Language

Figurative language is at the heart of poetry, allowing writers to craft vivid, imaginative and thought-provoking images. Beyond similes, metaphors, alliteration, personification, onomatopoeia, repetition and rhyme (covered in **Chapter 41**), many other literary devices enrich poetry. This chapter explores additional figurative language techniques, showing how AI can support their understanding, application and creative use.

Why Teach More Figurative Language?

Understanding and using a wide range of figurative language helps pupils to enhance their descriptive writing with deeper meaning and nuance and develop critical reading skills by identifying literary devices in poetry. When pupils engage with poetry creatively they can experiment with different techniques and use AI tools to generate, refine and analyse figurative language in their writing.

1. Hyperbole

Hyperbole is an extreme exaggeration used for emphasis or humour. For example, in "Gran, Can You Rap?" by Jack Ousby, the poet says, "She's the fastest, the grooviest gran in town!" which exaggerates her abilities for comic effect. Pupils can generate their own hyperboles using AI prompts such as:

> Prompt: "Write a hyperbole about how hungry someone is."
> Response: "I'm so hungry I could eat a mountain of spaghetti in one bite!"

Ask pupils to write their own hyperboles about different topics like weather, school or pets.

2. Idioms

Idioms are phrases where the meaning isn't literal but understood through common usage, such as, "you're on fire today!" "the elephant in the room" or "I'm keeping my eye on you."

In "The Boy Who Grew Dragons" by Andy Shepherd, we have "My heart was in my mouth." Meaning "I was really nervous."

Children use idioms without realising they do so, like "I just walked a million miles to get to school," but we use them too, like "I've asked you a thousand times to pick up that pencil." AI can also generate idioms for pupils to interpret.

Prompt: "Give me three idioms about emotions."
Response:

1. "Butterflies in my stomach." (Feeling nervous.)
2. "Over the moon." (Extremely happy.)
3. "Spill the beans." (Reveal a secret.)

Encourage pupils to use AI to explore idioms and incorporate them into their own poetry.

3. Symbolism

Symbolism uses objects, colours or actions to represent deeper meanings. In "The Highwayman" by Alfred Noyes, the red coat of the soldiers symbolises danger and bloodshed and the moonlight symbolises fate and mystery. Pupils can ask AI to generate symbolic meanings:

Prompt: "What does a key symbolise in literature?"
Response: "A key often symbolises knowledge, discovery, or unlocking secrets."

Pupils can create their own symbolic images using AI-generated ideas to inspire their writing, such as how golden light, rainbows or dark shadows can be used as symbols.

4. Assonance and Consonance

Assonance is the repetition of vowel sounds. Consonance is the repetition of consonant sounds. We see this in "The Tyger" by William Blake.

- "Tyger, Tyger, burning bright" (assonance of the long "i" sound)
- "Did he who made the lamb make thee?" (consonance of the "m" sound)

AI can generate examples of assonance and consonance for pupils to analyse.

Prompt: "Give me a sentence with assonance about the sea."
Response: "The waves played a lazy game on the bay."
Prompt: "Write a sentence with consonance about a storm."
Response: "The crackling clouds crashed and crumbled in the sky."

Pupils can experiment with these techniques in their own poems.

5. Oxymorons

An oxymoron combines two opposite ideas to create an effect. "Jabberwocky" by Lewis Carroll uses this oxymoron: "Frabjous day" (a mix of "fabulous" and "joyous"). AI can generate oxymorons for pupils to explore.

Prompt: "Give me three oxymorons."
Response:

1. Deafening silence.
2. Bittersweet memory.
3. Frozen fire.

Ask pupils to use these oxymorons in sentences for a poem. Then ask them to create their own oxymoron-based poem lines.

6. Enjambment

Enjambment is when a sentence or phrase continues beyond the end of a line, without a pause. In "The Listeners" by Walter de la Mare, we have:

> "Is there anybody there?" said the Traveller,
> Knocking on the moonlit door"

AI can create more examples of enjambment such as:

Prompt: "Write a poetic line using enjambment."
Response:

> "The river runs, its silver path weaving
> Through the sleeping hills, whispering secrets."

Encourage pupils to write their own lines using this technique.

Using AI to Explore Figurative Language

1. AI-Prompted Figurative Language Challenges

Pupils choose a literary device from **Chapter 41** or this chapter, they then ask AI to create an example, such as:

Prompt: "Write a simile and a metaphor about a storm."
Response:
"Simile: 'The storm raged like a furious beast.'
Metaphor: 'The storm was an angry drum, beating against the rooftops.'"

2. AI for Poetic Refinement

Pupils could write their own poem using as many kinds of figurative language as you set (depending on age, ability, understanding of the genre, etc.). They can use AI to check for these figurative elements or to suggest improvements.

3. AI-Assisted Analysis of Classic Poems

The children can input a classic poem and ask AI to identify literary devices. For example:

Prompt: "Analyse figurative language in "Daffodils" by William Wordsworth."

Response: "Personification: 'A host of golden daffodils' (The daffodils are given human-like qualities, as if they are hosting a gathering.)"

Children can do this with a range of different poems to check what kind of figurative language has been used.

Caution and Consideration

When using AI, consider:

- Encouraging originality: AI should inspire, not replace, pupil creativity.
- Balancing AI with hands-on learning: Pupils should also analyse and write without AI support.
- Checking AI accuracy: Review AI-generated content for relevance and age-appropriateness.

Recommended Tools

1. ChatGPT (free/paid) - Generates figurative language examples and poetry prompts.
2. Poem Generator (free) - Assists with structured and free verse poetry.
3. DeepL Write (free) - Helps refine poetic language and enhance descriptions.
4. RhymeZone (free) - Provides rhyming words, synonyms, and poetic structures.
5. Book Creator (freemium) - Allows pupils to compile AI-assisted poems into digital collections.

43 Writing Ballads

> Ballads are one of the most enduring forms of poetry, telling stories through rhythm, rhyme and repetition. They often feature dramatic events, heroic deeds or tragic tales, making them an engaging way to explore narrative poetry. AI tools can support pupils in writing ballads by generating story ideas, structuring stanzas and refining rhyme and rhythm patterns.

Why Teach Ballads?

Understanding and writing ballads helps pupils to develop storytelling skills by creating structured narratives. It also enhances rhythm and rhyme awareness through repeated patterns. By exploring ballads, children can investigate historical and folk traditions that have been passed down for generations. In this chapter, we will use AI tools to experiment with themes, structure, and language in their ballads.

1. Characteristics of Ballads

Ballads typically follow a clear structure such as:

- Quatrains: Four-line stanzas.
- Rhyme Scheme: Usually ABAB or ABCB.
- Strong Rhythm: Often written in iambic tetrameter (four beats per line) and iambic trimeter (three beats per line).
- Refrain/Repetition: Key lines or phrases are repeated.
- Dialogue: Characters often speak within the poem.
- Dramatic Events: Tales of adventure, tragedy or heroism.

In the ballad, "The Highwayman" by Alfred Noyes we have:

> The wind was a torrent of darkness among the gusty trees,
> The moon was a ghostly galleon tossed upon cloudy seas.

The vivid imagery and rhythm make it a memorable example of a ballad. Ask children to rewrite the lines describing the clouds and the sun during the day.

DOI: 10.4324/9781003621379-48

2. Exploring Ballads with AI

AI tools can help pupils generate and analyse ballads by:

- Providing examples of classic ballads.
- Generating story ideas based on prompts.
- Suggesting rhyming words to maintain ballad structure.
- Refining rhythm and repetition in student writing.

For example:

Prompt: "Give me an idea for a ballad about a lost treasure."
Response: "A sailor embarks on a journey to find a legendary treasure, but a storm and a ghostly warning stand in his way."

Pupils can use this AI-generated story idea to structure their own ballad.

3. Writing the First Stanza of a Ballad

To help pupils get started, encourage them to create a first stanza that establishes the setting and mood. For example:

The ship set sail at morning light,
Through misty seas and endless night.
A legend spoke of golden land,
But danger lurked beneath the sand.

We can use AI to give us an example of this:

Prompt: "Write the first stanza of a ballad about a knight on a quest."
Response:

"The knight rode out in armour bright,
To seek the sword of ancient might.
Through forests dark and mountains steep,
A promise made he vowed to keep."

Pupils can experiment with AI-generated stanzas and modify them to make them their own.

4. Using Repetition and Refrains

Repetition strengthens a ballad's musicality and emotional impact. Many traditional ballads repeat a phrase or chorus at key moments, such as in "The Ballad of Sir Patrick Spens" (a traditional Scottish ballad):

"Oh who is this has done this deed, and told the king of me?"

Prompt: "Write a refrain for a ballad about a lost city."
Response: "The city sleeps beneath the sea, lost in time, lost to me."

Pupils can write their own refrains and use AI for suggestions as inspiration.

5. Developing Conflict and Resolution in a Ballad

Ballads often tell of struggles, adventures or tragedies. Encourage pupils to include a conflict and resolution in their poem, such as in "The Ballad of Lucy Gray" by William Wordsworth (about a lost child).

> Yet some maintain that to this day,
> She is a living child;
> That you may see sweet Lucy Gray
> Upon the lonesome wild.

Prompt: "Write two lines of a ballad about a dragon and a hero."
Response:

> "The dragon roared, the flames arose,
> The hero stood and drew his sword."

Pupils can then expand these lines into full stanzas.

6. Creating Original Ballads with AI Support

Pupils can input a story idea into AI and request structured quatrains to help develop their poem, like this:

Prompt: "Generate a four-line stanza for a ballad about a lost king."
Response:

> "His throne stood empty, cold as stone,
> The crown lay deep in dust unknown.
> Yet echoes called from halls of old,
> A kingdom waiting to unfold."

Encourage pupils to use AI-generated stanzas as inspiration but modify them to fit their personal style.

7. Ballad Performance and Rhythm Check

Since ballads are often sung or recited, pupils should read their work aloud to ensure a smooth rhythm. Pupils could record their ballad using an AI speech-to-text tool to check for flow. The AI can suggest rhythm adjustments to enhance the poem's musicality.

Prompt: "Check the rhythm of this stanza:

> A lady wept beside the sea,
> Her lover lost, her heart set free."

Response: "Try adjusting to:

> A lady wept beside the shore,
> Her love would sail home nevermore."

This allows pupils to refine their ballads with AI feedback.

Using AI to Explore Ballads Further

1. AI-Generated Ballad Analysis

Pupils input a classic ballad and ask AI to break down its structure, rhyme scheme and repetition. For example:

> Prompt: "Analyse the rhyme scheme of 'The Highwayman.'"
> Response: "This poem follows an AABCCB rhyme scheme in its stanzas."

2. AI as a Ballad Brainstorming Partner

Pupils input story ideas and ask AI for quatrain starters, such as:

> Prompt: "Start a ballad about a lost dog."
> Response:
>
> > "Through fields of gold he ran away,
> > Beneath the sky so dark and grey."

3. AI for Synonyms and Descriptive Enhancements

Pupils use AI to enhance imagery in their ballads, like this:

> Prompt: "Give me a more vivid version of: 'The waves crashed on the shore.'"
> Response: "The waves thundered onto the jagged shore, spraying salt into the bitter wind."

Caution and Consideration

When using AI, consider:

- Encouraging personal creativity: AI should inspire, not replace, original thinking.
- Balancing AI-generated content with pupil effort: Pupils should craft their own ballads
- Reviewing AI accuracy: Ensure generated responses align with intended themes.

Recommended Tools

1. ChatGPT (free/paid) - Generates ballad ideas, stanzas, and rhyme suggestions.
2. Poem Generator (free) - Creates structured ballads based on user input.
3. RhymeZone (free) - Provides rhyming words and poetic phrases.
4. DeepL Write (free) - Enhances poetic language and rhythm.
5. Book Creator (freemium) - Allows pupils to compile ballads into digital collections.

44 Structured Poetry

> Structured poetry follows specific patterns, such as rhyme schemes, syllable counts or stanza structures. These forms help pupils develop discipline in writing while also encouraging creativity. AI tools can support structured poetry writing by suggesting formats, generating first lines and refining poetic structures.

Why Teach Structured Poetry?

Understanding structured poetry helps pupils to develop pattern recognition by following specific formats and enhances language control through syllable restrictions and rhyme schemes. In this chapter we will explore traditional poetry forms used across different cultures and periods and use AI tools to experiment with structure and receive instant feedback.

1. Haiku: Capturing Moments in Syllables

A haiku is a three-line poem with a 5-7-5 syllable structure, traditionally focusing on nature and fleeting moments. For example:

> An old silent pond,
> A frog jumps into the pond –
> Splash! Silence again.
> (by Matsuo Bashō)

We can use AI for Haiku generation like this:

Prompt: "Generate a haiku about a sunset."
Response:

> "Golden light fades low,
> Shadows stretch on rolling hills,
> Night whispers its song."

Ask pupils to experiment by generating their own haikus, focusing on different themes such as rain, animals or emotions.

2. Limericks: Adding Playfulness to Poetry

A limerick is a five-line poem with an AABBA rhyme scheme, known for its humorous and playful tone, such as:

> There once was a man from Peru,
> Who dreamt he was eating his shoe.
> He awoke in the night,
> With a terrible fright,
> To find that his dream had come true!

We can use AI for limerick writing too:

Prompt: "Write a limerick about a cat."
Response:

> "There once was a cat from the coast,
> Who loved eating jam on his toast.
> But one fateful day,
> It all blew away,
> And now he just stares at the post."

Challenge pupils to write their own limericks with AI-generated first lines or themes.

3. Sonnets: Expressing Deep Emotion

A sonnet is a 14-line poem written in iambic pentameter with a specific rhyme scheme. Shakespearean sonnets follow an ABABCDCDEFEFGG pattern, such as "Sonnet 18" by William Shakespeare. Here are the first two lines:

> Shall I compare thee to a summer's day?
> Thou art more lovely and more temperate.

When we use AI for sonnet analysis and writing we could say:

Prompt: "Generate the first two lines of a sonnet about the sea."
Response:

> "The ocean waves dance in the silver light,
> Their whispers echo through the moonlit night."

Encourage pupils to complete the AI-generated lines to build their own sonnet.

4. Acrostic Poems: Creating Meaning from Letters

An acrostic poem uses the first letter of each line to spell out a word or phrase, like this:

> Soft petals bloom wide,
> Under the golden sky,
> Never fading, standing tall.

We can ask AI to help with our acrostic poem inspiration:

Prompt: "Create an acrostic poem for the word 'RAIN.'"
Response:

"Rumbling clouds roll in,
A river swirls along the street,
In every drop, a story forms,
Nature hums its steady beat."

Pupils can create acrostic poems for their names, seasons or emotions.

5. Cinquains: Compact and Expressive Poems

A cinquain is a five-line poem with a specific syllable structure: 2-4-6-8-2, such as:

Winter,
Frosty, silent,
Snowflakes dance and whisper,
Blanketing the world in white dreams,
Sleeping.

Here's an idea for using AI for cinquain writing:

Prompt: "Generate a cinquain about a forest."
Response:

"Forest,
Misty, shadowed,
Branches twist and whisper,
Creatures stir beneath the thick leaves,
Hidden."

Pupils can write their own cinquains, experimenting with different topics, using the structure provided.

6. Free Verse with Structured Elements

Even without a rigid structure, poets can use elements of structured poetry in free verse. We can encourage pupils to apply rhyme, repetition or syllabic patterns to their work to enhance it and give it some structure.

In "The Sound Collector" by Roger McGough, we have:

The whistling wind, the gurgling drain,
The clinking clanking of a train.

Prompt: "Write a free verse poem with repetition about the night sky."
Response:

"The stars are watching,
The stars are waiting,
The stars whisper secrets to the silent moon."

Ask pupils to experiment by blending structured poetry techniques into free verse compositions.

Classroom Activities Using AI and Structured Poetry

1. AI-Assisted Poetry Writing Challenge

Pupils input a theme into AI and receive structured poetry prompts, for example:

> Prompt: "Give me a first line for a haiku about autumn."
> Response: "Crimson leaves drift down"

The children then continue the haiku using skills previously learnt.

2. AI-Based Poetry Analysis

Pupils input a classic structured poem and ask AI to identify its rhyme scheme, structure and key features, such as:

> Prompt: "Analyse the rhyme scheme of 'The Owl and the Pussycat.'"
> Response:
>
>> The rhyme scheme of 'The Owl and the Pussycat' by Edward Lear follows a consistent **AABCCB** pattern in each stanza. Here's how it works:
>> Example (First Stanza):
>>
>>> The Owl and the Pussy-cat went to sea *(A)*
>>> In a beautiful pea-green boat, *(A)*
>>> They took some honey, and plenty of money, *(B)*
>>> Wrapped up in a five-pound note. *(C)*
>>> The Owl looked up to the stars above, *(C)*
>>> And sang to a small guitar. *(B)*
>>
>> This same **AABCCB** rhyme pattern continues throughout the poem, giving it a musical and lyrical quality that makes it engaging for young readers.

3. AI as a Poetry Editing Tool

Pupils can submit their own structured poems to AI for rhythm and rhyme suggestions. You could ask the AI to "Make this limerick's rhythm smoother." Or "Can you suggest a stronger rhyme for the second line of my sonnet?" Or "Does my haiku follow the correct 5-7-5 syllable structure?"

Caution and Consideration

When using AI, consider:

- Encouraging originality: AI should inspire, not replace, pupil creativity.
- Checking AI accuracy: Ensure responses align with intended structures.
- Balancing AI with traditional learning: Pupils should practise writing structured poetry without AI assistance too.

Recommended Tools

1. ChatGPT (free/paid) – Generates structured poetry and prompts.
2. Poem Generator (free) – Provides templates for different poetry forms.
3. RhymeZone (free) – Suggests rhyming words and phrases.
4. DeepL Write (free) – Refines poetic language and metre.
5. Book Creator (freemium) – Allows pupils to compile structured poetry collections.

45 Free Verse

> Free verse poetry breaks away from traditional structures, allowing for creativity without strict rhyme schemes or syllable patterns. It focuses on rhythm, imagery and personal expression. Pupils can experiment with language, sound and shape, crafting poetry that feels natural and unrestricted. AI tools can support free verse writing by generating prompts, suggesting sensory details and providing feedback on rhythm and imagery.

Why Teach Free Verse?

Free verse helps pupils to express emotions freely without the constraints of rhyme or metre. They can also experiment with structure and pacing in a way that suits the poem's theme. This enhances creativity by focusing on word choice, imagery and meaning. We will use AI tools to develop ideas, refine language and provide structural feedback in this chapter.

1. Understanding Free Verse through Examples

Free verse does not follow a fixed pattern but often uses strong imagery and rhythm to create impact. In "The Red Wheelbarrow" by William Carlos Williams we have:

> so much depends
> upon
> a red wheel
> barrow
> glazed with rain
> water
> beside the white
> chickens.

This poem is simple but powerful, relying on imagery rather than rhyme or rhythm. We can use AI to analyse free verse like this:

> Prompt: "Analyse the use of imagery in 'The Red Wheelbarrow.'"
> Response: "The poem uses vivid yet minimal imagery to create a strong visual impact. The wheelbarrow, rain, and chickens form a single moment frozen in time, showing how small details in everyday life hold importance."

Ask pupils to find a free verse poem and use AI to analyse its use of imagery and structure.

2. Writing Free Verse Poetry

Since free verse has no fixed structure, we can encourage pupils to focus on:

- Line breaks and spacing for emphasis.
- Imagery and sensory detail to create mood.
- Repetition and rhythm for flow and effect.

For example:

> Prompt: "Write a free verse poem about a storm."
> Response:
>
>> "The wind howls, restless and fierce,
>> bending the trees into trembling shadows.
>> Rain hammers the earth,
>> tiny soldiers in an endless march.
>> Lightning slashes the sky,
>> a quicksilver dagger,
>> splitting the world in half."

We can then ask pupils to edit the AI-generated poem, changing words and adding personal imagery to make it their own.

3. Experimenting with Line Breaks and Structure

Line breaks influence meaning and emphasis in free verse poetry. For example:

> The wind speaks,
> in whispers
> through the golden fields.

A poem with long lines moves faster:

> The wind rushes over the golden fields, carrying the scent of summer rain and the warmth of the sun.

> Prompt: "How can I change the structure of this free verse poem to make it more dramatic?"
> Response: "Consider breaking longer lines into shorter fragments to increase suspense, or clustering related words together to create a strong visual impact."

Ask pupils to write a free verse poem and experiment with different line breaks to see how it changes the meaning and feel.

4. Using Repetition for Emphasis

Repetition in free verse can enhance rhythm and reinforce meaning. For example, in "The Sound Collector" by Roger McGough we have:

> The whistling wind,
> The gurgling drain,
> The clinking clanking of a train.

We can use AI to help with this writing exercise like this:

> Prompt: "Write a free verse poem with repetition about the night sky."
> Response:
>> "The stars are watching,
>> The stars are waiting,
>> The stars whisper secrets to the silent moon."

Ask pupils to write their own free verse poem, using repetition to highlight an important idea, but the children don't necessarily need to use the structure offered in this example. Free verse is all about being creative after being given examples.

5. Creating Mood and Atmosphere

Since free verse poetry isn't bound by structure, it relies heavily on mood and tone. In "A River" by Valerie Bloom, the poet says:

> The river's a wanderer,
> A nomad, a tramp,
> He never chooses one place,
> To set up his camp.

AI can help pupils explore different moods too:

> Prompt: "Write a free verse poem about a forest, but make it feel eerie."
> Response:
>> "Shadowed paths twist,
>> leaves rustle with unseen whispers.
>> Branches stretch like gnarled fingers,
>> grasping at the cold night air."

Pupils can edit the AI response to change the mood by making it peaceful, magical or tense.

Classroom Activities Using AI and Free Verse Poetry

1. AI-Assisted Free Verse Prompts

Pupils can input a theme into AI and receive a free verse prompt. For example:

Prompt: "Give me a first line for a free verse poem about the sea."
Response: "The endless tide hums a song only the moon can hear."
Prompt: "Now write a free verse line about a mountain."
Response: "The mountain stands silent, its ancient bones wrapped in mist."

Children can then add more prompts. Once they've found the response they like the most, they continue with the poem.

2. Free Verse Editing with AI

Pupils can write a first draft of a free verse poem and ask AI to suggest alternative imagery.

Prompt: "Make my free verse poem about rain more dramatic."
Original Line: "The rain dances on the rooftops, whispering secrets to the earth."
AI-Edited Line: "The rain crashes against the rooftops, drumming wild rhythms as the earth drinks deep."

Children could then use this dramatic tone as inspiration and as an example to edit the rest of their poem.

3. Collaborative Free Verse Writing

Pupils could take turns adding lines to a free verse poem too. AI can provide the first and last lines to frame the piece. Here's an example first and last line to work with:

AI example:
"First line:
The wind roars through the empty streets, carrying stories of distant places.
Last line:
And in the hush that follows, the world breathes once more."

We can see that the wind is the subject of the poem. It begins with a noisy roar and ends with a hush. The children write the other lines in between these, moving the free verse from being noisy to being calm.

Caution and Consideration

When using AI, consider:

- Encouraging original thought: AI-generated lines should inspire, but not replace, pupils' creativity.
- Checking AI responses: Ensure age-appropriate and meaningful output.
- Balancing AI with human editing: Pupils should refine their own work before relying on AI for revision.

Recommended Tools

1. ChatGPT (free/paid) - Generates free verse prompts and suggestions.
2. Poem Generator (free) - Provides free verse ideas and structures.
3. DeepL Write (free) - Helps refine poetic language and rhythm.
4. Book Creator (freemium) - Allows pupils to compile free verse poetry collections.
5. Wordtune (freemium) - Suggests alternative phrasing for poetic lines.

46 Poetry Prompts

> Writing poetry can sometimes feel like staring at a blank page, waiting for inspiration to strike. Poetry prompts offer a starting point, helping pupils unlock creativity by providing themes, first lines, structures or word lists to spark ideas. AI tools can support this process by generating tailored prompts, refining language choices and even suggesting alternative directions for poems.

Why Use Poetry Prompts?

Poetry prompts help pupils to overcome writer's block by providing a clear direction, and to experiment with new ideas they might not think of on their own. They can also develop children's written voices by exploring different tones, moods and styles. In this chapter we will explore how to refine pupils' language with AI-assisted word choices and phrasing suggestions. This chapter also explores how to create, use and refine poetry prompts, with AI playing a supportive role in generating fresh ideas and personalised challenges.

1. Sensory Poetry Prompts

Sensory details bring poetry to life, immersing the reader in sights, sounds, smells, tastes and textures. Pupils can use AI-generated sensory word lists to expand their descriptions. For example:

Prompt: "Describe a market using at least one sense in every line."
Response:

> "The scent of cinnamon lingers in the air,
> Coins jingle in the pockets of hurried hands,
> Sunlight glows golden on rows of ripe mangoes,
> The chatter of trader's hums like a melody."

Encourage pupils to modify and extend AI-generated sensory poems, like this one, making them more personal and expressive.

2. Emotion-Based Poetry Prompts

Emotions shape poetry, influencing word choice and rhythm. AI can generate emotional word banks to support pupils in expressing feelings through poetry, such as:

Prompt: "Write a poem where happiness feels like a place."
Response:

"Happiness is a golden meadow,
Where laughter rolls with the wind,
Where the sky stretches forever,
And worries dissolve like mist."

Pupils can experiment with different emotions. For example, what would sadness, fear or excitement feel like as a place?

3. First-Line and Last-Line Prompts

Starting and ending strong makes a poem memorable. AI can provide opening or closing lines to frame pupil writing, such as:

Prompt: "Begin a poem with 'The river remembers...'"
Response:

"The river remembers each stone it has touched,
The whisper of leaves on its restless back,
The footprints of those who paused to drink,
And the storms that carried it far from home."

Pupils can continue the poem in their own direction, shaping the story the river tells.

4. Object-Based Poetry Prompts

Everyday objects can become poetic subjects, revealing hidden meaning and significance. AI can provide unique perspectives by suggesting unexpected comparisons.

Prompt: "Write a poem from the perspective of an abandoned umbrella."
Response:

"Once I danced in the rain,
Twisting and twirling, shielding from storms.
Now I rest, forgotten and folded,
Waiting for the wind to call me home."

Pupils can take AI-generated ideas like this one and explore other objects, such as a lost key, a broken clock or a lighthouse waiting in the dark. They can rewrite the poems or extend them.

5. Contrast and Juxtaposition Prompts

Opposites create striking poetry. AI can help generate contrasting ideas to enhance a poem's impact, like this:

Prompt: "Describe the same place at dawn and at midnight."
Response:

"At dawn, the meadow hums with waking bees,
Soft golden mist clings to sleeping petals.
At midnight, the meadow breathes in silence,
Silver shadows curl under a blanket of stars."

Encourage pupils to explore how different times of day, seasons or emotions change a setting's feel. They can read their poems to each other for feedback too.

6. Rule-Based Poetry Challenges

Some poems follow constraints such as the use of certain words, lengths or patterns. AI can generate rule-based prompts to inspire creative problem-solving.

Prompt: "Write a five-line poem where every line includes the word 'wind.'"
Response:

"The wind hums a song through the empty street,
The wind lifts the kite higher than dreams,
The wind whispers secrets in restless trees,
The wind cools the earth with gentle hands,
The wind never stays, but always returns."

Pupils can create their own word-based challenges and test AI's ability to follow their rules.

7. Found Poetry Prompts

"Found Poetry" involves reshaping existing text into something new. AI can extract key phrases from passages to form poetic structures, like this:

Prompt: "Use lines from a news article, a book or a letter to create a poem."
Response (using an article about the sea):

"Waves rise and fall like the breath of the earth,
Tides pull the shore with invisible hands,
Beneath the blue, secrets wait in silence."

Pupils can try this with their favourite books or with newspaper articles, weaving rewritten lines into a fresh poetic piece.

Classroom Activities Using AI and Poetry Prompts

1. AI-Prompted Poetry Challenges

Pupils could input themes or emotions into AI to receive writing prompts such as:

Prompt: "Give me a first line for a poem about courage."
Response: "Courage steps forward when fear grips tight."

Pupils write their own poem using the AI-generated first line.

2. Poetry Expansion with AI

Pupils write a short poem and ask AI for suggestions to expand it.

Prompt: "How can I make my poem about the sea more descriptive?"
Response: "Try adding more sensory details such as what does the sea sound, smell and feel like?"

Pupils then edit their poem using AI's suggestions.

3. Collaborative Poetry Writing

One pupil writes a first line, then another adds the next, continuing in a chain. AI then provides the final line to bring the poem full circle.

Example:
First line: "The night wind carries lost voices home."
Second line: "Only to be heard behind closed curtains."
Last line (AI-generated): "And the dawn listens to their echoes."

Caution and Consideration

When using AI, consider:

- AI should enhance, not replace, creativity: Pupils should personalise AI-generated lines.
- Checking AI-generated prompts to ensure they align with classroom themes and age-appropriate content.
- Encouraging self-editing: AI can provide suggestions, but pupils should refine their own work.

Recommended Tools

1. ChatGPT (free/paid) – Generates poetry prompts and first/last lines.
2. Poem Generator (free) – Offers structured poetry prompts and themes.
3. DeepL Write (free) – Helps refine poetic language.
4. RhymeZone (free) – Provides rhyming word suggestions for poems.
5. Book Creator (freemium) – Allows pupils to compile poetry collections.

47 Rhyme

> Rhyme is one of the most recognisable features of poetry, creating rhythm, musicality and memorability. It can make poetry fun and engaging while reinforcing phonemic awareness in young readers. AI tools can help pupils explore rhyming patterns, generate new rhyming words and refine their poetry through structured feedback and creative prompts.

Why Teach Rhyme?

Rhyme plays a crucial role in poetry by enhancing sound patterns, making poems easier to remember and recite. It helps pupils develop word recognition skills and phonological awareness. Most importantly, rhyme makes poetry fun! This chapter will explore different types of rhyme and how AI can support both the analysis and creation of rhyming poetry.

Types of Rhyme

Rhyme can take many forms, and pupils can experiment with different types to understand their effects on poetry. Here are a variety of different types of rhyme:

End Rhyme

This is where words at the end of each line rhyme with each other such as in "The Quangle Wangle's Hat" by Edward Lear:

> On the top of the Crumpetty Tree The Quangle Wangle sat,
> But his face you could not see, on account of his Beaver Hat.

Internal Rhyme

This is where rhyming words occur within the same line:

> The cat sat happily on the mat,
> While the dog ran wild like a cheeky brat.

Slant Rhyme

This is where words sound similar but do not rhyme perfectly, such as:

> He stood alone upon the bridge,
> Still holding on to an old grudge.

In hip-hop music this is used frequently.

Eye Rhyme

This is where words look like they should rhyme but are pronounced differently, such as "love and move" or "laughter and daughter."

Exploring Rhyme with AI

AI tools can help pupils generate rhyming words, suggest alternative rhymes and refine rhythmic patterns, such as:

> Prompt: "Give me a list of rhyming words for 'sky.'"
> Response: "Sky, high, why, sigh, fly, try, lie, buy."

Pupils can then use these AI-generated lists to build rhyming couplets. For example:

> The bluebirds soar into the sky,
> Chasing clouds as they drift by.

AI can also offer alternative rhymes to improve fluency:

> Prompt: "Can you suggest a smoother rhyme for this line: 'The cat sat on the chair, licking his fluffy hair'?"
> Response:
>> "The cat sat on the chair,
>> grooming with gentle care."

This allows pupils to experiment with rhythm and refine their rhymes.

Writing Rhyme in Poetry

Once pupils understand rhyme types, they can start crafting their own rhyming poems. AI can assist by providing structured prompts.

1. Rhyming Couplets

Couplets are two-line stanzas where the end words rhyme, such as:

> The little mouse ran through the wheat,
> Looking for something tasty to eat.

We can ask AI to give us examples too:

Prompt: "Write a rhyming couplet about the moon."
Response:

"The moonlit sky so vast and bright,
Glows like a pearl in the deep of night."

Children can then have a go at writing their own after seeing a few examples. They could use the same rhyme but write their own line.

2. Limericks

Limericks follow a five-line pattern (AABBA) with a bouncy rhythm. For example, "There Was an Old Man with a Beard" by Edward Lear:

There was an Old Man with a beard,
Who said, 'It is just as I feared!'
Two Owls and a Hen, Four Larks and a Wren,
Have all built their nests in my beard!

We can ask AI for examples too:

Prompt: "Write a limerick about a wizard."
Response:
"There once was a wizard named Clyde,
Whose magic was quite bonafide.
With a flick of his wand,
He conjured a pond,
And swam with the fish far and wide!"

Children could then write their own limerick using a theme of their choice.

3. Rhyme in Narrative Poetry

Many ballads and narrative poems use rhyme to tell engaging stories. For example in "The Pied Piper of Hamelin" by Robert Browning we have:

Into the street the Piper stepped,
Smiling first a little smile,
As if he knew what magic slept
In his quiet pipe the while.

We could ask AI to write something following the same structure:

Prompt: "Write four rhyming lines about a pirate adventure."
Response:

"The pirate ship sailed through the misty deep,
Where mermaids and sea beasts lay hidden asleep.
With treasure in sight and a map in their hand,
They braved stormy waters to reach golden sand."

Children could then use this model to write their own narrative poetry.

Classroom Activities Using AI and Rhyme

1. Rhyme Challenges

Pupils are given a word and must generate as many rhymes as possible using AI, such as: Find five rhyming words for "tree."

2. Finish the Rhyme

AI provides the first line and pupils complete the couplet, such as:

"The old oak tree stood tall and proud…"

3. Rhyme Substitution

Pupils rewrite a line from a poem using a different rhyme suggested by AI.

Original: "The cat sat on the chair, licking his fluffy hair."
Response: "The cat curled up without a care, snoozing in the evening air."

Using AI to Analyse Rhyme in Famous Poems

Pupils can also input famous poems into AI and ask it to analyse the rhyme scheme. For example with "The Owl and the Pussycat" by Edward Lear we can ask:

Prompt: "What is the rhyme scheme of 'The Owl and the Pussycat'?"
Response: "The rhyme scheme follows an AABCCB pattern."

This analysis helps pupils recognise patterns and apply them to their own poetry.

Caution and Consideration

While AI is a great tool for exploring rhyme, pupils should also be encouraged to:

- Experiment with rhyme schemes rather than relying solely on AI suggestions.
- Read their poems aloud to check for natural flow and rhythm.
- Recognise that near rhymes and slant rhymes can also be effective in poetry.

Recommended Tools

1. RhymeZone (free) – Generates rhyming words and synonyms.
2. ChatGPT (free/paid) – Suggests rhymes and improves rhythm.
3. Poem Generator (free) – Helps structure rhyming poems.
4. DeepL Write (free) – Refines poetic language.
5. Book Creator (freemium) – Allows pupils to compile rhyming poems into digital collections.

48 Thematic Ideas

Poetry allows pupils to explore a wide range of themes, helping them to express thoughts, emotions and ideas creatively. A strong theme gives a poem focus and meaning, guiding word choice, imagery and tone. By engaging with different themes, pupils can deepen their understanding of the world around them while enhancing their poetic skills. AI tools can support thematic poetry by suggesting ideas, providing example poems and generating prompts to inspire writing.

Why Teach Thematic Poetry?

Thematic poetry helps pupils to develop deeper thinking by exploring universal ideas and enhance emotional expression by connecting personal experiences to their writing. It can also structure their work by focusing on a central idea. We can use AI tools to generate theme-based prompts, suggest imagery and refine pupils' poems.

Exploring Common Poetry Themes

1. Nature

Many poems celebrate nature, capturing its beauty and power. In "Wind" by Ted Hughes, we see how nature's force is personified:

> This house has been far out at sea all night,
> The woods crashing through darkness,
> The booming hills.

AI can help pupils explore nature themes like this:

Prompt: "Generate a line of poetry about a storm."
Response: "The thunder growled like an angry beast, shaking the sleeping sky."

Pupils can then extend this into a full poem about a natural event, such as a storm, a sunrise or the changing seasons.

2. Emotions and Feelings

Poetry is an excellent way for pupils to express emotions, from joy to sadness, fear to excitement. In "The Magic Box" by Kit Wright, emotions are woven into personal memories:

> I will put in the box,
> The last joke my grandfather told me.

AI can guide pupils to write about emotions:

> Prompt: "Suggest a first line for a poem about happiness."
> Response: "Laughter spills like golden light, warming the world with joy."

Pupils can then choose an emotion and write a poem expressing it through imagery and metaphor.

3. Friendship and Family

Relationships often inspire poetry, showing love, loyalty and connection. In "A Friend" by Gillian Clarke, we see friendship captured in a simple but powerful way:

> A friend is someone who touches your heart,
> And stays there forever.

AI can support writing about relationships:

> Prompt: "Write a simile about a best friend."
> Response: "A best friend is like a lighthouse, always guiding you home."

Ask pupils to create their own friendship poems, using similes, metaphors or personal memories.

4. Dreams and Imagination

Poetry often explores dreams, creativity and wonder. In "I Opened a Book" by Julia Donaldson, imagination takes centre stage:

> I opened a book and in I strode,
> Now nobody can find me.

AI can suggest prompts to spark imaginative poetry:

> Prompt: "Give me a magical first line for a poem."
> Response: "I found a door of golden light, and stepped into the stars."

Encourage pupils to build their own imaginative worlds in poetry, writing about time travel, mythical creatures or magical landscapes.

5. Identity and Belonging

Poems about identity help pupils reflect on their own experiences. In "Refugees" by Brian Bilston, identity and perspective are explored through clever wordplay:

> They have no need of our help,
> So do not be fooled by their tales.

AI can support identity poetry:

Prompt: "Suggest a metaphor for feeling out of place."
Response: "Like a lost note in a song, searching for its melody."

Pupils can write about their own identity, culture or sense of belonging, using personal reflections and descriptive language.

Using AI to Develop Thematic Poems

1. Generating Poetic Ideas

AI can provide inspiration by offering prompts and structured ideas:

Prompt: "Give me three ideas for a poem about kindness."
Response:

1. A tiny act of kindness that grows into something bigger.
2. A world where kindness is the most valuable currency.
3. A single smile that changes someone's day.

Pupils can choose an idea and develop it into a full poem.

2. Expanding Thematic Imagery

AI can also help pupils enhance their descriptions:

Prompt: "Describe the night sky using vivid imagery."
Response: "The sky is a velvet curtain, stitched with silver stars."

Ask pupils to use AI-generated imagery as inspiration for their own writing.

3. Experimenting with Poetic Form

Once pupils have chosen a theme, they can decide how to structure their poem. AI can help suggest different poetic forms:

Prompt: "How could I write a poem about the sea?"
Response:

1. A free verse poem that flows like waves.
2. A rhyming couplet poem that captures the sea's rhythm.
3. A shape poem where the words form the outline of a wave.

Encourage pupils to experiment with different forms based on their chosen theme.

Classroom Activities Using AI and Thematic Poetry

1. Theme-Based Poetry Challenge

Give pupils a theme (e.g. adventure, loneliness, discovery), then ask AI to generate a first line. Pupils can then continue the poem, exploring their own ideas.

2. Thematic Poetry Comparison

Pupils compare how different poets explore the same theme, for example:

> Prompt: "How does 'The Sea' by James Reeves compare to another ocean-themed poem?"
> Response: "James Reeves' 'The Sea' compares the ocean to a wild, hungry dog, emphasising its unpredictability, while John Masefield's 'Sea Fever' romanticises the sea as a place of freedom and adventure, with both poems using strong imagery and rhythm to capture its power."

AI can highlight stylistic differences in tone and imagery.

3. Collaborative Thematic Poem Writing

Pupils work in groups, each adding a line to a themed poem. AI can provide the first and last lines to frame the piece, for example:

> AI-Generated First Line: "The forest hums with secrets, hidden beneath the leaves."
> AI-Generated Last Line: "And when the wind sighs, it whispers them to the sky."

Caution and Consideration

When using AI, consider:

- Encouraging originality: Pupils should edit AI suggestions to reflect their own ideas.
- Checking AI output: Ensure responses are appropriate and meaningful.
- Balancing AI with personal creativity: AI should be a tool for inspiration, not a replacement for individual thinking.

Recommended Tools

1. ChatGPT (free/paid) – Generates theme-based poetry prompts and ideas.
2. Poem Generator (free) – Helps pupils explore different poetry themes.
3. RhymeZone (free) – Provides rhyming words for theme-based poems.
4. DeepL Write (free) – Refines poetic descriptions and structure.
5. Book Creator (freemium) – Allows pupils to compile thematic poetry collections.

49 Collaborative Ideas

> Poetry thrives when shared. Collaborative poetry activities encourage pupils to work together, sparking creativity, improving confidence and helping them see writing as a dynamic and interactive process. Whether co-writing lines, performing in groups or using AI to generate shared ideas, collaborative poetry fosters teamwork and enjoyment.

Why Use Collaborative Poetry?

Collaborative poetry allows pupils to develop ideas together, encouraging creativity and discussion. They can also learn from one another, gaining confidence and improving vocabulary. In addition, it allows children to experiment with different styles while sharing responsibility for a poem's structure and theme. We can use AI for inspiration, whether generating prompts, refining lines or co-writing poetry in real-time.

1. Round Robin Poetry

In this exercise, each pupil adds a new line to a growing poem. It encourages spontaneity, teamwork and active listening. For example, start with a first line:

"The river whispers secrets to the stones,"

The next pupil adds something like,

"As the wind hums through the trembling trees."

The poem continues until everyone has contributed. For support we can ask AI to suggest a first line to guide the poem. Pupils can then refine their additions using AI for synonyms, rhythm or imagery enhancement, like this:

Prompt: "Give me a first line for a group poem about the night sky."
Response: "The stars scatter silver secrets across the velvet dark."

2. Call-and-Response Poetry

Call-and-response poetry uses alternating lines where one pupil writes a line, known as the "call," and another responds, known as the "response." This builds rhythm and interaction, mirroring traditional oral poetry. Here's an example based on the ocean:

> Call: "The waves crash, restless and wild."
> Response: "The moon watches, silent and wise."

AI can support this by suggest contrasting or complementary response lines, helping pupils understand poetic balance. AI can also suggest alternative rhythms if the structure needs adjusting, like this:

> Prompt: "Give a response line to 'The wind sighs through the empty streets.'"
> Response: "Shadows stretch long beneath flickering lights."

3. Group Performance Poetry

Pupils can co-write and perform a poem, assigning different lines to individuals or small groups. This reinforces expression, pacing and tone. For example:

> Theme: A Storm Approaches
> Group 1: "Dark clouds gather, rolling, tumbling, colliding."
> Group 2: "The sky shudders, the trees shiver."
> Group 3: "Lightning slashes, thunder roars."

AI can help suggest performance cues, such as pauses, emphasis or dramatic delivery. AI can also provide synonyms to help pupils strengthen their word choices.

> Prompt: "Suggest a powerful last line for a group poem about a thunderstorm."
> Response: "And then – silence, as the storm swallows the sky."

4. Collaborative Poetic Forms

Structured poems like haikus, limericks or cinquains can be co-written, with different pupils contributing parts. For example, here we have a collaborative haiku:

- Pupil 1 (5 syllables): "Golden leaves tumble"
- Pupil 2 (7 syllables): "Soft whispers drift on the breeze"
- Pupil 3 (5 syllables): "Autumn hums its song."

AI can then check syllable counts to maintain poetic form and also provide thematic word banks to spark ideas.

> Prompt: "Give a five-syllable first line for a collaborative haiku about rain."
> Response: "Silver drops descend."

5. AI-Powered Poetry Relay

Pupils can also write a poem collaboratively with AI. Each pupil contributes a line and AI generates the next, helping guide structure and inspiration. You can give your chosen platform prompts like this:

> Prompt: "Continue this free verse poem: 'The mist curled over the empty road...'"
> Response: "A ghost of footsteps, echoing low."

Then take turns creating the poem, like this:

> Pupil: "A shadow moved beneath the trees."
> AI: "Silent steps traced paths unseen."
> Pupil: "The night air hummed with whispers low."
> AI: "Moonlight flickered, pale and keen."

Classroom Activities Using AI for Collaborative Poetry

1. AI-Assisted Prompt Generator

Pupils input a theme such as "friendship," "the sea" or "adventure" and AI generates a starting line. The children then continue the poem in groups and AI provides alternative endings or refinements.

> Theme: Adventure
> AI-Generated Opening Line: "Through tangled vines and golden sand, a hidden world awaits in our land."
> Pupils Continue the Poem (in groups):
>
>> Through jungle dark and mountains steep,
>> We climb so high, the rocks so deep.
>> A silver river twists and glows,
>> Where it leads – nobody knows.
>
> AI Offers Alternative Endings:
> Mystical Ending:
>
>> Beyond the hills, a castle stands,
>> With ancient spells and golden hands.
>
> Exciting Ending:
>
>> A roaring beast with fiery eyes,
>> Guards the treasure – our greatest prize!
>
> Reflective Ending:
>
>> But adventure's end is never clear,
>> For stories live when hearts hold dear.

2. Peer-Review Poetry Edits

Pupils write in pairs, swapping their lines for feedback. AI can suggest improvements in rhythm, vocabulary or line structure.

3. AI-Generated Word Lists for Inspiration

AI provides word banks for specific themes to assist collaborative writing. For example, for a poem about space, AI may suggest: nebula, eclipse, cosmic, infinity, silence.

Caution and Consideration

When using AI, consider:

- Balancing AI input with original thinking: AI should assist, not replace, pupil creativity.
- Encouraging discussion: Poetry is subjective: pupils should analyse AI's suggestions critically.
- Ensuring inclusivity: All voices should be heard in collaborative writing.

Recommended Tools

1. ChatGPT (free/paid) - Generates and refines poetic lines collaboratively.
2. DeepL Write (free) - Enhances language fluency and rhythm.
3. Poem Generator (free) - Provides structured and free verse poetry inspiration.
4. Book Creator (freemium) - Enables pupils to compile digital poetry anthologies.
5. Wordtune (freemium) - Suggests rewording for better poetic flow.

50 Poetry Analysis

> Poetry analysis helps pupils explore meaning, structure and literary devices within a poem. By closely examining a poem's themes, language and form, pupils can develop deeper comprehension and appreciation of poetic techniques. AI tools can assist in breaking down complex poems, generating discussion prompts and offering alternative interpretations to guide analysis.

Why Teach Poetry Analysis?

Poetry analysis enhances critical thinking by encouraging pupils to look beyond surface meanings. It builds comprehension by helping them decode figurative language and unfamiliar structures. It also develops appreciation by exploring the artistry of poetic expression. AI can support this process by generating explanations, suggesting alternative readings and prompting deeper reflection on poetic choices.

Analysing Meaning in Poetry

Understanding a poem's meaning requires looking at both the literal and figurative interpretations. Pupils can ask AI questions such as:

> What is the poem about on a basic level?
> What deeper themes or emotions does it convey?
> How does the poet's choice of language affect meaning?

For example, if we examine "Silver" by Walter de la Mare we can see that this poem describes the moon's light casting a silver glow over the world:

> Excerpt:
>
> > Slowly, silently, now the moon
> > Walks the night in her silver shoon

> Prompt: "What mood does the poem create and how does the imagery contribute to this?"
> Response: "The poem creates a peaceful and dreamlike atmosphere. The personification of the moon 'walking' and the repetition of 'silver' emphasise its quiet, magical presence."

We could ask pupils to apply this technique to another short poem, identifying the mood and the imagery of that one too.

Exploring Poetic Structure

The structure of a poem impacts its rhythm and meaning. Pupils could analyse the line length and stanza structure and ask how these affect pacing. Or they could look at enjambment vs. end-stopping and ask if the poem flows smoothly, or are there pauses. They could also examine rhyme scheme and rhythm and ask if they enhance the meaning. In "The Listeners" by Walter de la Mare we have:

> Is there anybody there?' said the Traveller,
> Knocking on the moonlit door

We could then ask AI:

> Prompt: "How does the structure of the poem build suspense?"
> Response: "The poem's rhythm, created by long and short lines, adds tension. The repetition of unanswered knocking and questions makes the reader feel the eerie silence."

Pupils can use AI to highlight structural choices in their own favourite poems and discuss their effects.

Examining Literary Devices

We can encourage pupils to identify and analyse how literary devices shape meaning. For example, in "A River" by Valerie Bloom we have:

> The river's a wanderer, a nomad, a tramp,
> He doesn't choose one place to camp.

> Analysis Prompt: "How does personification shape the description of the river?"
> Response: "The river is personified as a restless traveller, reinforcing its constant movement. The metaphor of a 'nomad' makes it seem free-spirited yet unpredictable."

We could ask pupils to apply AI-generated personification to another natural element, like the wind or the sun, to see how it changes the poem's effect.

Comparing Two Poems

Comparing poems deepens pupils' understanding of different poetic techniques and themes. When we compare "The Sea" by James Reeves vs. "The Ocean's Song" (a new AI-generated poem) we have:

> The Sea:
>
> > The sea is a hungry dog,
> > Giant and grey.

AI-Generated Poem:

> The ocean hums a lullaby,
> A vast and endless dream.

Comparison Prompt: "How do these poems present the sea differently?"

Response: "James Reeves describes the sea as wild and aggressive, using an animal metaphor, while the AI-generated poem makes it peaceful and dreamlike through soft imagery."

Ppils can use AI to generate alternative descriptions of natural elements and compare them to existing poems.

Applying Analysis to Pupils' Own Poetry

Pupils can also apply analysis techniques to their own writing. AI can suggest refinements in tone, imagery and rhythm.

Prompt: "Make this line more vivid: 'The wind blew across the field.'"

Response: "The wind raced across the golden field, bending the tall grass like waves on the sea."

Pupils can use AI tools to enhance their poetry with richer imagery and refined language.

Classroom Activities Using AI and Poetry Analysis

1. AI-Powered Poetry Breakdown

Pupils input a poem into AI and ask it to identify key literary devices such as:

Prompt: "Find examples of similes and metaphors in the poem 'The Moon' by Robert Louis Stevenson."

Response:
Poem Extract:

> The moon has a face like the clock in the hall;
> She shines on thieves on the garden wall,
> On streets and fields and harbour quays,
> And birdies asleep in the forks of the trees.

Simile: "The moon has a face like the clock in the hall."

- This is a simile because it compares the moon's face to a clock using the word "like."

Metaphor: "She shines on thieves on the garden wall."

- The moon is personified as "shining" on the thieves, implying it is an active observer rather than a mere object in the sky.

Now, pupils can take another poem and repeat this activity, looking for more similes and metaphors with AI assistance.

2. Theme Exploration Challenge

Pupils select another poem and use AI to generate questions about its themes. For example:

Prompt: "What is the theme of 'The Owl and the Pussycat'?"
Response: "The theme of 'The Owl and the Pussycat' by Edward Lear revolves around love and adventure, as it follows two unlikely companions who embark on a whimsical journey, overcoming differences and obstacles to find happiness together."

Children can then repeat this exercise for other chosen poems too.

3. AI-Generated Poetry Comparisons

Pupils can ask AI to rewrite a classic poem in a different style, for example:

Prompt: "Rewrite 'The Highwayman' in a modern setting."
Response:
"The Getaway Driver
(A Modern Retelling of The Highwayman)

> The engines roared in the neon night,
> Streetlights flickered dim.
> Down in the city, cold and bright,
> He waited, fast and slim.
> A leather jacket, dark as the sky,
> And eyes that burned with risk.
> He revved his bike as he whispered low,
> To the girl with the silver disc.
> She worked the tills in a corner store,
> Where shadows crept like thieves.
> She knew the codes, the backdoor locks,
> The nights when cash was heaved.
> The plan was set; at dead of night,
> He'd speed past just in time,
> And she would slip into the dark,
> A lookout for their crime.
> But someone heard – her manager, sly,
> Who whispered to the law.
> The officers waited in tinted cars,
> Silent, cold and raw.
> She heard the hum of his speeding bike,
> A signal in the air,
> Her heart beat fast – she had one chance,
> To warn him to beware.
> She darted out, her phone in hand,
> A text – one single word.

But blue lights flared before she could press,
Her warning went unheard.
The sirens howled, the tyres screamed,
His ride came skidding round,
A wall of steel, a flashing badge,
Then silence cloaked the sound.
They found her standing, pale and still,
Her phone clutched in her grip.
They told her he was gone for good,
A chase, a crash, a slip.
But still at night, when engines purr,
And city streets are bare,
A lone bike hums beneath the stars –
His ghost is riding there.

This version keeps the tragic romance, betrayal, and fate-driven action of 'The Highwayman' but places it in a modern city setting with a getaway driver and his accomplice."

Caution and Consideration

When using AI for poetry analysis, consider:

- Encouraging independent thought: AI should support, not replace, pupils' own ideas.
- Verifying interpretations: AI-generated responses may need cross-checking.
- Promoting creative discussion: Use AI to spark debate and refine understanding.

Recommended Tools

1. ChatGPT (free/paid) – Provides poetry breakdowns and alternative interpretations.
2. Poetry Foundation (free) – Provides access to classic and contemporary poetry.
3. RhymeZone (free) – Helps pupils identify and explore rhyme patterns.
4. DeepL Write (free) – Suggests stylistic improvements for poetry.
5. CommonLit (free) – Offers analysis tools for poetry comprehension.

PART 6
Non-Fiction

This final section equips teachers with ways to use AI in guiding pupils through the planning, research and writing of non-fiction texts. Whether developing a structured report, writing a conclusion, or crafting a narrative non-fiction piece, AI tools can support clarity, vocabulary, and engagement. Chapters cover summarising key information, distinguishing fact from opinion, and generating age-appropriate headings and captions. Pupils are encouraged to use AI to conduct safe, guided research and refine their writing for different audiences. Lesson planning ideas are provided for integrating AI into non-fiction writing tasks across the curriculum, such as science or history. With an emphasis on critical thinking, structure and independence, this part ensures that pupils not only consume information but communicate it effectively. Teachers will be given the opportunity to appreciate how AI can personalise feedback and assist with scaffolding without compromising pupil voice.

51 Structure

> Non-fiction texts are structured in different ways depending on their purpose. Whether explaining, persuading, informing or instructing, a well-organised structure ensures clarity and engagement. Teaching pupils about structure helps them to navigate texts with confidence and apply clear, logical organisation in their own writing. AI tools can support this process by analysing text structures, generating outlines and offering revision suggestions to refine non-fiction writing.

Why Teach Non-Fiction Structure?

Understanding structure helps pupils to improve comprehension by recognising how information is presented and develops writing skills by using clear frameworks for different types of texts. Children can also organise ideas effectively when producing their own non-fiction work. They can use AI to support identifying the structure of existing texts, generating structured writing prompts and providing feedback on logical flow.

Common Non-Fiction Structures

1. Chronological (Order of Events)

Some non-fiction texts follow a timeline to explain how something happens step by step. For example in *The Great Fire of London* by Emma Adams we follow the fire's progression from the bakery on Pudding Lane through its devastating spread across the city. We can use AI to support chronology of other historical events in texts too, like this:

> Prompt: "Identify the chronological markers in this passage about the Titanic [passage copied and pasted into the AI platform first]."
> Response: "Markers like 'At first,' 'Then,' 'Next,' and 'Finally' show the sequence of events."

Pupils could research a historical event, such as the first moon landing, and use AI to generate a timeline before writing a report in chronological order.

2. Cause and Effect

Using a cause-and-effect structure explains why something happens and the results of that event. In *How Plastics Harm the Ocean*, Jess French explores how plastic pollution enters the ocean, its impact on marine life and what can be done to prevent further damage. Pupils can read this text then ask AI to help explore the topic further, like this:

Prompt: "List five cause-and-effect relationships on how plastics harm the ocean."
Response:

1. "Cause: Plastic waste is improperly disposed of and enters waterways.
   Effect: Plastics accumulate in rivers and eventually flow into the ocean.
2. Cause: Ocean currents carry plastic waste across vast areas.
   Effect: Large garbage patches, like the Great Pacific Garbage Patch, form.
3. Cause: Plastics break down into microplastics due to sunlight and wave action.
   Effect: Marine animals mistake microplastics for food, leading to ingestion.
4. Cause: Marine animals consume plastic waste.
   Effect: Their digestive systems become blocked, leading to starvation or death.
5. Cause: Plastics release toxic chemicals as they degrade.
   Effect: These chemicals enter the food chain, harming marine life and potentially affecting human health."

Pupils could choose an environmental issue, such as deforestation, and use AI to generate a cause-and-effect outline before writing an informational piece.

3. Compare and Contrast

This structure highlights similarities and differences between two subjects. For example, in *Big Cats* by Nic Bishop the book compares lions, tigers, cheetahs and leopards, exploring how they are alike and different. We can use AI to explore this further for our particular year group.

Prompt: "Compare and contrast cheetahs and lions in a paragraph for a seven year old."
Response: "Cheetahs are the fastest land animals, while lions are stronger and hunt in groups. Both are carnivores that rely on speed and strength to catch prey."

Pupils could select two animals, countries or historical figures, then use AI to create a Venn diagram before writing a comparison.

4. Problem and Solution

This structure presents a problem and explores possible ways to solve it. In *Malala's Magic Pencil* by Malala Yousafzai, the story highlights Malala's challenge in accessing education and how she advocated for change. After reading the text we could ask the children what they would do if they had a magic pencil to draw things that would make others happy. We could then explore these issues further using AI.

Prompt: "Suggest three solutions to reduce food waste in schools."
Response: "1. Encourage composting, 2. Donate surplus food, 3. Teach portion control."

Pupils could then highlight a problem in their school, such as littering, and use AI to generate potential solutions before writing their argument.

5. Descriptive

Some non-fiction texts focus on detailed descriptions of a subject. In *A Year in the Wild* by Ruth Symons the author describes the changing seasons in different habitats around the world. We could ask AI to help us to do the same.

> Prompt: "Describe the Amazon Rainforest using sensory details."
> Response: "The air hums with the chirps of exotic birds, dense emerald leaves drip with moisture, and the scent of damp earth fills the air."

Pupils can research a habitat, generate an AI-supported description and write a detailed non-fiction passage using the example as a model text.

Using AI to Support Non-Fiction Writing

1. AI-Generated Outlines

Before writing, pupils can ask AI to generate an outline for their chosen topic, for example:

> Prompt: "Create an outline for an explanation text about volcanoes."
> Response:

1. "What is a volcano?
2. How do volcanoes form?
3. Types of volcanoes
4. Famous eruptions in history
5. How scientists study volcanoes"

The children then use their subject knowledge to write under each heading. The AI has then shown them how they can organise their non-fiction writing.

2. Editing for Structure

Pupils can input their writing into AI and ask for structural feedback, like this:

> Prompt: "Does my explanation text have a clear structure?"
> Response: "Your introduction is clear, but the middle paragraphs jump between ideas. Try grouping similar points together."

The children can then edit their work accordingly.

3. Generating Examples for Different Structures

Pupils who are struggling to organise their ideas can ask AI for an example based on their topic, such as:

> Prompt: "Write a short cause-and-effect paragraph about climate change."
> Response: "Burning fossil fuels releases carbon dioxide into the air, which traps heat and leads to global warming. As a result, ice caps melt, and sea levels rise."

The children can then use the AI response and expand upon it.

Classroom Activities Using AI and Non-Fiction Structure

1. Structuring Jumbled Information

Provide pupils with a set of jumbled sentences from a non-fiction text. They can input it into AI and ask for suggestions on organising it into a clear structure.

2. Collaborative Structure Challenge

Pupils could work in groups to write different sections of a structured non-fiction text. AI could then generate a concluding paragraph based on their work.

3. AI-Prompted Peer Review

Pupils can use AI to review a peer's non-fiction piece, focusing on structure. An example prompt could be: "Does this explanation text follow a logical order?"

Caution and Consideration

When using AI, consider:

- Encouraging originality: AI should support pupils, but their ideas should be their own.
- Checking AI-generated content: Ensure responses are accurate and relevant.
- Balancing AI with traditional methods: Pupils should still engage with printed texts and teacher-led discussions.

Recommended Tools

1. ChatGPT (free/paid) - Generates structured outlines and provides structural feedback.
2. DeepL Write (free) - Refines sentence flow and organisation.
3. Book Creator (freemium) - Allows pupils to structure and publish their own non-fiction books.
4. CommonLit (free) - Provides structured non-fiction texts for analysis.
5. QuillBot (freemium) - Helps restructure and refine non-fiction writing.

52 Research

> Research is a key skill in non-fiction writing, allowing pupils to gather information, evaluate sources and organise their findings effectively. Strong research skills help children write factually accurate and well-structured texts, whether they are producing reports, explanations or biographies. AI tools can support this process by suggesting reliable sources, summarising key information and helping pupils verify facts.
>
> Teaching research skills not only improves literacy but also develops critical thinking, ensuring children learn to question and cross-check information rather than accepting everything at face value. AI can act as a digital research assistant, guiding pupils through the process while still requiring them to engage actively with the material.

Why Teach Research Skills?

Understanding how to research helps pupils to find relevant information efficiently, distinguish between fact and opinion and also summarise and synthesise information. Research can develop independent learning habits and improve the accuracy and credibility of their writing. AI can assist with each stage of research, from identifying key ideas in a text to generating summaries and organising information into structured notes.

Types of Research in Non-Fiction Writing

1. Fact-Finding for Reports and Explanations

Reports and explanations rely on factual accuracy, so by using quality texts such as *The Street Beneath My Feet* by Charlotte Guillain (where readers explore layers of the earth through detailed illustrations and factual descriptions), we can help pupils write their own reports. AI can also help with conducting research for pupils' own explanation texts too. We can investigate volcanoes, habitats, historical events or any chosen topic by using prompts. Here's an example using *The Street Beneath My Feet*:

Prompt: "Summarise the key layers of the Earth in five bullet points."
Response:

- Crust – The thin outer layer where we live, made of rock and soil.
- Mantle – A thick layer of hot, flowing rock beneath the crust.
- Outer Core – A layer of molten (liquid) iron and nickel that surrounds the inner core.
- Inner Core – A solid, extremely hot ball of iron and nickel at the Earth's centre.
- Tectonic Plates – Large pieces of the crust that move slowly, causing earthquakes and volcanoes.

Pupils can compare AI-generated summaries with information from books and websites to check accuracy and depth.

2. Researching Biographies

When writing biographies, pupils must gather key details about a person's life, achievements and impact. *Fantastically Great Women Who Changed the World* by Kate Pankhurst introduces young readers to inspiring figures like Rosa Parks and Amelia Earhart. Pupils can use AI to support biography writing by structuring their research into clear sections, like this:

Prompt: "Create a structured biography outline for Florence Nightingale."
Response:

1. Early Life: Birthplace, childhood, education.
2. Career: Why she became a nurse, key moments.
3. Impact: How she changed hospital care.
4. Legacy: How she is remembered today.

This structure helps pupils organise their research before drafting their biography.

3. Comparing Sources and Fact-Checking

Encouraging pupils to compare sources builds their ability to evaluate information critically. In *Surprising Sharks* by Nicola Davies, the author dispels common myths about sharks, showing how research can challenge misconceptions. In addition to using texts like this one, AI can help pupils assess the reliability of different sources.

Prompt: "What are three common myths about sharks, and what are the facts?"
Response:

1. Myth: All sharks are dangerous to humans.
   Fact: Most sharks pose no threat; only a few species are aggressive.
2. Myth: Sharks must keep swimming or they die.
   Fact: Some sharks can rest on the ocean floor and still breathe.
3. Myth: Sharks eat humans.
   Fact: Sharks mistake people for prey but do not actively hunt humans.

Pupils can verify AI responses by cross-referencing books and trusted websites.

4. Organising Research Notes

Effective non-fiction writing requires well-organised notes. AI can help pupils categorise information and refine their ideas. In *Earth Heroes*, Lily Dyu profiles environmental activists and their efforts to protect the planet. Pupils can read this book, then use AI to summarise key points before writing about an activist of their choice, like this:

Prompt: "Summarise Greta Thunberg's climate activism in a paragraph."

Response: "Greta Thunberg is a Swedish activist who started the 'Fridays for Future' movement, encouraging students to protest climate change. She has spoken at the UN and inspired millions to take action against global warming."

Pupils can expand on this by adding details from their research and writing a full biography.

Using AI to Support Research

1. AI-Generated Research Outlines

Before beginning research, pupils can use AI to create an outline for their chosen topic, for example:

Prompt: "Create an outline for a non-fiction report about the Amazon Rainforest."
Response:

1. Introduction: What is the Amazon Rainforest?
2. Location & Climate: Where it is and what the weather is like.
3. Wildlife: Animals and plants that live there.
4. Threats: Deforestation and conservation efforts.
5. Conclusion: Why the rainforest is important.

This provides a clear structure for pupils to expand upon in their own writing.

2. AI for Summarising Information

Pupils can struggle with summarising large amounts of information. AI can help by condensing text into key points, like this:

Prompt: "Summarise this article about space exploration in three sentences." (Pupils copy and paste an article.)

Response: "Space exploration has led to discoveries about planets, stars and galaxies. Missions like Apollo 11 landed humans on the Moon, and modern technology allows for Mars exploration. Scientists continue to study space to understand our universe better."

Pupils can use this as a starting point before refining their summary with more details.

3. Fact-Checking with AI

AI can assist pupils in verifying claims, as it simultaneously checks multiple sources.

Prompt: "Is it true that Mount Everest is growing taller each year?"

Response: "Yes, Mount Everest grows by about 4 millimetres per year due to tectonic activity."

Encouraging pupils to cross-check with reputable sources reinforces the importance of verifying information.

Classroom Activities Using AI for Research

1. AI-Guided Research Challenges

Pupils work in pairs or small groups to research a topic of their choice, such as Ancient Egypt, endangered animals or space exploration. They then use AI to generate a summary of key points and compare it with their own research from books or websites. For example, if the topic was rainforests, then pupils can research the Amazon Rainforest using books, websites or teacher-provided materials. They then input a research prompt into AI, such as:

Prompt: "Summarise five key facts about the Amazon Rainforest."
Response:

1. The Amazon Rainforest is the largest rainforest in the world, covering nine countries.
2. It is home to over 400 billion trees and 10% of Earth's wildlife species.
3. The Amazon River flows over 4,000 miles, making it one of the longest rivers in the world.
4. The rainforest produces 20% of the world's oxygen, earning it the nickname "the lungs of the planet."
5. Deforestation is a major threat, with thousands of acres lost every year.

Pupils compare the AI-generated summary with their own findings. They then discuss if the AI missed any key points. Is there anything in the AI summary they disagree with? Did their own research include extra details? Pupils refine their research skills and evaluate AI's reliability as a tool.

2. Fact vs. Fiction Quiz

Pupils test their knowledge by inputting statements into AI and asking if they are true or false. This activity helps develop fact-checking skills and encourages pupils to verify information from multiple sources. For example, if we provide a mix of true and false statements about space exploration then pupils input the statements into AI, like this:

Prompt: "Are these statements true or false? Explain why.

1. The first human to walk on the Moon was Neil Armstrong in 1969.
2. Jupiter is the smallest planet in the Solar System.
3. There is no gravity in space."

Response:

1. "True. Neil Armstrong, an American astronaut, was the first person to walk on the Moon during the Apollo 11 mission in 1969.
2. False. Jupiter is actually the largest planet. Mercury is the smallest.
3. False. There is gravity in space, but astronauts experience microgravity, which makes them feel weightless."

Pupils then discuss which answers surprised them and use books or reputable websites to confirm AI's responses.

3. AI-Assisted Note-Taking

Pupils can gather research notes on a topic and use AI to help organise their information into categories, making it easier to structure their writing. For example, if they were writing an explanation text on volcanoes then the pupils gather information about volcanoes from books, websites or classroom materials. They input key facts into AI and ask it to organise the notes, like this:

Prompt: "Sort these volcano facts into categories: formation, types, eruptions, famous volcanoes.

- Mount Vesuvius destroyed Pompeii.
- Volcanoes are openings in the Earth's crust.
- There are active, dormant, and extinct volcanoes.
- Magma rises through cracks in the Earth.
- The largest volcano in the Solar System is Olympus Mons on Mars.
- When a volcano erupts, lava and gases are released."

Response:

- Formation: Volcanoes are openings in the Earth's crust. Magma rises through cracks in the Earth.
- Types: There are active, dormant, and extinct volcanoes.
- Eruptions: When a volcano erupts, lava and gases are released.
- Famous Volcanoes: Mount Vesuvius destroyed Pompeii. The largest volcano in the Solar System is Olympus Mons on Mars.

Pupils review and refine AI's organisation, adding any missing details from their research.

Caution and Consideration

When using AI, consider:

- Checking for accuracy: AI-generated information should always be cross-checked.
- Encouraging critical thinking: Pupils should question sources and verify facts.
- Maintaining originality: AI should be a tool, not a replacement, for pupils' own research.

Recommended Tools

1. ChatGPT (free/paid) - Assists with summaries, outlines, and research prompts.
2. Kiddle (free) - A child-friendly search engine for safe online research.
3. Google Scholar (free) - Provides access to reliable academic sources.
4. Book Creator (freemium) - Helps pupils compile research into published non-fiction texts.

53 Captions and Headings

Captions and headings are essential features of non-fiction writing. They help to organise information, make texts easier to navigate and guide the reader's understanding. Whether in information books, reports or explanations, captions and headings provide clarity, structure and engagement. Teaching pupils how to use effective headings and captions improves their ability to structure their writing and enhances their comprehension when reading non-fiction texts. AI tools can support this process by generating headings, suggesting captions for images and helping pupils evaluate whether their choices are clear and engaging.

Why Teach Captions and Headings?

Understanding how to use captions and headings helps pupils to navigate texts more easily by breaking information into clear sections, and to improve comprehension by identifying key ideas. This can also make their writing clearer by structuring information logically. It can also engage readers by making their work visually appealing. AI can assist pupils in learning these skills by suggesting headings, generating captions and helping pupils refine their choices to make them more effective.

Exploring Captions and Headings in Non-Fiction Texts

1. What Are Captions?

Captions are short descriptions that explain images, diagrams or illustrations. They provide extra information that helps readers understand the picture in context. In *The Big Book of the Blue* by Yuval Zommer, the illustrations of sea creatures include captions that provide fascinating facts, such as, "This fish can change colour to blend in with its surroundings." We can emulate this style of text by showing pupils an image related to a topic they are studying, such as a volcano, a Roman soldier or a rainforest animal, and then asking the children to generate their own captions like Zommer has done. Then, let them input the image description into AI and compare their captions with the AI-generated ones, for example:

> Prompt: "Write a short caption for an image of a chameleon hiding in a tree."
> Response: "This clever chameleon changes colour to stay hidden from predators."

Pupils can then discuss if the AI-generated caption matches the image well and how they could make it clearer or more engaging.

2. What Are Headings?

Headings divide non-fiction texts into sections, helping readers find information quickly and understand the main ideas. Good headings should be clear, concise and informative. In *The Street Beneath My Feet* by Charlotte Guillain, headings guide the reader through different layers of the Earth, such as:

- "Down Through the Soil"
- "The Rocky Crust"
- "Molten Rock Below"

These headings break up the information and make the book easier to navigate. Give pupils a short passage without headings and ask them to create suitable headings. Then, they can input the passage into AI and compare the AI's suggestions with their own, like this:

> Prompt: "Suggest three headings for a passage about how honeybees make honey."
> Response:
>
> 1 "Busy Bees at Work"
> 2 "From Nectar to Honey"
> 3 "Storing the Sweetness"

Pupils can then discuss which heading is the most informative and how they can make the headings clearer or more exciting.

Using AI to Support Captions and Headings

1. AI-Generated Headings

AI can help pupils create clear and engaging headings by suggesting ideas based on their writing, like this:

> Prompt: "Suggest a heading for a paragraph about the importance of recycling."
> Response: "Why Recycling Matters: Protecting Our Planet"

Pupils can compare this with their own heading and discuss whether it accurately represents their paragraph.

2. AI for Creating Captions

Pupils can practise writing captions by using AI to generate different examples and refining them to be more engaging, like this:

> Prompt: "Write a caption for an image of a lion resting in the sun."
> Response: "The mighty lion basks in the warm afternoon sun, gathering strength for the hunt."

Pupils can then adjust the tone (e.g. making it more scientific or poetic) and add extra details (e.g. mentioning the lion's habitat).

3. Improving Headings and Captions with AI Feedback

Pupils can input their own headings or captions and ask AI for feedback on how to improve them. For example:

> Prompt: "Is this a good caption? 'The bear is in the river.' How could I improve it?"
> Response: "Try adding more detail: 'The brown bear wades through the rushing river, searching for salmon to catch.'"

This encourages pupils to expand their descriptions and make them more engaging.

Classroom Activities Using AI for Captions and Headings

1. Headline Challenge

Pupils read a short article and write a headline or title. They can then use AI to generate alternative suggestions and discuss which is most effective. For example:

- Pupils write: "The Importance of Bees"
- AI suggests: "Why Bees Are the Tiny Heroes of Our Planet"

Pupils could then discuss which heading is more engaging and how the AI heading adds interest or clarity.

2. Editing AI-Generated Captions

Pupils improve AI-generated captions by adding detail, adjusting vocabulary or making them more engaging, for example:

> AI generates: "The panda eats bamboo."
> Pupils improve it: "The giant panda munches on fresh green bamboo, its favourite food."

This activity encourages pupils to evaluate and refine language choices.

Caution and Consideration

When using AI, consider:

- Encouraging originality: AI should assist, but pupils should create their own headings and captions.
- Checking AI-generated responses: Sometimes AI suggestions may be vague or lack important details.
- Discussing different styles of headings: Teach pupils how headings can be formal ("How Planets Form") or creative ("A Journey through the Solar System").

Recommended Tools

1. ChatGPT (free/paid) - Helps generate headings, captions, and summaries.
2. DeepL Write (free) - Assists with sentence clarity and fluency.
3. Canva (freemium) - Allows pupils to create captions for images in visual projects.
4. Book Creator (freemium) - Enables pupils to structure their own non-fiction books with headings and captions.

54 Lesson Planning

We know that in teaching we are often far too busy. AI can significantly reduce planning time by generating lesson outlines, suggesting engaging activities and offering differentiated tasks based on pupils' needs. Instead of starting from scratch, we can use AI to quickly develop structured plans, adapt resources and refine lessons. By integrating AI into lesson planning, we can save valuable time, personalise learning more efficiently and access a wide range of creative ideas to enhance classroom engagement.

Why Plan Lessons on Non-Fiction Writing?

Lesson planning for non-fiction writing helps pupils to develop key writing skills such as structuring reports, using captions and researching effectively. But it can also help children to understand different non-fiction text types, engage with real-world content, linking writing to subjects such as science, history, and geography, and build independence by learning how to structure their own writing logically. AI can enhance lesson planning by suggesting activities, offering writing prompts and helping teachers differentiate for varying abilities.

Key Elements of a Non-Fiction Writing Lesson Plan

A strong non-fiction writing lesson might include:

1. Learning Objectives – What will pupils achieve by the end of the lesson?
2. Model Texts and Examples – Using quality texts to illustrate key features.
3. Guided Practice – Scaffolding pupils through structured activities.
4. Independent Writing – Allowing pupils to apply what they've learned.
5. Assessment and Feedback – Checking understanding and providing support.

AI can support each of these stages by suggesting objectives, generating model texts and providing feedback on pupil writing, as we shall explore in this chapter.

Using AI to Support Lesson Planning

1. AI-Generated Lesson Outlines

AI can help create structured lesson plans quickly by suggesting key steps and activities. For example:

Prompt: "Create a brief lesson plan for teaching Year 4 pupils how to write a non-chronological report about rainforests."
Response:
"Lesson Title: Writing a Non-Chronological Report on Rainforests
Learning Objective: Pupils will understand the structure of non-chronological reports and write their own about rainforests.
Lesson Steps:

1. Introduction – Discuss non-chronological reports and show an example.
2. Model Text Analysis – Read 'Rainforests' by Catherine Barr and highlight key features.
3. Guided Practice – Pupils work in groups to organise facts under subheadings.
4. Independent Writing – Pupils draft their own report using a writing frame.
5. Plenary & Peer Review – Pupils share their work and use AI to check structure and clarity."

Pupils can use AI to generate subheadings, summarise research and check their report structure before submitting their final draft.

2. Generating Model Texts for Pupils

Pupils learn best when they see examples of high-quality writing. AI can generate model texts that demonstrate key features. In *The Street Beneath My Feet* by Charlotte Guillain, the author uses clear headings and factual descriptions to structure information. We can use AI to generate a short non-chronological report on a topic of study in this same style, then ask pupils to highlight the key features such as headings, paragraphs, and factual detail. For example:

Prompt: "Write a short non-chronological report about volcanoes for a Year 5 class."
Response:

"**Title: The Power of Volcanoes**

Volcanoes are openings in the Earth's surface where hot lava, gases, and ash escape. They can be found on land and under the sea.

Types of Volcanoes

There are three main types of volcanoes: active, dormant, and extinct. Active volcanoes erupt regularly, while dormant ones may erupt in the future. Extinct volcanoes are unlikely to erupt again.

Famous Eruptions

One of the most famous eruptions was Mount Vesuvius in AD 79, which buried the city of Pompeii in ash.

Pupils can analyse the AI-generated model and compare it to published texts to discuss strengths and areas for improvement. Also, as this response is brief, children can add more detail to each section.

3. Differentiation and Personalisation

AI can differentiate lesson activities based on pupils' abilities. We can adjust difficulty levels or generate alternative explanations for struggling learners. For example:

Prompt: "Simplify this paragraph about deforestation for Year 3 pupils.

Deforestation is the large-scale removal of trees, often to make space for farming, roads, buildings, or industries. When forests are cleared, animals lose their natural habitats, making it harder for them to find food and shelter. Many species, including tigers, orangutans, and parrots, are endangered because of habitat destruction. Deforestation also affects the environment in other ways. Trees help produce oxygen and absorb carbon dioxide, so cutting them down increases air pollution and contributes to climate change. Without trees to hold the soil in place, heavy rains can cause soil erosion and flooding. This not only damages the land but also makes it harder for new plants to grow. By planting new trees and protecting forests, people can help reduce the negative effects of deforestation and support wildlife, clean air, and a stable climate."

Response: "Cutting down too many trees is called deforestation. It happens when people remove forests for farming, roads, or houses. This can harm animals and the environment."

Pupils needing more challenge can be asked to expand AI-generated text, adding details from their own research.

Classroom Activities Using AI for Lesson Planning

1. AI-Assisted Writing Prompts

AI can generate engaging writing prompts to spark creativity, for example:

Prompt: "Give me three fun writing prompts for a non-fiction lesson about space."
Response:

1. Diary of an Astronaut – Write a day in the life of an astronaut in space.
2. Mars vs. Earth – Compare what life would be like on Mars versus Earth.
3. How to Build a Spacesuit – Explain the materials and design of a spacesuit.

We can then adapt the AI-generated prompts to suit our lesson objectives.

2. Quick Lesson Adaptations

Sometimes lessons need to be adjusted on the spot. AI can provide instantaneous alternative activities, like this:

Prompt: "My pupils are struggling with writing captions. Can you suggest a fun hands-on activity?"

Response: "Try a caption-matching game! Provide images and ask pupils to write their own captions before revealing the correct ones."

This allows us to quickly adapt our lessons to meet our pupils' needs.

Caution and Consideration

When using AI, consider:

- Ensuring AI-generated content aligns with curriculum goals: AI can provide useful ideas, but teachers should review and refine responses.
- Encouraging critical thinking: AI is a tool, but pupils should learn to question and improve AI-generated text.
- Using AI for time-saving, not as a replacement: AI can assist with planning, but teacher expertise remains essential.

Recommended Tools

1. ChatGPT (free/paid) - Generates lesson outlines, model texts, and writing prompts.
2. Twinkl PlanIt (paid) - Provides structured lesson plans for non-fiction writing.
3. TeachStarter (freemium) - Offers ready-made non-fiction resources.
4. Google Bard (free) - Assists with research and idea generation.

55 Topic-Related Vocabulary

Developing topic-related vocabulary is essential for helping pupils to write clear, informative and engaging non-fiction texts. When pupils understand and use precise vocabulary, their writing becomes more accurate and professional. Whether they are writing about volcanoes, space, animals or historical events, having access to relevant terminology allows them to communicate ideas effectively. AI can support vocabulary development by suggesting subject-specific words, providing definitions and examples, and helping pupils refine their word choices. By integrating AI tools into our vocabulary lessons, we can save time and provide pupils with instant access to high-quality, topic-specific language.

Why Teach Topic-Related Vocabulary?

Understanding key vocabulary in non-fiction writing helps pupils to improve their comprehension of non-fiction texts and write more precisely, using subject-specific terms. It can also develop confidence when discussing and explaining topics and help them organise their ideas more clearly. AI can assist by generating word lists, explaining meanings in simple terms and suggesting vocabulary appropriate for different age groups.

Using AI to Develop Topic-Related Vocabulary

1. Generating Word Lists for Specific Topics

AI can quickly create subject-specific vocabulary lists, saving us preparation time. For example:

Prompt: "List 10 key words for a Year 4 lesson on volcanoes."
Response:

1. Volcano – An opening in the Earth where lava erupts.
2. Lava – Melted rock that flows from a volcano.
3. Magma – Hot liquid rock inside the Earth.
4. Eruption – When a volcano releases lava, ash, and gases.
5. Crater – The hollow opening at the top of a volcano.

6   Ash Cloud – Tiny rock particles released during an eruption.
7   Tectonic Plates – Large pieces of the Earth's surface that move and cause earthquakes and volcanoes.
8   Dormant – A volcano that is not active but may erupt in the future.
9   Active – A volcano that erupts regularly.
10 Extinct – A volcano that is unlikely to erupt again.

We can display the vocabulary list and discuss each term. We could also ask pupils to use AI to help generate definitions in their own words. The children could then create a glossary page for their non-fiction writing.

2. Simplifying Complex Vocabulary

Pupils often encounter challenging subject-specific words in non-fiction texts. AI can help by simplifying definitions to make them more accessible. In *Earth Shattering Events* by Robin Jacobs, scientific vocabulary is used to explain natural disasters. AI can simplify these terms for younger learners.

> Prompt: "Explain 'plate tectonics' in a way that a Year 3 pupil would understand."
> Response: "The Earth's surface is like a big jigsaw puzzle made of giant pieces called plates. These plates move very slowly, and when they crash or slide past each other, they can cause earthquakes and volcanoes."

Classroom Activity:

- Give pupils a list of complex words and their AI-generated explanations.
- Pupils work in pairs to write their own simplified versions.
- Compare different explanations and discuss which ones are the clearest.

3. Using AI to Suggest Synonyms and Alternative Words

To enrich pupils' writing, AI can suggest synonyms and alternative phrases. This helps pupils avoid repetition and use more precise vocabulary.

> Prompt: "Suggest three alternative words for 'big' in a non-fiction report about elephants."
> Response:

1   Massive
2   Enormous
3   Gigantic

Pupils could then write a short paragraph about elephants using only simple words. They then use AI to replace basic words with stronger synonyms, and discuss how vocabulary changes affect the tone and accuracy of their writing.

4. Generating Vocabulary for Different Writing Styles

Different non-fiction writing styles require different vocabulary. AI can help pupils choose the right words for reports, explanations, and persuasive writing. In *Fantastically Great Women*

Who Changed the World by Kate Pankhurst, biographies use formal, descriptive language to highlight achievements.

Pupils could research a famous historical figure and write a biography introduction. AI then suggests alternative phrasing to make their writing more engaging and informative.

> Prompt: "Rewrite this sentence in a more formal way: 'Florence Nightingale helped lots of people in hospitals.'"
> Response: "Florence Nightingale revolutionised hospital care, improving conditions and saving countless lives."

Pupils then compare versions and discuss which one sounds more authoritative.

Classroom Activities Using AI for Topic-Related Vocabulary

1. AI-Powered Word Sort

- Pupils receive a list of mixed-topic words (e.g. science, history, geography).
- They use AI to sort them into categories.
- This helps them recognise which words belong to different non-fiction genres.

> Prompt: "Sort these words into categories: volcano, eruption, king, queen, oxygen, carbon dioxide."
> Response:

- Geography: Volcano, eruption
- History: King, queen
- Science: Oxygen, carbon dioxide

2. AI-Generated Word Banks for Writing Support

- Pupils working on a non-fiction report can ask AI for word suggestions related to their topic.
- This helps them include specialist vocabulary without struggling to think of terms.

> Prompt: "Give me a list of words to use in a non-fiction report about the rainforest."
> Response:

1. Canopy
2. Biodiversity
3. Habitat
4. Deforestation
5. Ecosystem

Pupils incorporate these words into their writing, ensuring their vocabulary is precise and appropriate.

3. AI-Assisted Vocabulary Challenge

- Pupils write a short non-fiction paragraph using basic vocabulary.
- AI suggests stronger, more precise words.
- Pupils edit their work using the new vocabulary.

Example:

Basic sentence: "Lions live in Africa. They are very big and strong."
AI-enhanced sentence: "Lions inhabit the African savannah. They are powerful predators, known for their strength and hunting skills."

Pupils could then discuss how vocabulary choices improve clarity and engagement.

Caution and Consideration

When using AI, consider:

- Encouraging pupils to think critically about AI suggestions: Not every AI-generated word is appropriate for the context.
- Balancing AI use with traditional methods: Pupils should still engage in dictionary work and reading to build vocabulary naturally.
- Ensuring age-appropriate language: AI may suggest complex terms, so teachers should guide pupils in choosing the right words for their writing level.

Recommended Tools

1. ChatGPT (free/paid) – Generates word lists, definitions, and sentence examples.
2. WordHippo (free) – Provides synonyms and alternative words.
3. DeepL Write (free) – Helps refine sentence structure and improve word choice.
4. Oxford Learner's Dictionary (online) – Offers clear definitions and example sentences.

56 Fact vs. Opinion

> Understanding the difference between fact and opinion is a key skill in non-fiction writing. Facts are statements that can be proven true, while opinions express personal beliefs, feelings or viewpoints. Teaching pupils to distinguish between the two helps them read critically, write more accurately and evaluate the reliability of information. AI can support this process by generating examples of facts and opinions, helping pupils verify claims and suggesting ways to strengthen fact-based writing. By integrating AI into lessons, we can save time while equipping our pupils with essential literacy and critical thinking skills.

Why Teach Fact vs Opinion?

Teaching pupils to identify facts and opinions helps them to read critically by questioning information and identifying bias. But it can also help children to write persuasively by using strong evidence to support their arguments and to understand the role of opinions in non-fiction (e.g. reviews, debates, persuasive writing). This then develops their research skills by helping them to verify facts using reliable sources. AI can assist by generating fact-based statements, identifying opinion-based language and guiding pupils in writing well-supported arguments.

Fact vs Opinion in Non-Fiction Texts

Non-fiction texts often contain both facts and opinions. Understanding the difference helps pupils evaluate information critically. In *The Great Fire of London* by Emma Adams, the book presents historical facts about the fire but also includes personal perspectives from people who experienced it. For example, if we were to read the book and then say, "The fire started in a bakery on Pudding Lane in 1666," we can confirm that this is a fact that can be proven with historical records. However, if we were to say, "The fire spread because people were careless," this is a viewpoint that cannot be proven.

To further explore this with our pupils, we can read a short passage and highlight facts in one colour and opinions in another. AI can be used to generate more examples for practice too.

Prompt: "Give me three facts and three opinions about space travel."
Response:

✓ Facts:

1   The first human to walk on the Moon was Neil Armstrong in 1969.
2   The International Space Station orbits Earth at about 28,000 km per hour.
3   Mars is the fourth planet from the Sun.

✗ Opinions:

1   Space travel is the most exciting scientific achievement.
2   Astronauts have the most dangerous jobs.
3   One day, humans will definitely live on Mars.

Pupils can then discuss why the first three statements are facts and why the last three statements are opinions.

Using AI to Identify Fact vs Opinion

1. AI for Fact-Checking

AI can help pupils verify facts by checking against reliable sources. For example:

Prompt: "Is it true that Mount Everest is growing taller every year?"
Response: "Yes, Mount Everest grows by about 4 millimetres per year due to tectonic activity."

Pupils could then input more statements into AI and check if they are fact or opinion. They can use books and websites to confirm AI's accuracy.

2. AI for Writing Fact-Based Sentences

AI can also help pupils strengthen their writing by turning opinions into fact-based statements, like this:

Prompt: "Rewrite this opinion as a fact: 'Dogs are the best pets.'"
Response: "Many people consider dogs to be excellent pets because they are loyal and can be trained to assist humans."

Pupils can write five opinion-based sentences and use AI to turn them into factual statements. You can then discuss how adding evidence makes writing more reliable and persuasive.

3. AI for Recognising Opinion-Based Language

Pupils often struggle to spot opinion-based words in writing. AI can highlight words that indicate opinion, such as think, believe, feel, prefer, probably, should, best, worst, etc. In *Fantastically Great Women Who Changed the World* by Kate Pankhurst, facts about historical figures are combined with personal perspectives. This text could be read as an example. But then we can also input sentences into AI and ask which words show opinion, like this:

> Prompt: "Identify the opinion words in this sentence: 'Leonardo da Vinci was one of the most brilliant artists in history.'"
>
> Response: "The phrase 'one of the most brilliant' is an opinion because it expresses a viewpoint rather than a fact."

Pupils can then rewrite the sentence to make it fact-based, e.g. "Leonardo da Vinci was a famous artist known for painting the Mona Lisa."

Classroom Activities Using AI for Fact vs Opinion

1. AI-Powered Fact vs Opinion Quiz

Pupils could input mixed statements into AI and ask if they are fact or opinion. AI explains why, helping pupils understand the differences.

> Prompt: "Which of these sentences are facts and which are opinions?
> - 'The cheetah is the fastest land animal.'
> - 'Football is the most exciting sport.'
> - 'Water boils at 100°C.'
> - 'Chocolate is the tastiest dessert.'"
>
> Response: "Here's the breakdown of facts vs opinions for each sentence:
>
> ✓ Facts:
> 1. 'The cheetah is the fastest land animal.' → Fact (This can be scientifically measured and proven.)
> 2. 'Water boils at 100°C.' → Fact (This is a scientific fact under standard atmospheric conditions.)
>
> ✗ Opinions:
> 1. 'Football is the most exciting sport.' → Opinion (Excitement is subjective; different people have different preferences.)
> 2. 'Chocolate is the tastiest dessert.' → Opinion (Taste is based on personal preference and cannot be proven as fact.)"

Pupils could then rewrite the opinion sentences as factual statements.

2. Fact vs Opinion Sorting Game

AI generates 10 mixed statements on a topic. Pupils sort them into two columns: fact and opinion. For example:

> Response: "Here are 10 mixed statements about Ancient Egypt in a random order:
> 1. The Great Pyramid of Giza was built over 4,500 years ago.
> 2. The pyramids are the most impressive ancient structures in the world.

3   Pharaohs were considered both political rulers and religious figures.
4   Cleopatra was the most powerful ruler of Ancient Egypt.
5   Ancient Egyptians used hieroglyphics as their writing system.
6   The Sphinx is the most mysterious monument in history.
7   The Ancient Egyptians believed in over 2,000 gods and goddesses.
8   Hieroglyphics are more beautiful than modern writing systems.
9   The Nile River was essential for farming and trade in Ancient Egypt.
10 Life in Ancient Egypt must have been very difficult."

After pupils have sorted the statements into fact and opinion, they can use AI or research to verify the factual statements, then rewrite opinion statements as factual ones by adding evidence.

3. AI-Enhanced Persuasive Writing

Pupils could write a short persuasive paragraph then ask AI to identify opinion-based words. Pupils could then rewrite the sentences to include facts to support opinions. For example:

Opinion-Based Sentence: "School uniforms are bad because they are boring."
Fact-Supported Version: "Some students feel school uniforms are restrictive, but research shows they help reduce bullying and create a sense of equality."

Caution and Consideration

When using AI, consider:

- Encouraging critical thinking: AI-generated responses should be checked against reliable sources.
- Teaching balanced writing: Opinions can be included in non-fiction, but they should be supported by facts.
- Ensuring age-appropriate AI use: Pupils should be guided in using AI responsibly and thoughtfully.

Recommended Tools

1   ChatGPT (free/paid) - Identifies facts vs opinions and provides examples.
2   Google Fact Check (free) - Helps pupils verify claims.
3   CommonLit (free) - Provides non-fiction texts for fact vs opinion analysis.
4   DeepL Write (free) - Helps refine fact-based writing.

57 Summarising

> Summarising is a vital skill in non-fiction writing, helping pupils condense large amounts of information into clear, concise points. While **Chapter 10** explored summarising texts, this chapter will focus on how pupils can summarise their own research, findings and writing, which is a crucial skill when producing non-fiction reports, explanations and biographies.
>
> AI can assist in this process by helping pupils extract key details, suggesting concise wording and providing structural guidance to ensure their summaries are effective.

Why Teach Summarising in Non-Fiction Writing?

Summarising helps pupils to avoid unnecessary detail while keeping key facts, and to clarify their understanding by identifying the most important points. It also helps children to write concisely, especially when creating reports and explanations, and to develop strong research skills by extracting relevant information. AI can support this process by generating bullet-pointed summaries, suggesting alternative phrasing for overly long explanations and helping pupils identify key information in their writing.

Summarising Research Findings

Before writing a non-fiction text, pupils often gather information from books, articles or online sources. They need to sort through details and summarise key points to avoid copying full sections. For example, in *Sharks* by Nicola Davies, the author presents detailed facts about different shark species. If pupils were researching sharks, they might read several pages of information before needing to summarise it. Once pupils have gathered this information they can input the key facts into AI and ask it to summarise in three bullet points, like this:

Prompt: "Summarise this paragraph about sharks in three bullet points:

'Sharks have been around for over 400 million years, making them older than dinosaurs. They have a cartilaginous skeleton instead of bones, which makes them lightweight and fast swimmers. There are over 500 species of sharks, ranging from the tiny dwarf lantern shark to the enormous whale shark.'"

Response:
1. Sharks have existed for over 400 million years, predating dinosaurs.
2. Their skeletons are made of cartilage, making them lightweight and fast.
3. There are more than 500 species, including the dwarf lantern shark and whale shark.

Pupils can then compare the AI-generated summary with their own and discuss if the AI picked the most important points and consider if any key facts are missing. They might then improve the wording.

Summarising a Biography

When writing a biography, pupils must summarise a person's life and achievements in a few sentences, rather than including every detail. In *Little People, Big Dreams: Amelia Earhart* by Maria Isabel Sánchez Vegara, the book provides key milestones of Amelia Earhart's life. After reading the text, pupils might gather all of the information they have learnt and then use AI to condense it into a short summary, like this:

Prompt: "Summarise this paragraph about Amelia Earhart's achievements in two sentences.

'Amelia Earhart was the first woman to fly solo across the Atlantic Ocean in 1932. She later attempted to fly around the world but disappeared during the journey. She inspired many women to pursue careers in aviation.'"

Response: "Amelia Earhart became the first woman to fly solo across the Atlantic in 1932. Her groundbreaking achievements inspired future generations of female aviators."

Pupils could then discuss what details were kept or removed. They could also discuss if they think that the summary is still clear and what they would add back into the text.

Summarising Explanations and Reports

Pupils sometimes write long explanations about a topic before needing to summarise key points in a conclusion. In *A Seed Is Sleepy* by Dianna Aston, the book explains in detail how seeds grow into plants. Pupils summarising a plant life cycle would need to extract key stages without too much unnecessary detail. Here's an example summary:

A plant's life cycle begins when a seed is planted in soil and absorbs water, waking it from dormancy. As it germinates, a small root grows downward to anchor the plant and absorb nutrients, while a shoot emerges upward seeking sunlight. The young plant, or seedling, develops leaves that help it produce food through photosynthesis. As it matures, the plant flowers, attracting pollinators like bees, which help create seeds. Once seeds are dispersed by wind, animals or water, they settle into soil and begin the cycle again.

Pupils can then input their work into AI and ask it to summarise in one sentence.

Response: "A plant's life cycle begins with a seed absorbing water and germinating, growing roots and a shoot, developing into a seedling that matures, flowers, produces seeds, and restarts the cycle through seed dispersal."

Pupils then refine the AI response, ensuring accuracy and clarity.

Using AI to Support Summarising Skills

1. AI for Condensing Overly Long Sentences

Pupils can sometimes write overly long, unclear sentences. AI can help shorten and clarify them.

> Prompt: "Rewrite this sentence to make it clearer and more concise. 'The Amazon Rainforest, which is one of the biggest rainforests in the whole world, produces a large amount of the Earth's oxygen, which is why it is sometimes called the "lungs of the planet".'"
>
> Response: "The Amazon Rainforest, one of the world's largest, produces much of Earth's oxygen, earning it the nickname 'lungs of the planet'."

Pupils could write three long sentences and use AI to shorten them while keeping key details. They could then compare versions and discuss which is clearer and more effective.

2. AI-Generated Bullet-Point Summaries

AI can convert paragraphs into bullet points, helping pupils see key ideas more clearly. For example:

> Prompt: "Turn this paragraph about deforestation into three bullet points.
>
> 'Deforestation happens when people cut down too many trees in forests to make space for farms, roads, and buildings. Trees are important because they give us oxygen to breathe, provide homes for animals, and help keep the air clean. When too many trees are removed, animals lose their homes, and the Earth gets hotter because trees help cool the planet. We can help by planting new trees and protecting forests so animals and people can have a healthier world.'"
>
> Response:
>
> - Deforestation happens when too many trees are cut down for farms, roads, and buildings.
> - Trees give us oxygen, clean the air, and provide homes for animals, so losing them harms nature.
> - Planting new trees and protecting forests helps keep the planet healthy for animals and people.

Pupils then compare AI's version with their own and decide which summary is better and why.

3. AI for Editing Summaries

Pupils can write their own summaries, then ask AI for suggestions to improve clarity and conciseness.

> Prompt: "How can I improve my paragraph on deforestation?"
> Response:
> "Adding Specific Examples – Mentioning specific animals affected (e.g. orangutans, tigers) or places (e.g. the Amazon Rainforest) would make the explanation more relatable.
> Clarifying the Impact on Climate – Instead of just saying the Earth gets hotter, explain how trees absorb carbon dioxide and help reduce climate change.

Using More Engaging Language – Adding a simple cause-and-effect connection (e.g. 'When forests disappear, animals struggle to find food and shelter.') can make the explanation clearer.

Encouraging Action – Ending with a call to action like "We can help by recycling paper and planting trees!" gives children a way to make a difference."

Pupils can then edit their work based on the feedback.

Caution and Consideration

When using AI, consider:

- Encouraging original thinking: AI should support summarising, but pupils must still think critically.
- Checking AI-generated summaries: Pupils should compare AI results with their own work to improve their skills.
- Ensuring accuracy: AI can sometimes oversimplify or leave out key details, so pupils must verify information.

Recommended Tools

1. ChatGPT (free/paid) – Helps generate concise summaries.
2. SummarizeBot (freemium) – Extracts key details from long texts.
3. DeepL Write (free) – Refines sentence structure for clarity.
4. CommonLit (free) – Provides structured non-fiction texts for summarising practice.

58 Explaining Features

Explaining features is a key skill in non-fiction writing, helping pupils describe, clarify and define important details about a topic. Whether writing about animals, historical events, scientific processes or geographical landmarks, pupils must learn to clearly explain features so that readers understand their significance. AI can support this process by helping pupils identify key features, generate clear explanations and refine their descriptions. Using AI, pupils can also check if their explanations are easy to understand, logically structured and factually accurate.

Why Teach Explaining Features?

When pupils learn to explain features effectively, they improve their clarity in writing, develop stronger research and analytical skills and also enhance their ability to organise information logically. This then can support factual writing with well-structured descriptions.

AI can assist with this by generating explanations for features of a topic, suggesting ways to improve clarity in pupils' writing and providing structured templates to help pupils organise their ideas.

What Are Features in Non-Fiction Writing?

A feature is a key aspect or characteristic of something. Pupils might explain the features of an animal, a landmark, a machine, a historical event or a scientific process. In *Shackleton's Journey* by William Grill, the book describes the features of the ship *Endurance*, explaining how it was specially designed for icy conditions. Once pupils have read this text, they could write about a chosen feature and then use AI to generate a short explanation for this same feature and compare it to their own. For example:

> Prompt: "Explain how the Endurance ship's hull was designed and why it was important."
> Response: "The Endurance had a reinforced wooden hull to withstand the crushing pressure of Antarctic ice, allowing it to travel through extreme conditions."

Pupils can then discuss if the explanation fully describes the feature, whether it is clear and easy to understand and if it could be improved with more detail.

Explaining Features in Different Types of Writing

1. Scientific Features

In *A Seed Is Sleepy* by Dianna Aston, the book explains the features of seeds and how they grow into plants. Pupils choose a plant from the book and explain one of its features. They can then use AI to refine their explanation and check for clarity.

> Prompt: "Explain how a cactus stores water and why this is important."
> Response: "A cactus has thick, fleshy stems that store water, allowing it to survive in dry deserts where rainfall is rare."

Pupils can then discuss how they could make this more detailed and even clearer using their knowledge from the book. They can also write about another chosen plant in the same style.

2. Geographical Features

In *Rivers* by David Lindo, the book explains the features of a river system, such as the source, tributaries and mouth. After reading this book pupils could write a paragraph explaining this geographical feature to consolidate their knowledge. They could then use AI to shorten or clarify their explanation, like this:

> Prompt: "Explain what a river delta is and how it forms."
> Response: "A river delta is a landform created where a river meets a larger body of water, like an ocean. It forms when the river slows down and deposits sediment, creating fertile land."

Pupils can then compare and edit their own work based on the AI description.

3. Historical Features

In *Egyptology* by Dugald Steer, the book explains the features of the pyramids, including how they were built and their purpose. Pupils can research another historical structure or invention and explain one key feature using the book as a model. For example:

> Prompt: "Explain why the Great Wall of China was built."
> Response: "The Great Wall of China was built to protect China from invaders, acting as a barrier to keep out enemy forces."

Pupils can evaluate this answer by comparing it to Steer's book. They could examine if the AI response fully answers the question, then decide if they should add more detail for better clarity.

Using AI to Support Explaining Features

1. AI for Expanding or Simplifying Explanations

Pupils can ask AI to expand their explanations by adding more detail, or simplify complex ideas to make them easier to understand. Here's an example for expansion:

> Prompt: "Make this sentence more detailed: 'A cheetah is built for speed.'"
> Response: "A cheetah is built for speed because it has long legs, a lightweight body, and powerful muscles that help it run up to 70 miles per hour."

Pupils could then discuss if they think the expanded version is better and also examine if it explains "how" and "why."

2. AI-Generated Templates for Explaining Features

AI can provide structured templates for pupils who struggle to organise their ideas, like this:

> Prompt: "Give me a template for explaining a feature of an animal."
> Response: "[Feature] is important for [animal] because it helps them [purpose]. For example, [explanation of how it works]. This allows the animal to [benefit].
> For example:
>> 'Fur is important for a polar bear because it helps them stay warm in freezing temperatures. For example, their thick fur traps heat and repels water. This allows the polar bear to survive in icy conditions.'"

Pupils can use this template to structure their own explanations.

Classroom Activities Using AI for Explaining Features

1. Feature Sorting Game

Pupils could receive a mix of well-explained and poorly explained features like these:

> "A volcanic eruption happens when pressure builds up inside the Earth, forcing molten rock (magma) to escape as lava, along with ash and gases.
> The Eiffel Tower is really tall and famous.
> A penguin's feathers are tightly packed and coated with oil to create a waterproof and insulated layer, helping them stay warm.
> The Eiffel Tower is a 330-metre iron structure designed by Gustave Eiffel in 1889, built to withstand strong winds and serve as a landmark for the World's Fair.
> Volcanoes erupt when lava comes out.
> Penguins have feathers to keep them warm."

Pupils then use AI to revise any unclear explanations.

2. AI-Powered Editing Challenge

Pupils write a rough explanation of a feature, such as, "Giraffes have long necks so they can reach food." They then put this into an AI platform and ask it to explain more fully:

> Response: "Well-Explained Feature (After Revision): 'A giraffe's long neck helps it reach leaves high up in trees, allowing it to find food that other animals cannot reach. This adaptation is especially useful in the African savannah, where tall trees provide a primary food source.'"

Pupils can write more rough explanations for a feature of an animal, plant or object, then use AI to help refine their explanation. They can compare their original and the AI-revised version and discuss what was missing from their rough explanation, and examine how AI improved the clarity and the detail. They could then refine it even further.

3. AI-Generated "What Am I?" Riddles

AI writes a riddle describing a feature such as:

> I have strong roots but never move, I drink up water to help me grow. My leaves stretch towards the sky. What am I?
> Answer: A tree
> I keep you dry when rain pours down, held above but never worn. What am I?
> Answer: An umbrella
> I dig through the soil without any eyes, helping plants grow as I wiggle inside. What am I?
> Answer: A worm

Pupils create their own riddles and test them with their peers.

Caution and Consideration

When using AI, consider:

- Ensuring AI-generated explanations are factually correct.
- Encouraging pupils to refine AI responses rather than relying on them completely.
- Using AI as a tool to support learning, not to replace independent thinking.

Recommended Tools

1. ChatGPT (free/paid) - Generates explanations and suggests improvements.
2. BBC Bitesize (free) - Provides fact-based explanations for various subjects.
3. DeepL Write (free) - Helps refine sentence structure.
4. Kiddle (free) - A child-friendly search engine for fact-checking.

---

59 Creating Narrative Non-Fiction

> Narrative non-fiction blends real facts with storytelling techniques, making factual writing more engaging and immersive for readers. This genre is especially useful as it helps pupils connect with historical events, scientific discoveries and biographies through a structured, story-like approach. AI can support the creation of narrative non-fiction by suggesting engaging openings, structuring events chronologically and refining storytelling elements while maintaining factual accuracy. By incorporating AI into lesson planning, we can save time while guiding pupils in crafting compelling factual stories.

Why Teach Narrative Non-Fiction?

Teaching pupils how to write narrative non-fiction helps them to engage readers by presenting facts in a vivid and memorable way. It also improves structuring skills, as stories have clear beginnings, middles and endings. It can develop children's empathy by experiencing historical events or real-life situations from a personal perspective. It can strengthen research skills too while learning to weave facts into engaging storytelling.

AI can assist by suggesting narrative openings to hook the reader, structuring information chronologically to improve flow and providing feedback on clarity and engagement.

What Is Narrative Non-Fiction?

Narrative non-fiction tells true stories but uses descriptive language, dialogue and character perspectives to make the information engaging. *The Man Who Walked Between the Towers* by Mordicai Gerstein narrates the true story of Philippe Petit's tightrope walk between the Twin Towers, using vivid storytelling while maintaining historical accuracy. Once pupils have read this book we can discuss how storytelling techniques are used in it. They can then use AI to turn a simple factual event into a narrative opening in the same style. For example:

Prompt: "Turn this fact into a story introduction: 'In 1969, Neil Armstrong became the first person to walk on the Moon.'"

Response: "Neil Armstrong stepped onto the Moon's surface, his heart pounding inside his space suit. 'That's one small step for man, one giant leap for mankind,' he declared as his boots left their first imprint on the dusty lunar ground. Millions of people watched from Earth, holding their breath in amazement."

We can then discuss how this introduction makes the event more engaging and examine what descriptive details make it feel like a story. The children could then add their own details to improve it.

Structuring Narrative Non-Fiction

A good narrative non-fiction piece follows a clear structure like this:

1 Introduction – Hooks the reader with an engaging opening.
2 Main Events – Presents factual details in a story-like format.
3 Resolution – Concludes the story while reinforcing the key facts.

Pupils can research a historical event and use AI to structure it into a narrative format. For example:

Prompt: "Create a three-part outline for a narrative about the Great Fire of London."
Response:

1 Introduction: It was a warm September night in 1666, and the streets of London were quiet. In a small bakery on Pudding Lane, a tiny spark flickered in the darkness...
2 Main Events: The fire spread quickly, leaping from house to house as people ran for their lives. The sky glowed orange, and thick smoke filled the air. Samuel Pepys, a Londoner, wrote in his diary about the chaos unfolding before his eyes.
3 Resolution: After four days, the fire finally died down. Most of London was destroyed, but from the ashes, the city was rebuilt with stronger buildings.

Pupils can use this structured outline to write their own version of the story but adding new facts that they have learnt while studying the topic.

Adding Descriptive Elements

1. Using Dialogue to Bring History to Life

Dialogue makes historical events and real-life moments more immersive. In *I Am Amelia Earhart*, Brad Meltzer uses imaginative dialogue to place the reader in the perspective of Amelia Earhart. Pupils could research a different famous figure and create a short dialogue exchange based on real events. AI can then help refine their dialogue to make it more realistic, like this:

Prompt: "Write a short dialogue between Florence Nightingale and a patient during her time in the Crimean War."
Response:

Patient:	"Miss Nightingale, thank you for helping us. The hospital feels cleaner already."
Florence Nightingale:	"Every soldier deserves proper care. Cleanliness is the first step to recovery."

Pupils can expand on this dialogue and use it in their narrative non-fiction piece.

2. Using Sensory Details for Immersion

Strong narrative non-fiction paints a picture using the five senses. *The Street Beneath My Feet* by Charlotte Guillain uses detailed sensory descriptions to describe underground life. Using that text as a model, pupils could describe a real place or event using at least three senses, then AI can help refine descriptions.

> Prompt: "Describe the eruption of Mount Vesuvius in 79 AD using sensory details."
>
> Response: "The ground trembled beneath the people of Pompeii as a deep rumbling echoed through the streets. A towering cloud of ash darkened the sky, turning day into night. Thick, choking air filled their lungs as molten lava flowed down the mountain's side, crackling like thunder."

Pupils compare AI's version to their own and discuss what makes the description vivid. They can then examine if they could add more sensory details to make the description even more engaging.

Using AI to Support Narrative Non-Fiction Writing

1. AI for Generating Story Openings

AI can suggest engaging introductions to help pupils start their narratives. For example:

> Prompt: "Give me an engaging opening for a story about the first Olympic Games in Ancient Greece."
>
> Response: "The scorching sun beamed down on the dusty track as thousands of spectators filled the grand stadium of Olympia. The year was 776 BC, and the air buzzed with excitement as the best athletes from across Greece prepared for the first Olympic Games. Barefoot runners stood at the starting line, their muscles tense, waiting for the trumpet's signal. The honour of victory was not just for themselves – it was for their city, their gods, and their legacy in history."

AI provides a starting point and pupils can then refine it with their own ideas.

2. AI for Structuring Events Logically

Pupils can list key events of a real-life moment and AI can help organise them into a clear structure. For example:

> Prompt: "List the key events in Neil Armstrong's moon landing."
>
> Response:
>
> 1. Apollo 11 Launches (July 16, 1969) – Apollo 11 blasts off from Kennedy Space Centre with Neil Armstrong, Buzz Aldrin, and Michael Collins aboard.
> 2. Journey to the Moon – The spacecraft travels 240,000 miles in four days toward the Moon.
> 3. Lunar Module 'Eagle' Lands (July 20, 1969) – Armstrong and Aldrin pilot Eagle to a safe landing in the Sea of Tranquillity.

4. First Steps on the Moon – Armstrong steps onto the Moon, saying "That's one small step for man, one giant leap for mankind."
5. Buzz Aldrin Joins – They explore, collect samples, plant the flag, and conduct experiments.
6. Return to Lunar Module – After 2 hours and 15 minutes, they re-enter Eagle and prepare for liftoff.
7. Reuniting with Collins – Eagle launches and docks with Columbia in lunar orbit.
8. Return to Earth (July 24, 1969) – Apollo 11 splashes down in the Pacific Ocean and is recovered by the USS Hornet.

Children could then add to each event as they learn more about the topic.

3. AI for Checking Engagement and Clarity

Pupils can input their story into AI and ask:

Prompt: "Is my story engaging? How can I make it better?"

AI provides feedback on pacing, detail, and clarity.

Caution and Consideration

When using AI, consider:

- Ensuring historical accuracy: AI-generated narratives should always be fact-checked.
- Encouraging original writing: AI should support, not replace, pupils' creativity.
- Discussing ethical storytelling: Pupils should consider how real people and events are represented.

Recommended Tools

1. ChatGPT (free/paid) – Generates story openings and structures narratives.
2. DeepL Write (free) – Refines sentence flow for engaging storytelling.
3. CommonLit (free) – Provides real-world texts for inspiration.
4. Google Bard (free) – Helps with research-based storytelling.

---

60 Writing Conclusions

A strong conclusion is an essential part of non-fiction writing, helping to wrap up ideas clearly and leave a lasting impression on the reader. Unlike summarising, which focuses on condensing key information (as discussed in **Chapter 10**), a conclusion brings closure, reinforces the main points and sometimes encourages further thinking or action. AI can assist pupils in crafting effective conclusions by suggesting sentence starters, checking clarity and refining wording. By integrating AI into conclusion writing, we can help pupils develop a structured approach to ending their non-fiction texts effectively.

Why Are Conclusions Important?

Teaching pupils how to write strong conclusions helps them to provide closure by signalling the end of their writing, and reinforce key ideas without unnecessary repetition. This then makes their writing more memorable by leaving a final thought or by encouraging reflection or action (where relevant).

AI can support pupils by generating conclusion sentence starters, suggesting ways to improve clarity and helping pupils to ensure their ending matches the tone and purpose of their writing.

What Makes a Good Conclusion?

A well-written conclusion should:

1. Summarise the main idea without repeating everything.
2. Give a final thought, reflection, or key message.
3. Encourage further thinking or action if appropriate.

In *One Plastic Bag* by Miranda Paul, the conclusion highlights the impact of reducing plastic waste and encourages readers to think about their own actions. Pupils can read the conclusion and discuss how it provides closure. They can also consider if it leaves the reader with a final thought or action. AI can be used to suggest improvements to conclusions copied and pasted into it.

Different Types of Conclusions

1. Restating Key Ideas

This type of conclusion briefly reminds the reader of the main points. For example, in *The Big Book of the Blue* by Yuval Zommer, the book ends by reinforcing the importance of ocean life and how readers can protect it.

Once pupils have written a conclusion for a non-fiction text, they can use AI to compare their own conclusion with an AI-generated one. Here's an example based on rainforests:

Prompt: "Write a conclusion for a non-fiction report about why rainforests are important."

Response: "Rainforests are home to millions of species and play a key role in keeping our planet healthy. Protecting them is important for the environment, animals, and future generations."

Pupils could discuss if this conclusion reinforces the main idea. They could make it stronger by adding a final thought.

2. Encouraging Action

This conclusion type inspires readers to do something after reading. In *Greta and the Giants* by Zoë Tucker, the conclusion encourages young readers to help protect the environment. Pupils could write a conclusion for a persuasive text that encourages action. This could be something environmental as in *Greta and the Giants*, perhaps about reducing plastic waste, then AI could suggest ways to make it more powerful.

Prompt: "Improve this conclusion to make it more persuasive: 'People should use less plastic because it harms the environment.'"

Response: "Every piece of plastic we refuse to use makes a difference. By choosing reusable bags and bottles, we can help protect the planet for future generations."

Pupils can then discuss how this conclusion might make the reader want to take action. Perhaps they could make it more persuasive by adding more facts or emotive language.

3. Leaving the Reader Thinking

Some conclusions leave the reader with a thought-provoking question or idea. In *If Sharks Disappeared* by Lily Williams, the book ends by asking what the ocean would look like without sharks, making readers think about conservation. Pupils could write a conclusion in the same style for a text about a topic of your choice. AI can then help to make it more thought-provoking.

Prompt: "Rewrite this conclusion to leave the reader thinking: 'Space exploration is important because we learn more about our universe.'"

Response: "As we continue to explore space, what new worlds might we discover? Could life exist beyond Earth? The future of space exploration is full of possibilities."

You could then discuss with your class what the new version might make the reader think. Then ask the children to make it even stronger by adding more detail.

Using AI to Support Writing Conclusions

1. AI for Generating Conclusion Sentence Starters

AI can provide sentence starters to help pupils begin their conclusion effectively, such as:

Prompt: "Give me three sentence starters for a conclusion about climate change."
Response:

1. "In conclusion, protecting our planet is essential for future generations."
2. "The evidence shows that taking action against climate change is more important than ever."
3. "Now that we understand the impact of climate change, it's time to make a difference."

Pupils can choose a sentence starter and complete their conclusion.

2. AI for Checking Clarity and Strength of Conclusions

Pupils can input their conclusion into AI and ask:

Prompt: "Does my conclusion clearly wrap up my writing? How can I improve it?"

AI gives feedback on clarity, structure and effectiveness.

3. AI for Editing Word Choice in Conclusions

Pupils can use AI to make their conclusions more impactful by refining word choice, like this:

Prompt: "Make this conclusion more powerful: 'Saving the rainforest is important.'"
Response: "Rainforests are the lungs of our planet, and their survival depends on us. Every tree we save protects wildlife, the climate and future generations."

Pupils could evaluate which words make the conclusion stronger and use this vocabulary to edit their own conclusions.

Caution and Consideration

When using AI, consider:

- Encouraging pupils to think independently: AI can provide ideas, but conclusions should reflect their own writing.
- Ensuring AI-generated conclusions match the tone of the writing: Some AI responses may be too formal or informal.
- Checking factual accuracy: AI should be used as a support, not a replacement for real research.

Recommended Tools

1. ChatGPT (free/paid) – Generates sentence starters and suggests refinements.
2. DeepL Write (free) – Improves clarity and word choice.
3. Book Creator (freemium) – Helps pupils structure and present their writing.
4. CommonLit (free) – Provides well-structured non-fiction texts for analysis.

REFERENCES

Please note that the sources listed below are provided as examples only. The exercises throughout this book are designed to be flexible and can easily be adapted to suit a wide range of materials, allowing you to use any resources that best fit your classroom needs.

Adams, E., & Lewis, J.W. (2016). *The Great Fire of London*. Wayland.
Alexander, L. (1964). *The Book of Three*. Dell.
Alexander, L. (1984). *The Chronicles of Prydain*. Dell.
Almond, D. (1999). *Skellig*. Delacorte Press.
Anderson, S. (2018). *The House with Chicken Legs*. First US edition. Scholastic Press.
Anderson, S. (2020). *The Girl Who Speaks Bear*. First US edition. Scholastic Press.
Applegate, K. (2012). *The One and Only Ivan*. HarperCollins.
Aston, D.H., & Long, S. (2007). *A Seed Is Sleepy*. Chronicle Books.
Barr, C., & Samels, R. (2023). *The World's Wildest Waters: Protecting Life in Seas, Rivers, and Lakes*. First US edition. DK Publishing.
Bell, A., & Tomić, T. (2018). *The Polar Bear Explorers' Club*. First edition. Simon & Schuster Books for Young Readers.
Bell, P.G., & Sorrentino, F. (2018). *The Train to Impossible Places: A Cursed Delivery*. Usborne.
Bilston, B., & Sanabria, J. (2022). *Refugees*. Palazzo Editions Ltd.
Blake, William, 1757-1827 (2002). *The Tyger*. Spoon Print Press.
Bloom, V. (2024). "A River" from *The River's A Singer: Selected Poems*. Macmillan Children's Books.
Brown, P. (2016). *The Wild Robot*. Little, Brown and Company.
Bryon, N., & Adeola, D. (2019). *Look Up!* Puffin.
Burnett, F.H., & Tudor, T. (1987). *The Secret Garden*. First Harper Trophy edition. HarperCollins.
Carroll, L. (1993). *Alice's Adventures in Wonderland*. Dover Publications.
Carroll, L., & Stewart, J. (2003). *Jabberwocky*. Candlewick Press.
Cowell, C. (2017). *The Wizards of Once*. First US edition. Little, Brown and Company.
Dahl, R. (1988). *Matilda*. Penguin.
Dahl, R. (2016). *Fantastic Mr Fox*. Puffin.
Dahl, R., & Blake, Q. (1981). *The BFG*. Puffin Books.
Dahl, R., & Blake, Q. (1981). *The Twits*. Viking Penguin.
Davies, B. (2014). *The Storm Whale*. First US edition. Henry Holt and Company.
Davies, N., & Croft, J. (2008). *Surprising Sharks*. Candlewick Press.
De la Mare, W. (1912). 'The Listeners': *The Listeners and Other Poems*. Constable and Company, Ltd.
DiCamillo, K., & Ering, T.B. (2003). *The Tale of Despereaux: Being the Story of a Mouse, a Princess, Some Soup, and a Spool of Thread*. Walker Books
DiCamillo, K., & Ibatoulline, B. (2006). *The Miraculous Journey of Edward Tulane*. Candlewick Press.
Donaldson, J., & Scheffler, A. (2004). *The Gruffalo's Child*. Macmillan Children's Books.
Dyu, L., & Lay, J. (2019). *Earth Heroes: Twenty Inspiring Stories of People Saving Our World*. Nosy Crow.
Edge, C. (2019). *The Infinite Lives of Maisie Day*. First US edition. Delacorte Press.
Elphinstone, A. (2018). *Sky Song*. Simon & Schuster Children's UK.
Farook, N. (2021). *The Girl Who Stole an Elephant*. First edition. Peachtree Publishing Company Inc.
Gerstein, M. (2003). *The Man Who Walked Between the Towers*. Roaring Brook Press.
Gold, H. (2021). *The Last Bear*. HarperCollins.

Grahame, K. (1961). *The Wind in the Willows*. Charles Scribner's Sons.
Green, B., & Skuse, J. (2018). Teach Your Monster to Read. Popleaf.
Guillain, C., & Zommer, Y. (2017). *The Street Beneath My Feet*. Words & Pictures.
Hawking, L., Hawking, S., Galfard, C., & Parsons, G. (2007). *George's Secret Key to the Universe*. First US edition. Simon & Schuster Books for Young Readers.
Hughes, T. (1957). "Wind" from *The Hawk in the Rain*. Faber and Faber.
Hughes, T. (2001). *The Iron Man*. Faber and Faber.
Ibbotson, E. (2001). *Journey to the River Sea*. First US edition. Puffin Books.
King-Smith, D. (2001). *Babe: The Gallant Pig*. Dell Yearling.
Kipling, R. (2009). *The Jungle Book*. Puffin Classics.
Kirtley, S. (2020). *The Wild Way Home*. Bloomsbury Children's Books.
Lear, E., & Brett, J. (1991). *The Owl and the Pussycat*. Putnam.
Lear, E., Mendelson, E., & Huliska-Beith, L. (2001). *The Complete Nonsense and Other Verse*. Sterling Pub. Co.
Leonard, M.G., Sedgman, S., & Paganelli, E. (2020). *The Highland Falcon Thief*. Macmillan Children's Books.
Lewis, C.S. (1994). *The Lion, the Witch, and the Wardrobe*. First Harper Trophy edition. HarperCollins.
Llenas, A. (2021). *The Colour Monster: A Story About Emotions*. Little, Brown and Company.
MacKenzie, R. (2015). *The Nowhere Emporium*. Kelpies.
Magorian, M. (1986). *Good Night, Mr. Tom*. First Harper Trophy edition. Harper & Row.
Mayer, M., & Browning, R. (1987). *The Pied Piper of Hamelin*. First US edition. Macmillan.
McGough, R. (2005). *The Sound Collector*. Poetry.com. Retrieved 17 April 2025, from https://www.poetry.com/poem/58704/the-sound-collector.
McKay, H. (2018). *The Skylarks' War*. First edition. Macmillan.
Mojang Studios (2011). *Minecraft*. Mojang Studios.
Morpurgo, M. (1997). *The Butterfly Lion*. Viking.
Morpurgo, M. (2000). *Kensuke's Kingdom*. Egmont and Harper.
Murphy, J. (2007). *The Worst Witch Saves the Day*. Candlewick Press.
Noyes, A., & Keeping, C. (1981). *The Highwayman*. Oxford University Press.
O'Brien, R.C., & Bernstein, Z. (1972). *Mrs. Frisby and the Rats of NIMH*. Puffin.
Pankhurst, K. (2016). *Fantastically Great Women Who Changed The World*. Bloomsbury Children's Books.
Paul, M., & Zunon, E. (2015). *One Plastic Bag: Isatou Ceesay and the Recycling Women of the Gambia*. Millbrook Press.
Pearce, P., & Einzig, S. (1958). *Tom's Midnight Garden*. J.B. Lippincott.
Pennypacker, S. (2017). *Pax*. HarperCollins.
Potter, B. (2002). *The Tale of Peter Rabbit*. Warne.
Pullman, P. (1996). *The Firework-Maker's Daughter*. Corgi Yearling.
Pullman, P. (2007). *The Golden Compass*. Laurel-Leaf.
Pullman, P., & Roberts, N. (2001). *Northern Lights*. Scholastic.
Raúf, O.Q., & Curnick, P. (2019). *The Boy at the Back of the Class*. First US edition. Delacorte Press.
Rogers, L J., & Groenink, C. (2019). *16 Words: William Carlos Williams and "The Red Wheelbarrow"*. First edition. Schwartz & Wade Books.
Rowling, J.K. (2014). *Harry Potter and the Philosopher's Stone*. Bloomsbury Children's Books.
Rundell, K. (2015). *The Wolf Wilder*. First edition. Simon & Schuster Books for Young Readers.
Rundell, K. (2017). *The Explorer*. Simon & Schuster Books for Young Readers.
Sachar, L. (2015). *Holes*. Bloomsbury Children's Books.
Said, S.F., & McKean, D. (2003). *Varjak Paw*. First US edition. D. Fickling Books.
Sánchez Vegara, M.I., Mariadiamantes, M., & Plitt, R. (2016). *Amelia Earhart*. Frances Lincoln Children's Books.
Shepherd, A., & Ogilvie, S. (2018). *The Boy Who Grew Dragons*. Piccadilly Press.
Steer, D., Andrew, I., Harris, N., & Ward, H. (2004). *Egyptology: Search for the Tomb of Osiris, Being the Journal of Miss Emily Sands, November 1926-*. First US edition. Candlewick Press.
Stevenson, R.L., & Pearson, T.C. (2006). *The Moon*. Farrar, Straus & Giroux.
Thompson, L.I. (2017). *The Goldfish Boy*. Scholastic Press.
Tolkien, J.R.R. (1973). *The Hobbit: Or, There and Back Again*. Ballantine Books.
White, E.B. (1974). *Stuart Little*. Collins.
White, E.B., & Williams, G. (1952). *Charlotte's Web*. First edition. Harper & Brothers.
Wordsworth, W. (1958). *Selected Poems of William Wordsworth*. (R. Sharrock, ed.). Macmillan.
Wright, K. (2010). *The Magic Box: Poems for Children*. Macmillan Children's Books.
Zommer, Y., & Taylor, B. (2018). *The Big Book of the Blue*. Thames & Hudson.

For Product Safety Concerns and Information please contact our EU
representative GPSR@taylorandfrancis.com
Taylor & Francis Verlag GmbH, Kaufingerstraße 24, 80331 München, Germany

www.ingramcontent.com/pod-product-compliance
Lightning Source LLC
Chambersburg PA
CBHW080411170426
43194CB00015B/2777